CW00971698

The Cher Bible: 2018 Ultimate Edition

Daniel Wheway

Published by Daniel Wheway, 2018.

While every precaution has been taken in the preparation of this book, the publisher assumes no responsibility for errors or omissions, or for damages resulting from the use of the information contained herein.

THE CHER BIBLE: 2018 ULTIMATE EDITION

First edition. July 1, 2018.

Copyright © 2018 Daniel Wheway.

ISBN: 978-1722450120

Written by Daniel Wheway.

Introduction

Rightfully coined the "Goddess of Pop", Cher has conquered music, film and television during her 50-year showbiz career, selling 100-million records, grossing $650-million on tour, drawing $700-million at the U.S. Box Office and winning Oscar, Grammy, Emmy and Golden Globe Awards.

She is one-half of highly-successful duo Sonny & Cher, a multi-million-selling doll, multi-million-selling fitness icon, hit songwriter, enduring sex symbol, award-winning television producer, film director, video director, award-winning fashion icon, author, model, humanitarian, mother, daughter, and of course the idol of a highly diverse fan base.

The Cher Story

1946-1969

I Got You Babe — Sonny & Cher Top The Charts

Cher's mother, Georgia Holt, was an aspiring actress who headed to Hollywood during adolescence to find fame. However, showbiz success evaded Georgia, and by 1945, she was in a penniless marriage to Armenian truck driver John Sarkisian, with whom she was now expecting a baby.

Georgia's mother pressured her to have an illegal abortion but she backed out on the abortion table — she gave birth to her daughter Cherilyn "Cher" Sarkisian on 20 May 1946.

John took Georgia and an infant Cher to Pittsburgh before bailing on them, thus leaving Georgia to raise Cher alone in the city whilst working for tips as a waitress in an all-night diner. A struggling Georgia placed her daughter in a Catholic orphanage for a small time but found herself having to fight in order to get Cher back when the nuns there deemed her an "unfit mother".

"I remember my mom, she was pretty outlandish for her time. She was a model and she was beautiful and she was on the cutting edge."

– Cher

"We were dead poor", Cher has since recalled. Georgia raised Cher whilst frequently relocating homes but at one point settled down for a while with new husband Gilbert LaPiere — whom Cher learned to call "Dad".

Cher had entertainment running through her veins from the get-go. A three-year-old Cher ran around the house singing, naked, whilst a four-year-old Cher developed a desire to be on the big screen when she was taken to a theatre to watch classic feature-length animation *Dumbo*. Inspired by her mother's Broadway musical cast albums, a five-year-old Cher was already putting on small performances for her mother and her new baby sister, Georganne LaPiere.

> **Trivia:** The first song Cher learned was *Hey, Good Lookin'* by Hank Williams; and the first record Cher ever bought was *Tequila* by The Champs.

It came at little surprise then that during fifth grade, 1956-'57, Cher was gathering girls from her grammar school to help her put on a performance of *Oklahoma!* for her class and teacher. Even then, Cher had a low voice, which came in handy when she was void of boy volunteers for her show, thus performing all the male parts herself.

Cher had inherited her dark looks from her Armenian father, who she did not meet until a visit from him after turning eleven years of age. She felt let down by her father — he was addicted to heroin and pawned Georgia's jewellery. By fifteen years of age, Cher had become uncomfortable with her dark hair, eyes and skin, having been surrounded by her blond mother's blond family. However, 1961's *Breakfast At*

Tiffany's finally gave her a fellow non-blond and "irregular"-looking idol in the shape of its star Audrey Hepburn.

In 1962, Cher began a brief loveless sexual romance with 25-year-old actor Warren Beatty, dropped out of school and began acting classes. In November, she met and befriended struggling songwriter Salvatore Bono, known to most as "Sonny", in a Los Angeles coffee shop.

> "I got my first look at Salvatore Phillip Bono. I will never forget it, because everyone else in the room disappeared, just washed away into some fuzzy soft focus."

– Cher

Sonny had tried — and failed — to gain success as a recording artist since 1955, and after meeting Cher, he landed a job working for now-legendary record producer Phil Spector as a promotion man at Gold Star Studios in Hollywood, before adding "percussionist" and "background singer" to his job title. Rooting from a friendship, Cher and Sonny became romantically involved, and next time Beatty called her — after eight months of no contact — she told him that she was now in love with Sonny.

Up until that point, Cher aspired to be an actress, like her mother, whom had now landed minor TV and film roles. However, Sonny, who was enjoying some success as a songwriter with his co-penned *Needles & Pins* by Jackie DeShannon (US#84), introduced Cher to Spector, who provided her with the job of a "baby-sitter" for his girlfriend Ronnie Bennett.

Spector eventually hired Cher to perform alongside Sonny, and others, as a background singer at the Gold Star Recording Studios in July 1963 when one of his usual background singers, Darlene Love, could not make it in time to record Spector's latest masterpiece: The Ronettes' classic *Be My Baby*. The US#2 hit was Sonny & Cher's first joint professional recording, alas as background singers.

Sonny and Cher were background singers on virtually every Spector recording until October 1964, when they sang back-up on another masterpiece — The Righteous Brothers' US and UK #1 *You've Lost That Lovin' Feelin'*. Other classics that feature Sonny and Chers' background vocals are The Ronettes' Transatlantic Top 40 hits *Baby I Love You* and *Do I Love You?,* and Darlene Love's festive favourite *Christmas (Baby Please Come Home)*.

"She was so loud, so powerful, she was louder than everybody in this studio. So Phil would keep telling her 'OK move back... Move back Cher... Move back Cher. One time I said, 'You're gonna move her back so far, she's gonna be in the alley in a minute.'"

– Darlene Love

Meanwhile, the couple emerged as a musical duo under the name of "Caesar & Cleo", playing gigs of cover hits, whilst releasing a cover of Don & Dewey's little-known *The Letter* on Vault Records in February 1964 — which stirred some interest in California. Sonny — whose *Needles & Pins* had just been revived into a UK#1 hit by The Searchers — persuaded

Spector to record Cher. Her March debut solo single *Ringo, I Love You* — an ode to Ringo Starr with elements of The Beatles' *She Loves You* — was released under the pseudonym "Bonnie Jo mason" on the newly-formed Annette Records label. It went by unnoticed.

> "Elvis was really my biggest inspiration, because my voice was so not girly (first record I put out was called 'Ringo, I love you', and they wouldn't play it because they thought I was a guy). He was the only artist I could really identify with."

> **– Cher**

Still as "Caesar & Cleo", the duo signed with Reprise Records and released another overlooked single: a rousing cover of Mickey & Sylvia's *Love Is Strange*. Almost simultaneously — and with a name change to "Sonny & Cher" under a new contract — they released Sonny-original *Baby Don't Go*, which, due to its small popularity in California and Texas, finally gave them an appearance on a Billboard music chart, alas the Billboard "Bubbling Under" chart — a chart of the week's best-selling singles that missed the main Billboard Hot 100. An attempt to get a cover of Bobby Freeman's *Do You Want To Dance* onto the Netherlands music chart failed.

Sonny was determined to get him and/or Cher a proper hit record, and just prior to the year's end, he penned a solo Cher song called *Dream Baby,* which too was a minor hit in California. A February 1965 attempt to get *Baby Don't Go* onto the UK charts failed but a switch to Atco Records saw another US single release — April's Sonny-written Spector-sound-a-like *Just You*. Like the duo's last single, it was a minor hit in California and Texas. Meanwhile, they were playing gigs up and down the West Coast, making appearances on Television shows *Shivaree* and *Shindig!* and were back in the recording studio to record Sonny's latest composition, *I Got You Babe*.

The hard work started to pay off: July saw Cher's cover of Bob Dylan's *All I Really Want To Do* enter the lower part of Billboard's Hot 100 — becoming her first hit record. Meanwhile, After several failed attempts to catch a proper big break in the US, Sonny & Cher took the advice of The Rolling Stones (who were in the US on their first West Coast tour) of moving to England to hit it big.

"I loved songs that weren't as big of hits. I loved *Just You*. I loved *All I Really Want to Do* too; that was fun. Everyone thought that was a Sonny & Cher record because they didn't know I could jump the octaves that easily."

– Cher

Sonny and Cher and their managers Charlie Greene and Brian Stone sold their cars to raise cash for the plane tickets. In protest of their hippie appearance, the London Hilton hotel turned Sonny and Cher away from its premises the morning that they arrived, and photographers captured the display as the hotel staff proceeded to escort them out the door (Cher later heard that Greene had arranged the whole thing for a publicity stunt). As a result, Sonny & Cher were on the front page of the British papers later that same day. Whilst the London Hilton objected to the couple's alternative image, it captured the rest of the British nation's interest.

"When I was young we got beaten up for looking the way we looked. No one even dared to look different. The Beatles had nice hair cuts and were in suits. The Stones were kind of on the fringe."

– Cher

The duo had become an overnight sensation as interview and photoshoot requests came flooding in the next day for the pair. More importantly, London deejays discovered and began to spin their latest recording, *I Got You Babe*. Sonny & Cher were quickly snapped up to make promotional appearances for the song on UK television shows *Ready Steady Go* and *Top of The Pops*. *Babe* knocked the Beatles' *Help!* off the top of the UK single charts near the end of August and stayed there for a second week.

Sonny & Cher returned home to America where they were greeted at the airport by roughly five-thousand new American teenage fans. Also greeting them was the presence of *I Got You Babe* at the top of the US charts — where it would spend three weeks. It even crossed over to reach #19 on the R&B Singles chart. The classic sixties duet has since sold over three-million copies worldwide.

Cher's *All I Really Want To Do* had to battle The Byrd's version of the same song in the charts. The group's version rose

to #40 in the US and #4 in the UK. Cher's version performed arguably better, reaching the Top 20 on both sides of
the Atlantic: #15 in the US and #9 in the UK.

Baby Don't Go was re-released, reaching #1 in Canada, #8 in
the US and #11 in the UK, as was *Just You*, which hit #20
in the US. With the addition of Sonny's solo self-penned
Laugh At Me (US#10, UK#9, Canada#1), the overnight
sensations had an impressive *five* hits on the US Hot 100
chart simultaneously. Before long, a re-issue of *The Letter* also made an appearance at #75 on the US Hot 100.

The duo's 3-million-selling Gold-certified debut album *Look
At Us* spent a staggering *eight* weeks at #2 on the Billboard
200, whilst reaching #7 in the UK. It hit #3 in Australia
where track *Sing C'est La Vie* was issued as a single, reaching
#2 (and #1 in Belgium). Cher's million-selling debut album
All I Really Want To Do, fuelled solely by its title track,
reached #7 in the UK and #16 in the US (where it spent an
impressive six months on the chart). A Reprise label compilation album featuring songs by "Sonny & Cher and Friends"
titled *Baby Don't Go* reached #69 in the US: it featured
their "Caesar & Cleo" recordings alongside songs from other
artists on the label's roster, namely Bill Medley, The Lettermen and The Blendells.

Sonny was writing, producing and arranging the majority
of their material — most of which was folk-rock. Meanwhile, Cher had fast become a trendsetter for millions of
teenage girls, who imitated her unique image: the jet-black
straight hair; the Cleopatra-style eye liner; the equally-bold

mascara; the furry waistcoats; and the often-striped bell-bottom trousers. Cher would remain a trendsetter for her whole career.

September saw the couple appear on some of the biggest television shows in America, such as *Where The Action Is*, *Hullabaloo* and perhaps most excitingly, *The Ed Sullivan Show*. On the latter show, the host pronounced Cher's name incorrectly, like "Chur", and thus led her to style her name as "Chér" for most of the next ten years. Cher performed new Sonny-penned teenage angst-themed solo single *Where Do You Go* (US#25) whilst the duo performed their new single *But You're Mine* (UK#15, US#17). Sonny & Cher appeared as themselves in the film *Wild on the Beach*, singing the *I Got You Babe* B-side and *Look At Us* album track *It's Gonna Rain*.

February 1966 saw Sonny & Cher take on popular ballad *What Now My Love* as their new single, which showcased that Cher's deep voice was certainly powerful enough to fit comfortably alongside other great female singers of the time, such as Dusty Springfield and Petula Clark. It reached #16 in the US and #13 in the UK — the only Transatlantic Top 20 version of the much-covered song. It came from their new album *The Wondrous World of Sonny & Chér*, which reached #34 on the US Billboard 200 when released in April, and #15 in the UK.

Cher's new single *Bang Bang (My Baby Shot Me Down)* became her first million-selling solo single, reaching #2 in the US and #3 in the UK. It became one of Sonny's most-covered compositions, eventually being reworked by Stevie

Wonder, Petula Clark, Cliff Richard, Nancy Sinatra, Frank Sinatra and Lady Gaga among *many* others. It was lifted from Cher's second solo studio album *The Sonny Side of Chér* (US#26, UK#11).

Have I Stayed Too Long failed to become a Top 40 hit single for the duo, reaching #49 in the US and #42 in the UK, but the outlandish couple were nominated at the 1966 Grammy Awards for 'Best New Artist' alongside the likes of The Byrds, Herman's Hermits and eventual winner Tom Jones.

In September, *Little Man* — written by Sonny and sang mostly by Cher — was released, becoming a million-selling European smash-hit for the duo despite only reaching #21 in the US. It became their second UK Top 5 hit in the UK (#4).

Cher's third album *Chér* followed maybe a little too quickly and stalled at #59 in the US and became her first album not to chart in the UK. It did, however, contain the UK Top 75 chart hits *Sunny* (Bobby Hebb cover, #32 — and a #2 hit in multiple European countries) and *I Feel Something In The Air* (Sonny composition tackling unwanted pregnancy, #42), as well as the US#32 hit *Alfie* (played during the closing credits of that year's hit Michael Caine-starring movie of the same name).

After the November 1966 disappointing performances of the duo's *Living For You* (UK#42, US#87), Cher's *Behind The Door* (US#97) and her *Mama (When My Dollies Have Babies)* (US#124 — though #70 on Billboard Hot 100's rival Cash box Top 100 Singles chart), Sonny unleashed a new song for the duo in January 1967: *The Beat Goes On* (UK#29). The song propelled the duo back to the Top 10 (#6) of the US singles charts.

Meanwhile, Sonny & Cher became briefly controversial in Pasadena, California in January for siding with the "Sunset Strip Rioters" — teenagers protesting the city's new curfew — and as a result, were removed from their promised position of honor in the next day's *Tournament of Roses Parade*. That same month, they entered Italy's San Remo song festival with two songs — the duo's Il cammino di ogni speranza and Cher's solo *Ma piano (Per non svegliarmi)* — but failed to reach the final rounds.

> "It's a good thing that we were so entertained by each other because we were constantly together."
>
> **– Cher**

Despite the inclusion of *The Beat Goes On*, Sonny & Cher's March album *In Case You're in Love* only peaked at #45 on the US Billboard 200. It did not chart in the UK at all. That same month, they appeared in acting roles on an episode of NBC's TV series *The Man From U.N.C.L.E.*. A month later, they released *A Beautiful Story*, which peaked at #53 on the US Hot 100.

Sonny was inspired to make a film for the duo to star in despite Cher's unenthusiasm about the project. Directed by William Friedkin and co-starring George Sanders, the movie was titled *Good Times* and released in April 1967. It premièred in Austin, Texas — where it did well. However, elsewhere, it was a commercial and critical failure. The following month, they released the soundtrack album to the film, which fared arguably better, charting at #73 in the US. In the following months, they released the small hit singles *Plastic Man* (US#74, and notably #49 in France) and taken from the aforementioned soundtrack album, fan-favourite *It's The Little Things* (US#50).

Sonny & Cher released their first greatest hits package in August, *The Best of Sonny & Chér*. The collection was highly successful, reaching #23 on the US Billboard 200, on which it would chart for an impressive forty-seven weeks. Their upbeat December 1967 single *Good Combination* reached #53 on the US Hot 100. However, it would be their final hit single of the decade. Following the release of her Jim Hendrix-cover *Hey Joe* (US#94) and new studio album *With Love, Chér* (US#47), the female-half of the duo enjoyed a solo comeback with December's *You Better Sit Down Kids* (US#9), a song about divorce — an unusual subject for a pop song at the time. However, despite once again achieving Top 10 status, that would be *her* final solo hit of the decade.

"By 1968, Sonny and I had fallen off the charts. It was a different time, a different sound."

– Cher

Sonny & Cher's pop ditties (*Circus* and *You Gotta Have A Thing of Your Own*) stopped reaching the US Hot 100 as the anti-drug duo became disconnected with the majority of the record-buying public, which had turned on to acid-rock as part of the in-full-swing drug culture (American actress Lily Tomlin recalls Cher's anti-drug stance: "She and I went out to dinner and someone famous came over to our table and literally laid lines of coke on the table and Cher was appalled".) In a bid to recover their career, Sonny thought up plans to write and produce a film for Cher to star in, entitled *Chastity*. He placed all of the duo's savings into making the movie. During its production, Cher announced that she was pregnant.

Despite the dried-up record sales, Sonny & Cher were still hitting some popular events in 1968 including April's *40th Annual Academy Awards*, June's *Martin Luther King Benefit* at Madison Square Garden and August's *Newport Pop Festival* — the first ever music concert to have more than 100,000 paid attendees.

Cher's July album *Backstage* was her first to not chart in the US, or produce any Billboard hit singles (despite attempts with *The Click Song*, which *did* hit #78 on the Cash Box Top 100 Singles chart and #84 on further US Hot 100 rival Record World 100 Top Pops, and *Take Me For A Little While*). Her first solo compilation album, titled *Golden Greats*, was released before the year's end. It contained all of her US and UK Top 40 hits but reached a very low #195 on the US Billboard 200 chart.

In February 1969, Cher's stand-alone single *Yours Until Tomorrow* failed to chart and went by unnoticed. On 4 March, Cher (whom up to this point had experienced four miscarriages) and Sonny had their first child; a daughter whom they named Chastity Sun Bono, after their new feature film. Devastatingly for Cher, when Chastity was six-weeks-old, Sonny revealed to her that they were in debt by $270,000 to the IRS.

Before long, Sonny and Cher got married. Their relationship was moving forward but their career and finances were in danger. The film *Chastity* opened in theatres on 24 June 1969 to mixed reviews and was a Box Office failure. Its predominantly-instrumental soundtrack album of the same name unsurprisingly did not chart, and contained the Cher track *Chastity's Song (Bands Of Thieves)*, which became a flop single.

Cher — who had begun to grow out her 1960's trademark bangs/fringe — also released a new studio album in June entitled *3614 Jackson Highway*. It received critical acclaim but only charted at #160, and none of its singles (*I Walk On Guilded Splinters*, and Bob Dylan-cover *Lay Lady Lay*) reached the US Hot 100, despite Billboard predicting that her cover of Buffalo Springfield's *For What It's Worth* would become one of her biggest hits. A follow-up album was recorded — including non-charting single *You've Made Me So Very Happy* — but was not released (until 2001).

1970-1980
Living In A House Divided – TV's Sonny & Cher Separate

Sonny & Cher had hit hard times. They were in worryingly heavy debt, and thus had to perform at nightclubs. By no choice of their own, Sonny & Cher had to reinvent their image for the nightclub circuit. Sonny was required to wear tuxedos, Cher was required to wear evening dresses. Just years ago, the duo were selling out 30,000-seat arenas. Now, on a good night, they were playing to a couple of hundred. Steadily, and accidentally, somewhat due to the disinterest of their small audiences, they incorporated humour into their act in-between songs.

The changes to their stage show proved to be a success as audience numbers grew steadily thanks to positive word-of-mouth. Requests came in for the duo to do guest spots on television shows, such as *The Barbara McNair Show*, which gave them extensive airtime to showcase their stage act. They even fronted their own 1970 one-off variety hour, *The Sonny & Cher Nitty Gritty Hour*, containing a mix of slapstick comedy, skits and live music.

Although their recording career was still at a low, with a pre-Carpenters *Superstar* and Sonny-penned ballad *Classified 1A* not reaching the US Hot 100 for Cher and *Get It Together* missing out for the duo, Sonny & Cher were offered a chance to guest-host *The Merv Griffin Show*. When their potential was spotted by CBS head of programming Fred Silverman, he offered them the opportunity to do something much more substantial than guest hosting: a chance to star in their own television series.

The Sonny & Cher Comedy Hour premièred on 1 August 1971 and aired weekly for six shows as a summer replacement show. It was a huge ratings success. Millions of viewers per week enjoyed the variety show's mixture of memorable comedy sketches, famous guests and of course, Sonny & Cher's music.

Having released single *Real people* just a couple of months ago in June 1971 to zero success, the duo saw the opportunity to turn their successful, and now televised, stage act into album sales. In September, as their variety show was closing its very successful run on television, Sonny & Cher took advantage and revived their music career — swapping their folk-rock beginnings for adult contemporary material. They released the album *Sonny and Cher Live*. It contained live versions of old hits and covers, and was a success, charting at #35 on the Billboard 200 and ultimately going Gold. Cher's new single, the story song *Gypsy's, Tramps & Thieves* marked a humongous return to success for her, reaching the #1 spot on the US Hot 100 and enjoying a two-week stay there. The song, which some listeners speculate has rape and prostitution in its narrative, also became her biggest UK hit in five years (#4), and eventually sold 3 million copies worldwide. She also released her new album: originally entitled *Chér* then unsurprisingly re-titled *Gypsys Tramps & Thieves*, it was her highest-selling solo album yet, reaching #16 in America (where it spent 45 weeks on the chart).

The husband-and-wife's joint comeback single, October's *All I Ever Need Is You*, was also a massive success. It became their second transatlantic Top 10 single, reaching #7 in the US and #8 in the UK. It sold over a million copies worldwide.

Due to the high ratings of their summer series, their variety show *The Sonny & Cher Comedy Hour* returned full-time to US television with a second series in late-December and was an immediate hit. The show's theme tune was an instrumental version of their 1967 US Top Ten hit *The Beat Goes On* and at the end of most episodes, they would sing their signature hit *I Got You Babe*. Old hits aside, the duo would perform their latest releases during the series, giving their records great exposure — something that was reflected in their sales at the time.

Early 1972 provided more success for the pair. Cher's ballad *The Way Of Love* was another major success, reaching #7 on the US Hot 100 and selling close to a million copies. Titled after their recent hit, the couple's new album *All I Ever Need Is You* became their highest-charting US album since their debut, peaking at #14 — and selling a million copies. Their next single *A Cowboy's Work Is Never Done* was another US top ten hit, reaching #8 and *again*, was a million-seller. At the 1972 Grammy Awards, single *Gypsies, Tramps & Thieves* was nominated for Best Female Pop Vocal Performance and single *All I Ever Need Is You* was nominated for Best Pop Vocal by a Duo or Group.

Superpak, a compilation of Cher's 1960's recordings, hit #92 on the Billboard 200. And 1967's *The Best of Sonny & Cher* returned to the charts for another 17 weeks — bringing its Billboard 200 weeks-on-chart tally to a whopping sixty-four weeks.

Due to the variety show's success, Cher had once again become a major trend-setter. Dressed every week in lavish Bob Mackie-designed gowns and now often sporting various outlandish wigs — something that she would stick with throughout the rest of her career — millions of women watched the show to see what she was wearing. Notably, Cher was the first woman to expose her navel on US television. Moreover, she graced the front cover of fashion magazine *Vogue* five times from April 1972 to February 1975.

"Maybe some people thought I looked ridiculous, but that was okay by me. Look, I'd started out as a skinny little kid from the Valley. And now I'd become a one-named enigma called Cher."

– Cher

In addition to recording music and making a television series, Sonny & Cher were also hitting the road in the little spare time they had on an American tour.

The variety show's second series finished in late March and would not return until September with its third series. While off-air, Sonny & Cher's latest records did not sell as well as their predecessors. Their July 1972 single-only release *When you Say Love* performed moderately, reaching number 32 on the US Hot 100. Cher's solo May ballad about separation *Living In A House Divided* settled at number 22 and its

July parent album *Foxy Lady* stopped at #43. However, when the show returned in September, sales failed to pick-up despite the show's ongoing success. Cher's September solo up-tempo single *Don't Hide Your Love* (penned by Neil Sedaka, who "loved" her interpretation) failed to hit the Top 40 (US#46).

A compilation album consisting of Sonny & Cher's early material, titled *The Two of Us*, reached #122 on the Billboard 200 album chart. Cher's *Superpak Vol.II* reached #97 on the Billboard 200.

Sonny & Cher's fortunes were mixed: their television career was booming; their latest record sales were once again dwindling; and unbeknownst to fans, the couple's relationship was in serious trouble. By November, their marriage had experienced a long slide into crisis and Cher told Sonny — whom had had multiple affairs throughout their relationship — that she wanted to leave him. However, Sonny convinced Cher that she should continue to appear alongside him publicly as a happily married couple for their career's sake.

Trivia: Cher's favourite films are *Godfather* and its sequel *Godfather II.*

The duo made an appearance at the *30th Golden Globe Awards* in January 1973, and whilst the third series of *The Sonny & Cher Comedy Hour* ended in March 1973, the duo made an appearance at the *The 45th Annual Academy Awards* to present the award for 'Best Original Song'.

Sonny & Cher released the lengthy-titled single *Mama Was A Rock And Roll Singer, Papa Used To Write All Her Songs*. It reached just #77 in the US. Its identically-titled parent album only reached #132 — their least successful studio album to-date.

Cher's new album *Bittersweet White Light* was released the next month. It marked a very temporary departure in Cher's recording style; the album consisted mostly of covers of American standards. It only reached #140. Its sole single *Am I Blue* missed out on the US Hot 100 but did reach #79 on the Cash Box Top 100 Singles chart.

If their latest chart showings were anything to go by, Sonny & Cher's music seemed to be falling out of favour with the public once again. However, Cher's next single breathed new life into her solo output: July's *Half Breed* — a story-song about a girl facing racism. It became her third overall #1 hit on the US Billboard Hot 100, spending two weeks there during a 20-week run on the chart. It sold a staggering two-million copies worldwide. Sonny & Cher's new single *The Greatest Show on Earth*, however, failed to chart. Behind closed doors, Sonny's new girlfriend moved in to live under the same roof as Sonny, Cher and Chastity. By the end of the month, Cher found solace in entertainment magnate David Geffen, whom she began dating.

Trivia: Cher owned an appaloosa horse named Red Mark

Cher's latest album, *Half-Breed*, was released in September and would ultimately hit #28 on the US Billboard 200 with a 25-week chart run and a Gold certification from the RI-AA. Cher's career was back on a massive high. Her January 1974 single *Dark Lady* became her third million-selling solo US#1 hit in less than two-and-a-half years, and she won the 'Best Actress – Musical or Comedy Series' Golden Globe award that month for *The Sonny and Cher Comedy Hour*.

"For the year-and-a-half that we did *The Sonny & Cher Comedy Hour* after our separation I didn't have much of a social life. That was a deal I made with Sonny, that I wouldn't go out in public without him."

– Cher

Sonny & Cher's records however, as a duo, remained struggling. *Live in Las Vegas Vol.2*, a sequel to the duo's 1971 US Top 40 live album, only crawled to #175 and their *Greatest Hits* (though just 1970's material) stalled at #146 on the US Billboard 200.

Whilst David Geffen checked over Cher's contract, he pointed out that Sonny had constructed their business so that contractually Sonny owned 95% of *everything* they earned, with the other 5% going to their lawyer. Even worse, Cher was tied up in this contract for two more years. The only way she could be free of the contract was via divorce.

On 20 February 1974, Cher filed for divorce.

Although the *Sonny & Cher Comedy Hour* was expected to return in October, it was cancelled when it became apparent that the duo could no longer work together on the series, despite it being among the Top 10 (#7) top-rated primetime television series of the 1973-74 season as measured by Nielsen Media Research. Unsurprisingly, the divorce of America's most popular showbiz couple became big news.

After receiving a total of fifteen Emmy Award nominations, the last ever episode of *The Sonny & Cher Comedy Hour* aired in March. Two months later, Cher scored another moderate hit with *Train of Thought* (US#27) and then *I Saw A Man & He Danced With His Wife* (US#42) in August.

In September, Sonny starred in his own variety show named *The Sonny Bono Comedy Revue*. As his show began, Cher revealed plans for her own variety show.

In October, Cher's record company released a *Greatest Hits* album. Featuring just solo hits from the last four years, the album only reached #152 on the Billboard 200 Chart. Two Cher singles were issued in November: *Carousel Man* missed out on the US Hot 100 but reached #111 on the Record World 100 Top Pops and #88 on the Canadian singles charts; and *A Woman's Story*, a stand-alone single produced in a reunion with ex-employer Phil Spector, again failed to reach the US Hot 100 but reached #66 on the Cash Box Top 100 Singles chart and #83 on the Canadian singles chart. By the end of the year, Cher's romantic relationship with Geffen had ended — but they remained firm friends and Geffen signed up to be producer of her upcoming solo series. She instead began dating rocker Gregg Allman of the Allman Brothers Band.

Cher's solo show, simply titled *Cher*, debuted on 12 February 1975 with a television special featuring Elton John, Flip Wilson and Bette Midler. The variety show was being produced by Geffen and was an instant success. It showcased Cher in comedy sketches, musical spots and the star herself interviewing other celebrities. By the time the show had debuted, Sonny's show had been cancelled.

"With David Geffen producing, the *Cher* show was a huge success. It knocked off *The Wonderful World of Disney* on Sunday night, which Freddie Silverman and CBS had been trying to do since the year dot."

– Cher

Cher received an Emmy Award nomination for Outstanding Variety, Music or Comedy Series for *Cher,* and in March, her cover of Fontella Bass' 1965 classic *Rescue Me* reached #84 on the Cash Box Top 100 Singles chart and #82 on the Canadian singles chart. Another single from her recent studio sessions with Phil Spector was released in April — a cover of Martha Reeves & The Vandella's *A Love Like Yours (Don't Come Knocking Every Day)*, a duet with *Without You*-singer Harry Nilsson. The lush production failed to chart.

April also saw the release of Cher's new album, *Stars*. Although the album was warmly received by critics, and promoted well, it only reached #153 in America (though has since become a fan-favorite). Its single *Geronimo's Cadillac* failed to chart.

On 30 June, three days after her divorce from Sonny became final, Cher married Gregg Allman. Nine days later, Cher famously filed for divorce when she realized that Allman had serious alcohol and drug problems. Allman instead promised that he would become clean.

In December, Allman himself filed for divorce. He retracted this decision when he and Cher realized that she was pregnant. Before the year's end, Cher ranked at #9 in People Magazine's *25 Most Intriguing People*.

In Jan 1976, season 2 of *Cher* came to an end after 15 episodes. Cher decided not to make any further episodes and surprisingly decided to reunite with Sonny for a new variety show. Less than a month later, in February, Sonny and Cher returned to television sets together in *The Sonny & Cher Show*. The variety show was not much different from their original *The Sonny & Cher Comedy Hour* but instead featured all-new characters and sketches. It opened to high ratings — but these began to steadily decline as the season approached its April finale.

On 10 July, a day after recording finished for a new album, Cher and Gregg Allman's son was born. He was named Elijah Blue Allman. Sometime following his birth, Cher had mastopexy — breast-lift surgery.

"When I was pregnant with Elijah I had a gigantic chest. After the birth, I didn't like the way my breasts looked. And my clothes didn't fit anymore. So I had them just kind of ... tighten up the skin."

– Cher

The Sonny & Cher Show returned in September. In an effort to recapture viewers that it had lost during season one, popular features from their 1971-1974 show were brought back, such as Cher's character Laverne and the famous *Vamp* sketches.

In October, Cher returned to releasing music with her new single *Long Distance Love Affair* and its poorly-promoted parent album, *I'd Rather Believe In You*. Both failed to chart. However, even with record sales at a low and TV viewership decreasing, Cher was highly-popular among the doll-buying public. Toy-makers Mego sold more than 2,000,000 Cher dolls in 1976, making it the company's best-selling toy of 1976.

In January 1977, Cher released her new single *Pirate*. It brought her back to the US Hot 100, alas only to #93. In March, with guest Tina Turner, the season 2 finale of *The Sonny & Cher Show* aired. It would be the last ever episode as the variety show was not renewed for a third season.

The next month, Cher released another album, *Cherished*. Cher was unhappy with the album, only recording it for contractual reasons. It was barely publicized and was ignored by critics and the public, thus not charting. Unsurprisingly, May's single *War Paint and Soft Feathers* failed to enter the charts.

Despite Cher's reluctance, Sonny & Cher reunited to make a single before the year was over. *You're Not Right For Me* — as it was titled — went by unnoticed. It would be their last.

Cher's focus was on her new husband-and-wife duo. In November, she and Gregg Allman released an album together entitled *Two The Hard Way*, under the name "Allman & Woman". The pair embarked on the worldwide *Two The Hard Way Tour*. However, in December, Cher left Allman for good, leaving him in Europe and returning to America with her children, after realizing that he had resumed his alcoholic behaviour. The album was critically-panned and despite the tour, it sold poorly, with no chart appearances.

"By 1978, I was a working single parent with two children and loads of debt. I had to go back to the clubs, and this time on my own."

– Cher

Cher's last three albums had failed to chart and whether she could still attract big numbers on TV was to be tested: on 3 April 1978, Cher starred in her own television special, fittingly entitled *Cher... Special*. The show featuring A-list guest stars Rod Stewart and Dolly Parton, and at one point, Cher playing all the characters in a *West Side Story*-remake. It was a ratings success for its television network, ABC, and was ranked among the top ten most watched programs of the week. Around this time, Cher *legally* changed her full name from Cherilyn Bono Allman to just, amazingly, "Cher".

"I settled on Cher Bono Allman, because I didn't want either of my children to feel left out. One day I woke up and thought *screw this — I don't want either of these names.*"

– Cher

In February 1979, Cher — with full support from her new record label Casablanca — swerved her recording career into a new direction with the release of disco single *Take Me Home*. The new sound was a success as the single climbed all the way to #8 on the US Hot 100, being certified Gold a few months down the line for shifting a million copies. Its identically-titled parent album, consisting mainly of disco songs, was released that same month and was also a big success — it rose to #25 on the American charts, also collecting a Gold certification. One of its tracks was co-written by Cher and another included brief guest vocals by Kiss-rocker Gene Simmons — who Cher was now in a relationship with.

ABC television special *Cher... and Other Fantasies* showcased some of Cher's new album when it hit the small screen in March 1979. The second single from the LP, May's *Wasn't It Good*, proved to be a a moderate success, peaking just inside the Top 50 at #49 in the US.

Cher then began three years of concerts with her first solo tour, *The Take Me Home Tour*, which featured a dozen costume changes, elaborate choreography, two female impersonators and a mechanical bull. The show initially hit the road before taking residence at Las Vegas's Caesars Palace in August.

Cher made a temporary departure from her new-found disco sound with her album's third single, Dolly Parton-cover *It's Too Late (To Love Me Now)*, which gave her a #87 placement on the Billboard Hot Country Singles Chart. Cher made her first proper music video — notably pre-MTV — to promote new single *Hell On Wheels*. Unfortunately, the video, which latched onto the roller-skating trend, didn't help the single to climb any higher than #59 on the US Hot 100. Its parent album *Prisoner* boasted perhaps her most-risqué album cover ever (almost nude, draped in chains). Unfortunately, the album did not chart, despite being released in the same year as its Gold-certified predecessor. *Hell On Wheels* also featured in that year's Linda Blair-starring movie *Roller Boogie* and on its soundtrack album.

Chastity's teacher advised Cher to have her ten-year-old daughter evaluated because she suspected that she may have a learning problem — not only did Cher find out that Chastity had dyslexia, but also that she had it herself.

"They told me that I was dyslexic, too. It was like a big, 'Ohhh...'. Now I understood everything, why I had so much trouble at school. It all fit together."

– Cher

A self-penned disco song, *Bad Love*, appeared in February 1980's Jodie Foster-starring movie *Foxes* and on its soundtrack album — the whole album reached #30 on Billboard's Dance Club Songs chart. The next month, Cher failed to grab another US Hot 100 placement with disco single *Holdin' Out For Love*.

Meanwhile, fellow star Diana Ross was gearing up to release her disco album *Diana* but was unsure about its potential black-and-white minimal un-Diana cover photo. She turned to Cher for advice, whom told her, "You ain't never looked that good". A convinced Ross stuck with it, and the album became her biggest-selling studio set, and thus the cover shot remains iconic.

Cher herself returned to her rock 'n' roll roots, and assembled rock band Black Rose featuring herself on lead vocals and eventual-boyfriend Les Dudek (The Steve Miller Band) on guitar. Despite song-writing credits from Bernie Taupin, Mike Chapman, David Foster and Carole Bayer Sager, their November self-titled album failed to reach the charts, as did lead single *Young and Pretty*, despite a supporting mini-tour and some television promotion. Black Rose's second single *Never Should've Started* also failed to chart when released in February 1981. That same month, American cable channel HBO aired *Standing Room Only: Cher in Concert* — a recording of her ongoing solo tour.

Cher was back at Caesar's Place in January 1981 for her solo *The Take Me Home Tour*, although at some point, it transformed into *A Celebration at Caesar's Place* — a different show with an updated setlist, new costumes, and evidently, a name change. Cher revealed that she was earning $320,000 a week for her performances there. Before her final show at the venue in July, one date was recorded, and later broadcast in 1983 as *Cher: A Celebration at Caesar's* on American cable channel Showtime.

"I was making a fortune on the road, but I was dying inside. Everyone kept saying, 'Cher, there are people who would give anything to have standing room only at Caesar's Place. It would be the pinnacle of their careers.' And I kept thinking, 'Yes, I should be satisfied, I've got to be satisfied. But I wasn't satisfied.'"

– Cher

1981-1995
Working Girl — Cher Earns Hollywood Acclaim

November 1981 saw a surprise return to the UK charts for Cher when she duetted with Meat Loaf, alas uncredited, on the uptempo rock single *Dead Ringer For Love*. Taken from his UK#1 album *Dead Ringer*, the single became his biggest hit in the country, reaching #5 and spending an impressive seventeen weeks on the chart. Cher also featured alongside Meat Loaf in the single's music video, in an all-black leather rock-chick get-up.

Cher had spent five years trying to score an acting role, but Hollywood was evidently against the idea with nobody offering her a chance to read for a part. Cher's ambition to act finally caught the attention of someone willing to give her a chance: unconventional director Robert Altman. He offered her — and Cher accepted — a starring role alongside Sandy Dennis and Karen Black in his Broadway play *Come Back To The 5 & Dime, Jimmy Dean, Jimmy Dean*, which ran from February to April 1981.

Meanwhile, Cher was attempting to rejuvenate her solo music career by releasing the uptempo March single *Rudy*. Unfortunately, the poorly-promoted upbeat pop-rock single failed to chart.

By the end of August, Cher had completely wrapped up the Caesar's Palace performances, and was releasing her next —

and ultimately un-charting, though promoted — single *I Paralyze*.

Starring the same trio as the play, Cher starred in the movie adaptation of Robert Altman's *Come Back To The 5 & Dime, Jimmy Dean, Jimmy Dean*. It premièred in the US in September at the Chicago International Film Festival, after which it reportedly received a ten-minute standing ovation and won the festival's Best Film Award. Altman disallowed major US studios from handling the film, instead allowing newly-found independent film company Cinecom to handle its distribution. This resulted in the film being showed in just four venues across North America, but it still reached #18 at the Box Office. Its $840,958 US gross wasn't the only reflection of the film's reception, as come Golden Globe Awards time, it received a nomination for Best Supporting Actress in a Motion Picture — for Cher.

The release of the new movie coincided with the release of Cher's new pop/rock studio album *I Paralyze*, which failed to chart and would remain her last album for five years, whilst she concentrated on movies.

Cher — who had begun to wear braces to straighten her teeth — was then asked by director Mike Nichols to star alongside Meryl Streep and Kurt Russell in his upcoming film *Silkwood*, based on the last years of labor activist Karen Silkwood. Without knowing what the role was, Cher immediately said "yes" when offered the chance to star alongside Streep in a movie. Through Streep, Cher met actor Val Kilmer, whom she began a relationship with.

Silkwood premièred in December 1983 and reached #1 at the U.S. Box Office before racking up a total gross of $35-million. Come awards season, it scored an array of major nominations, with Cher's portrayal of Karen's unglamorous lesbian friend Dolly Pelliker — a composite of two real-life characters — scooping nominations for Best Supporting Actress at the Oscars, Best Actress in a Supporting Role at the BAFTA's and Best Supporting Actress in a Motion Picture at the Golden Globes. The latter she won. After the film's première, Cher underwent a rhinoplasty procedure to reduce the size of her nose.

Trivia: Meryl Streep and Cher once saved a girl from a huge male mugger in New York City — whilst two male onlookers did nothing.

Cher then scored a leading role in *Mask*, another film based on a real-life character. Directed by Peter Bogdanovich, it told the story of a young boy called Rocky Dennis, played by Eris Stoltz, that suffered from craniodiaphyseal dysplasia — a disorder which causes facial disfigurement and reduces life expectancy. The film, which also starred Sam Elliot, ranked at #2 for three weeks (behind *Police Academy 2: Their First Assignment*) at the U.S. Box Office Chart when released in March 1985. It eventually grossed $48-million and scored high praise. Cher — who was about to begin a brief relationship with actor Tom Cruise — won the Best Actress award at the May Cannes Film Festival and received a nomination for Best Actress in a Motion Picture, Drama at the Golden Globes. It was likely she would receive a Best Actress nomination at the Oscars.

"I didn't get nominated. And the reasons people gave had
nothing to do with my acting. They said I wasn't 'serous'
enough, or I didn't have a last name or that I dated young
men and I didn't dress like a 'serious actress.'"

– Cher

However, reportedly for not being "a serious actress", Cher
was snubbed at the Oscars and so (alongside boyfriend
Joshua Donen, whom she was living with) donned a head-
line-grabbing Mohawk Indian outfit to the March 1986
awards ceremony, where she took to the stage to present an
award, quipping, "As you can see, I got my Academy hand-
book on how to dress as a serious actress".

During a night out at New York club *Heartbreak* in May
1986, Cher met Robert Camilletti — a bagel shop worker
— whom she was to begin a serious relationship with. A few
days later, Cher caused a stir during an appearance on *Late
Night With David Letterman*: when Letterman asked Cher
why she hadn't been on the show before, she answered, "Because I thought you were an a**hole", encouraging applause,
boos and whistles from the studio audience.

In October, Elton John included a song co-written with
Cher, *Don't Trust That Woman*, on his UK-Gold-certified album *Leather Jackets*.

Soon after, Cher — who was now almost-always sporting
black curly wigs in public — began work on a new film, *The
Witches of Eastwick* — a role she had to fight for when director George Miller told her that co-star Jack Nicholson

deemed her "not sexy enough" for it. Cher played the role of one of three witches (the others being Michelle Pfeiffer and Susan Sarandon) opposite Nicholson in the dark comedy/ fantasy film. It topped the U.S. Box Office Chart in June and grossed $63-million.

Trivia: Jack Nicholson helped Cher through a panic attack just before the lunch scene in *The Witches of Eastwick*.

With another two films in the pipeline, someone suggested to Cher that she ought to get back into the recording studio.

October 1987 saw Cher star in the courtroom thriller *Suspect* alongside Dennis Quaid, which ranked at number 3 on the US Box Office Chart and grossed $18-million. That same month, Cher released her first single in five years, with Geffen Records. *I Found Someone*, previously a minor hit for Laura Branigan, became Cher's first US top ten single in the US since 1979, reaching #10. It also reached #5 in the UK, and sold a million copies worldwide. Its music video — which was directed by Cher and co-starred boyfriend Camilletti — was nominated for Best Female Video at that year's MTV Video Music Awards.

In November, she released her own fragrance, *Uninhibited*, which reportedly grossed around $15-million in it first year.

In December, Cher starred in the Norman Jewison-directed romantic comedy *Moonstruck* alongside Nicholas Cage, whom she had personally picked to be her co-star. The film was a tremendous success, grossing $80-million and ending up as the fifth highest-grossing film of the year. Cher's performance as Italian-American accountant Loretta Castorini was highly-praised, and she was bombarded with awards for the role, including Best Actress at the Golden Globe Awards, and even greater, Best Actress at that year's Academy Awards — beating among others, friend Meryl Streep, who jumped up for joy as Cher was announced the winner. During filming of the movie, Cher fell in love with Camilletti, whom joined her as she attended the Oscars. During her speech whilst collecting her golden statuette, after losing an earring on her walk up to the podium, Cher stated, "I don't think this means that I am somebody, but I guess I'm on my way".

Trivia: "During her Oscar acceptance speech, a nervous Cher thanked the likes of her hairstylist and make-up artist but forgot to thank her director, Jewison. She quickly realized and decided to take drastic steps to recognize him. The next day, she took out a full-page ad in Variety thanking the director."

"MGM hated the film and they didn't want to put it out. They said it had no appeal to the audience. They only released it because the movie they decided to release tanked, and we were the only film they had."

– Cher, on *Moonstruck*

Meanwhile, Cher's new pop/rock *Cher* rose to #32 on the US Billboard 200 and was eventually certified Platinum for a million sales. Moreover, it reached #26 in the UK where it received a Gold certification. She was voted #10 in People Magazine's 25 Most Intriguing People of 1987. Before the year's end, it surfaced that all her hard work may have been doing wonders for career, but it was taking its toll on her health — she was diagnosed with fatigue syndrome Epstein-Barr Virus.

In February 1988, Cher appeared once again on *Late Night With David Letterman*, this time in a memorable on-screen reunion with Sonny Bono. After Cher performed her latest hit *I Found Someone*, and took a seat next to old partner Bono for a sit-down interview, Sonny & Cher were asked to musically reunite to sing their signature tune *I Got You Babe*. The appearance won a TV Land Award for Greatest TV Music Moment 19 years on.

Cher's next single, April's *We All Sleep Alone*, peaked at #14 in the US. Again, its (steamy) video co-starred Camilletti. September's dance single *Skin Deep* reached number 79 on the US Hot 100.

Cher made another music video starring Camilletti and herself for the album's fourth single, December's pop/rock ballad *Main Man*, which she had performed during September's MTV Video Music Awards. However, it failed to chart.

Cher turned her focus onto her next Geffen studio album. Lead single *After All* was a duet with Chicago front-man Peter Cetera and was used as the love theme for a new movie entitled *Chances Are*, starring Robert Downey, Jr. and Cybill Shephard. The film was not a hit but the single was. It reached #6 on the US Hot 100, #1 on the Billboard Adult Contemporary chart and received a Gold certification for shifting 500,000 copies. It went on be nominated at the Academy Awards for Best Original Song.

> "He said to me, 'I can't bear to be under the microscope all the time. I love you, but I need to go back home - I miss my life.'"

> **– Cher**

In June, Cher announced that boyfriend Camilletti had split with her after he had a much-publicized altercation with paparazzi — landing him in jail, with a fine, and with community service — and struggled with public life. She rebound with Bon Jovi guitarist Richie Sambora.

Album *Heart of Stone* was released in July and took Cher into the Top 10 (#10) of the Billboard 200 — where she'd never been before solo. It would eventually be certified Triple-Platinum in the US, and has sold over 4.5-million copies worldwide. It topped the albums chart in Australia (where it went Quadruple-Platinum) to become Cher's first ever #1 album. It also received a Platinum certification in the UK, where it reached #7, plus Quadruple-Platinum status in Canada. No doubt about it, much of its success rooted from the album's second single, the Diane Warren-penned *If I Could Turn Back Time*.

> "*If I Could Turn Back Time*... I said, 'I'm not doing this song Diane.' She said, 'I'll pay for it'. Well, she's the cheapest girl in the world. If she's willing to do it, then she must believe in it so much, and I just... I'm gonna do it. I got in the studio and it sang itself."

The rock-ish number featured a risqué music video, with Cher sporting a flesh-bearing body-stocking. In other parts, Cher could be seen straddling a cannon. Daytime airings of the video were banned by MTV, whom ordered for it to be played only after 9PM. The single: reached #3 on the US Hot 100 and went Gold; reached #6 in the UK; #1 in Australia for 6 weeks, where it went Double-Platinum; and sold over 2 million copies worldwide. It became her second consecutive and third overall #1 on Billboard's Adult Contemporary chart. Cher performed the song wearing the music video's outfit at the 1989 MTV Video Music Awards. Cher was then named Favorite All-Around Female Star at People's Choice Awards.

Cher embarked on an 8-date mini-tour, *The Heart of Stone Tour*, in the US in support of the album before releasing new hit singles *Just Like Jesse James* (million-seller, US#8, UK#11, despite no music video) and *Heart of Stone* (US#20). Her Epstein-Barr virus came into full play as she struggled to shoot new movie *Mermaids* but fought it enough, with help from antibiotics, to resume her tour in March 1990, taking it around the world and grossing $40-million along the way. However, she was left physically exhausted, had multiple bouts of pneumonia — which almost killed her — and was forced to seriously wind back her working hours.

"By the time I made *Mermaids*, in 1990, my immune system was completely shot. My glands were always swollen, and I was on and off antibiotics for two years straight."

– Cher

She starred in ABC special *An Evening With... Friends of the Environment* alongside Bette Midler, Goldie Hawn, Meryl Streep, Olivia Newton-John and Robin Williams. In June, she provided track *Trail of Broken Hearts* for the hit soundtrack album of Tom Cruise's movie *Days of Thunder*. Around this time, she became the spokesperson and a key donor of Children's Craniofacial Association - a charity which helps individuals, and the families of those, with facial anomalies.

Co-starring Bob Hoskins, Winona Ryder and Christina Ricci, Cher's new movie — 1960's-based comedy/drama *Mermaids* — finally opened just before Christmas. With competition from the likes of *Home Alone*, *Look Who's Talking Too* and *Edward Scissorhands*, the film only opened at #6 at the US Box Office and garnered a so-so total gross of $35-million.

The film saw Cher play a glamorous and eccentric single mother in her early 30's (despite being 43 in real-life during shooting) whom frequently relocates homes with her daughters — Cher only had to look at her real mother for inspiration for the role. It was supported by a moderately successful (US#65) soundtrack album. For it, Cher recorded renditions of 1960's much-covered classics *Baby I'm Yours* and *The Shoop Shoop Song (It's In His Kiss)*. The former was released in the UK but did not chart in the Top 75. The latter peaked at a decent #33 in the States but was a *triumphant* success in Europe, especially in the UK where it spent 5 weeks at number one and became the top-selling female song of the year. The song sold well over a million copies worldwide.

In Januray 1991, she released a book co-authored with nutritionist Robert Haas called *Forever Fit: The Lifetime Plan For Health*, which reportedly sold 100,000 copies that year. In February, the Emmy Award-nominated *Cher ...At The Mirage* — a taping of her recent tour — was broadcast on CBS, gaining 17.5-million viewers. (A video release of it followed the next year.)

Cher was back in June 1991 with a new single and studio album. *Love & Understanding* reached #17 in the US and #10 in the UK. Parent album *Love Hurts* saw contrasting chart performances on each side of the Atlantic: it reached a disappointing #48 in the US (though was certified Gold) but spent 6 weeks at number 1 in the UK, becoming the top-selling female studio album of the year there. It achieved big success across Europe and sold over two-million copies worldwide.

Cher's decline in record sales in the US was largely attributed to her appearing in an array of infomercials for health, beauty and diet products. Aired repeatedly every day on US television, they made Cher an easy target for comics, with Cher herself even stating that they were "a smarmy thing to do".

"The backlash was huge. I was riding so high after the Academy Award. Now I was a joke. There's nothing like an infomercial to slam-dunk your ass."

– Cher

She released one of the most-successful and fastest-selling fitness videos of all-time, *CherFitness: A New Attitude*, which sold 1.5 million copies in the US and 300,000 in the UK. *Save Up All Your Tears* — previously a minor hit single by Bonnie Tyler — was Cher's next single, charting at #37 on both sides of the Atlantic. A rock ballad version of the much-covered ballad *Love Hurts* (most famously by Nazareth) (UK#43) and *Could've Been You* (UK#31) followed in the UK whilst *When Lovers Become Strangers* became a Top 40 hit in Canada.

1992 saw Cher win an ECHO Award in Germany (their version of the Grammy's) for Best International Female Artist. She appeared as herself in a cameo role in Robert Altman's critically-acclaimed movie *The Player* starring Tim Robbins, as the one guest to turn up in a red dress at a shindig with a black-and-white dress-code. She also released a second fitness video, *CherFitness: Body Confidence*, which became the best-selling fitness video of 1993 in the UK, selling 350,000 copies. The same year, she was unveiled as one of Madame Taussauds Wax Museum's "5 Most Beautiful Women of History".

Cher began her *Love Hurts Tour* in April — the tour faced numerous postponements and cancellations due to Cher's

Epstein-Barr Virus. A total of 26 shows were played, with US dates being postponed for five months. It eventually grossed a healthy $20-million.

In November, she released a cover of sixties classic *Oh No Not My Baby*, which reached #33 in the UK. It was one of three unreleased songs from the Geffen label vaults that appeared on that same month's album, *Cher's Greatest Hits: 1965-1992*. The collection spent a massive 7 weeks at #1 in the UK, achieved Triple-Platinum status there with sales above one-million and was the best-selling female album of the year. It sold over 1.5-million copies worldwide. The other two new songs *Many Rivers To Cross (Live From The Mirage)* (UK#37) and *Whenever You're Near* (#72) hit the UK singles chart in early 1993. For the second consecutive year, she was nominated for Best International Female Star at Germany's ECHO Awards.

In March 1993, Cher's first music video collection, namely *The Video Collection*, was released. Sonny & Cher's *I Got You Babe* made a brief return to the UK charts in May 1993 due to its repeated presence in that year's $70-million-grossing Bill Murray-starring movie *Groundhog Day*. June 1994 saw Cher team up with popular cartoon characters Beavis & Butt-head for a cover of that same song. It was supported by a video starring the two animated characters alongside the real Cher in a biker get-up. It hit the British Top 40, reaching #35. Cher also teamed up with musician Larry Adler for a jazzy cover of *It Ain't Necessarily So* for his multi-artist UK#2 album *The Glory of Gershwin*. The song was given a limited single release.

In December, Cher played herself for a second time in a cameo role in a Robert Altman movie — this time, in the poorly-received *Pret-a-porter*, starring Marcello Mastroianni and Sophia Loren.

Before the year's end, Cher journeyed to a songwriter's retreat in France to write a new album. However, Rob Dickins, head of Warner Music UK, refused to release the album on its WEA label — which Cher was now signed to — for it being "not commercial". Therefore, the album, an acoustic-rock collection, got shelved. She also started a mail-order catalogue business called *Sanctuary*, selling Gothic-themed products

March 1995 saw British charity Comic Relief ask Cher, Chrissie Hynde and Neneh Cherry — along with Eric Clapton on guitar — to perform their 1995 charity single *Love Can Build A Bridge*. It spent one week at #1 in the UK. In April, Cher's daughter Chastity "came out" as a lesbian with LGBT magazine *The Advocate*.

"When I found out that Chas was gay, I went ballistic! What added insult to injury was finding out that everyone else in the solar system knew but me!"

– Cher

Cher returned to the recording studio to record an album of mostly covers (of mostly male songs) entitled *It's A Man's World*. Lead single, October's *Walking In Memphis* — a cover of Marc Cohn's self-penned 1991 hit — reached #11 in the UK. The album, released in November, reached #10 in the UK (and eventually went Gold) as its second single, January 1996's *One By One*, also became a Top Ten hit (#7).

In April, the album's third UK single, *Not Enough Love In The World*, reached #31. That same month, Cher starred in the Paul Mazursky-directed dark-comedy movie *Faithful* alongside Ryan O'Neal and Chazz Palminteri, based on the latter actor's screenplay. Cher was unhappy with the final product and refused to promote it — resulting in a poor performance at the US Box Office, grossing just $2.1-million. Cher has since always excluded the film from her filmography during her tour's movie sections.

June saw *It's A Man's World* finally get its US release, though remixed with an R&B flavour. Although a brave move, the gamble did not pay off, as it stalled at #64. The remixed version of *One By One* peaked at a low #52, but was played over the closing credits of September 1996 HBO television movie *If These Walls Could Talk*, which had three half-hour segments: one starring Demi Moore; one Sissy Spacek; and one Cher, as Dr. Beth Thompson. 50-year-old Cher, who directed her segment and wrote some of its script, was nominated for Best Supporting Actress in a Series, Mini-Series or Motion Picture Made for TV at the Golden Globe Awards and Satellite Awards. About abortion in different eras, it became the highest-rated movie in HBO history, pulling in 6.9-million viewers.

July saw the album's fourth UK single, a cover of The Walker Brothers' dramatic *The Sun Ain't Gonna Shine Anymore*, reach #26 in the UK. In December, *Paradise Is Here* (a cover of a 1986 Tina Turner track) was released as the album's second-and-final US single — it failed to enter the US Hot 100.

Cher's music played a large role in the November 1997 *The X-Files* episode *The Post-Modern Prometheus*, which concerned a deformed man who adored Cher because of her role in *Mask*. The episode attracted 18.68-million viewers — the 11th most-watched programme of the week.

1998-2018
Believe – Cher Claims Her Goddess Of Pop Title

Cher received a telephone call from daughter Chastity in January 1998, telling her that Sonny had passed away. On January 5 1998, 62-year-old Sonny — now a successful politician — died of injuries from hitting a tree whilst skiing in Lake Tahoe. Cher was asked to give the eulogy at his funeral. Unbeknownst to her, it was to be broadcast live on television. Tearfully speaking, Cher stated that without Sonny, there would not have been Cher, before adding that Sonny was "The most unforgettable character I've ever met."

"When you've known someone your entire life, you don't think of them being able to leave you. Even if you're angry with one another, or you move to Africa, or they join some religious cult, they're never just going to not be there. This is how I felt about Son."

– Cher

In May, Sonny & Cher were honoured with a "star" on the Hollywood Walk of Fame for their television work. Cher also starred in CBS television special *Sonny & Me: Cher Remembers*, providing a look at their years together. The special was the 13th most-watched programme of the week, attracting 9.9-million viewers. And in November, Cher released her autobiography, *The First Time*, which she dedicated to "Son".

The book was a collection of personal and career first experiences as opposed to being a showbiz tell-all.

"I was at a really low point in my career and I'd been dropped by my record company. The head of Warner UK, this amazing man named Rob Dickens, he gave me the chance to have a career again. I went there alone because my manager had left me. I was liking a singing Lazarus."

– Cher

In October, Cher headed in a different music direction with new dance single *Believe*. The song became Cher's best-selling single of all-time, selling a whopping 7-million copies. It topped the singles charts in over 20 countries including the US (4 weeks) and the UK (7 weeks). It remains the best-selling single by a female solo singer in the UK (1.8-million copies) and Cher remains the oldest solo female singer to top the singles chart on both sides of the Atlantic. The single gave her the US record of largest gap between US#1's (25 years) plus the longest span of #1's (34 years). It received nominations at the Grammy Awards for Record of The Year and Best Dance Recording — the latter it won, becoming Cher's first Grammy Award win. It also won a Billboard Music Award for Single Of The Year. The song is notable for being the first hit single to use auto-tune for effect — since nicknamed "the cher effect".

Her new album, also called *Believe*, was released in October too. Similarly, it became her best-selling album of all-time, selling over 11-million copies worldwide and gaining at least

Gold status in 39 countries including 6-times-Platinum status in Canada, 5-times-Platinum in Denmark and 4-times-Platinum in Spain. It took her to a new solo high of #4 on the Billboard 200 in the US (where it was certified 4-times-Platinum) plus topped the charts in Germany (where it sold a million copies) and reached #7 in the UK, where it was certified Double-Platinum. It received a nomination at the Grammy Awards for 'Best Pop Album'.

Cher began 1999 by performing a solid rendition of US national anthem *The Star Spangled Banner* at that year's Super Bowl, which was watched by 83.7-million viewers. She won a World Music Award for Lifelong Contribution to the Music Industry, at a ceremony which saw Britney Spears perform *The Beat Goes On* as a tribute, and also won an American Fashion Award for her Influence in Fashion.

February 1999 saw the release of Cher's next single, the disco-influenced *Strong Enough*. It sold over a million copies worldwide and reached #5 in the UK but only reached #57 in the US — although (like predecessor *Believe*) it topped the Billboard Dance Club Songs chart.

The next month, Cher starred alongside British film icons Judi Dench and Maggie Smith in Franco Zeffirelli's BAFTA-nominated semi-autobiographical period movie *Tea With Mussolini*. It received a so-so reception at the US Box Office, grossing $14-million.

April saw Cher performing *If I Could Turn Back Time* and *Believe*, and *Proud Mary* with Tina Turner and Elton John, on the fund-raising VH-1 special *Divas Live '99*, which became the network's most-watched show ever with 9-million viewers. The show's DVD and CD releases were both certified Gold in the US.

June saw the release of dance-pop single *All or Nothing*, which was a moderate hit, reaching #12 in the UK and again, topping Billboard's Dance Club Songs chart. Its music video consisted of concert footage taken from Cher's new *Do You Believe? Tour*. The 121-date tour took her to 1.5-million fans across North America and Europe to gross $160-million. Its August companion HBO special *Cher: Live in concert - From the MGM Grand in Las Vegas* attracted 6-million viewers, becoming the network's highest-rated original programme of the year. It received seven Emmy Award nominations — including Individual Performance in a Variety or Music Program for Cher — and was turned into a successful DVD, *Live In Concert*.

If I Could Turn Back Time — Cher's Greatest Hits, containing previously unreleased Geffen-era track *Don't Come Cryin' To Me*, was released in the US in August, where it only reached #57 but went on to score a million sales and a Gold certification. October single — and the last from Cher's latest studio album — *Dov'è L'Amore* became another moderate hit, reaching #21 in the UK. Upon hearing the track before the albums' release, an impressed Madonna declared that it must be the album's first single and stated that she wanted to direct its music video, which never came to fruition.

In November, *The Greatest Hits* was released outside the US to great success. It went Top Ten in over a dozen countries, including the UK (#7) and became her second consecutive #1 album in Austria, Denmark and Germany.

Cher's 1994 self-written shelved album — that was rejected by her label for being "not commercial" — was finally released in 2000, online, with the fitting title *Not.com.mercial*. Cher won a Blockbuster Entertainment Award that year for Favorite Female Artist.

In November, she appeared as herself in an episode of US comedy *Will & Grace,* entitled *Gypsys, Tramps & Weeds* — it became the show's second-highest-rated episode, with 22-million viewers, and was ranked #7 in Q Magazine's Top 10 Greatest Rock Star Cameos.

In 2001, Cher won a Bambi Lifetime Achievement Award in Germany whilst readers of A&E's *Biography Magazine* ranked Cher #3 in a poll of their favourite actress of all-time. She co-wrote duet *Più Che Puoi* with Italian singer Eros Ramazzotti for his multi-million-selling album *Stilelibero*. It was released as a single, becoming a top 20 hit in Belgium, Switzerland and Italy.

In November — and now often sporting blond wigs — Cher released new single *The Music's No Good Without You*. The auto-tune-laden dance number reached #8 in the UK — giving her UK Top Ten singles in five consecutive decades. Its parent album *Living Proof* was also released that month. It surprisingly stalled at just #46 in the UK but reached #9 in the US when released in February 2002. The US's lead single from the album was the 9/11-dedicated *Song For The Lonely*, which peaked at #85, and #18 in Canada. It reached #1 on Billboard's Dance Club Songs chart.

Trivia: Cher's favorite song from her own discography is *Song For The Lonely*.

In May, Cher returned to *Will & Grace*, for a cameo in hour-long episode *A.I.: Artificial Insemination*, which attracted 23.7-million viewers and saw her perform upcoming single *A Different Kind of Love Song*. The next month saw her return to VH1's *Diva* series, in *Divas Las Vegas* and its accompanying CD and DVD releases. July's *A Different Kind of Love Song* became Cher's fifth Billboard Dance Club Songs chart #1. Meanwhile, *Alive Again* became a Top 30 hit in Germany .

She was named Dance Club Songs Artist of the Year at the 2002 Billboard Music Awards, where she also received an Artist Achievement Award — one of only four artists to do so.

"Touring is really difficult, it's lonely. Going from one city to another, the isolation is rough. The show is the fun part."

– Cher

In June, she kicked off her *mammoth* 326-date *The Farewell Tour*. During it, Cher performed some of her greatest hits to over 5.88-million fans in 20 countries whilst grossing a whopping $250-million. It finished as the top-grossing tour ever by a female artist. A television special of it was broadcast on NBC, where it was watched by 17-million viewers — easily making it the #1 concert special of the 2002/03 TV season. For it, Cher was given her first Emmy Award, for Outstanding Variety, Music or Comedy special. A DVD of it was then released in August, which has sold over 600,000 copies worldwide and has Triple-Platinum status in the US and 8-times-Platinum in Australia.

"It defies the laws of pop gravity. Most people who she started out with are dead or way off the map of pop culture."

- – David Wild

- Contributing Editor, *Rolling Stone Magazine*

February 2003 saw the release of double A-side single *When The Money's Gone / Love On Another*. Neither were promoted but the former song became Cher's 6th #1 on Billboard's Dance Club Songs chart and the latter received a Grammy Award nomination for Best Dance Recording.

The Very Best of Cher was released in April 2003 and became a huge hit in the US, where it reached #4 and was certified Double-Platinum. It received a Gold certification in the UK — Cher's 9th consecutive album to do so. It sold over 3 million copies worldwide. Her first solo live album *Live - The Farewell Tour* was released in August, hitting #40 in the US. Both albums were also compiled together as *The Very Best of Cher - Special Edition*, reaching #83 on the US Billboard 200.

In December, Cher played a diva-ish version of herself in the comedy film *Stuck On You*, starring Matt Damon and Greg Kinnear. It grossed $65-million worldwide and peaked at #3 on the US Box Office chart. A new track *Human* featured in the film and on its end credits. Before year's end, Cher did a duet of show tune *Bewitched, Bothered & Bewildered* with Rod Stewart, which hit #17 on Billboard's Adult Contemporary chart, and was featured on his Multi-Platinum album *As Time Goes By: the Great American Songbook, Volume II*.

Containing the majority of Cher's music videos, the seemingly-hastily-released DVD *The Very Best of Cher: The Video Hits Collection* appeared on store shelves in June 2004. It went Platinum in the US and Australia.

In March 2005, Cher was awarded the VH1 Music First Award — recognizing legends in music — at the first MTV Australia Video Music Awards. She remains the sole winner of the award. The next month, she completed her *The Farewell Tour* and went into retirement.

In October, An All-Star Tribute To Cher was released, an album featuring covers of Cher songs by other singers, such as *The Beat Goes On* by Tiffany, *Take Me Home* by Anita Pointer, *Just Like Jesse James* by Lynn Anderson and *Save Up All Your Tears* by Freda Payne.

Cher — who had been very active every year for the last forty years — was seldom seen in 2006 and '07. September 2006 saw her being voted by the British public as the country's favourite female pop star on TV show *Battle Of The Popstars Live.*

She was back in May 2008 to began an almost-three-year residency at Caesar's Palace in Las Vegas, entitled *Cher At The Colosseum*, in which she performed her hits and covers in an elaborate and very technical stage show. 192 shows were played, grossing $97-million. The show was promoted in a special Cher and Tina Turner episode of *The Oprah Winfrey Show*. Cher was given a Legend Award at the Armenian Music Awards before year's end.

Between 2008 and 2010, Sonny and Cher's daughter Chastity Bono underwent a gender transition to become male and adopted the name Chaz Bono.

"I called one day and the answering message came on and it was Chaz as a girl. I thought 'oh my god, I am never going to hear that voice again'. It was a sense of mourning. I said to Chaz is there any way I can keep that and 'Chaz said I don't think so, Mum'. Now it doesn't make any difference as I don't feel a loss at all. The loss I thought I was going to feel, I don't feel one iota."

– Cher

In 2010, Cher starred as Tess alongside Christina Aguilera in her first musical film *Burlesque*. It opened at #3 at the US Box Office and grossed $89-million worldwide. The film's soundtrack album contained two Cher songs: *Welcome To Burlesque* and the Golden Globe Award-winning ballad *You Haven't Seen The Last of Me*. The album was a worldwide success: it was certified Platinum in Australia (#2), Gold in the US (#18), Canada (#16) and Japan (#8), and Silver in the UK. It reached #1 on the Taiwan International Albums Chart, where it was certified Double-Platinum. The afore-mentioned Cher ballad, written by *If I Could Turn Back Time*-composer Diane Warren, was remixed and became her 7th #1 on Billboard's Dance Club Songs chart — which granted her the record of having Billboard #1 hits in six con-secutive decades.

As well as Lifetime Achievement Award honours at the Glamour Women of the Year Awards and Spain's Los Pre-mios 40 Principales, Cher was honoured with a hand and footprint ceremony at Grauman's Chinese Theater — the same theatre in which she had watched *Dumbo* sixty years earlier.

In early 2011, Cher and her family members appeared in her son's Emmy Award-nominated and GLAAD Media Award-winning documentary *Becoming Chaz*. In July 2011, she voiced character Janet the Lioness in the family comedy film *Zookeeper* starring Kevin James — it grossed $169-million worldwide. She also sang Boston's *More Than A Feeling* with the cast over its closing credits. In October, Cher revealed that she was working on a Broadway play based on her life: one actress will portray a "young" Cher from the 1960's that "asks for stardom"; a second one will portray Cher in the middle portion of her career; whilst the third will play cur-rent Cher whom "asks for guidance".

In 2012, Cher unearthed a shelved 1980's album recorded by her mother Georgia Holt and simultaneously began working on a documentary about her mother's life. They both turned into commercial products the following year: album *Honky Tonk Woman* hit #43 on Billboard's Top Country Charts; and TV special *Dear Mom, Love Cher* aired on US cable channel LifeTime, attracting 1.2-million viewers, and later winning Cher a Women's Image Network Award for Best Show Produced By A Woman whilst being nominated for Outstanding Documentary Film. The album included a duet between Georgia and Cher, namely *I'm Just Your Yesterday*, which the pair performed on *The Ellen DeGeneres Show*.

In October 2012, a portion of Cher's planned comeback single, the dance anthem *Woman's World*, was leaked online, which forced the singer to make plans of releasing it sooner. However, the single was not released until June 2013. She performed it on NBC's *The Voice* and it became her 8th #1 hit on Billboard's Dance Club Songs chart. In September, she released her first studio album in 12 years, *Closer To The Truth*. It gave Cher her highest debut ever on the Billboard 200 (#3), her highest solo position on the chart (again, #3), and expanded her span of US Top 3 albums to 48 years. The album also brought Cher back to the UK Top Five for the first time since 1992's *Cher's Greatest Hits: 1965-1992*, and was later certified Silver. It also reached #4 in Canada and was certified Gold.

"Now it's crazy, everyone takes your picture and it's like in two seconds on Instagram and Facebook and I don't like

that. I don't really like that at all. That's the only thing I
don't like about my job"

– Cher

October single, ballad and Miley Cyrus-cover *I Hope You
Find It* (UK#25), made her the oldest female artist to score
a UK Top 30 hit with a new recording and increased her
span of UK Top 40 solo hits to *six* consecutive decades before becoming her 31st hit on Billboard's Adult Contemporary chart. That month, she offered $500,000 for the release
of an elephant named Billy from confinement in Los Angeles Zoo to a sanctuary.

In November, she performed *I Hope You Find It* and signature hit *Believe* whilst guest-judging on a Cher-themed
episode of ABC's *Dancing With The Stars* — watched by
13.7-million viewers. November's co-written *Take It Like A
Man* became a #2 hit on the Billboard Dance Club Songs
chart as did 2014's bango-led P!nk-penned *I Walk Alone*.
Ballad *Sirens* from Cher's latest studio set was included on
the multi-artist US#28 digital album *Songs For The Philippines*, released in aid of Typhoon Haiyan victims.

In March 2014, Cher came out of touring retirement and
embarked on her North American *Dressed To Kill Tour*. It
ended its first leg with a gross of $55-million, becoming the
world's top grossing female tour in the mid-year chart. However, Cher had to postpone the tour due to having an infection that affected her kidney function.

"Every once in a while I think, 'Jesus, you're so old! How did
this happen?' I haven't looked in the mirror in years. The only time I was happy with the way I looked was when I was,
like, 40 to 45."

– Cher

Cher was honoured with the amfAR Award of Inspiration
at the fifth annual Inspiration Gala São Paulo in April 2015.
The following month, Cher made a surprise appearance on
the final season of *Late Show With David Letterman* — donning the same outfit as she did on the show during Sonny
& Cher's 1987 reunion episode. At 69-years-old, Cher mod-
elled for Marc Jacobs' Fall 2015 advertising campaign.

Cher recorded vocals for hip-hop group Wu-Tan Clan's new
studio album *Once Upon a Time in Shaolin...* — of which only one copy was made and auctioned off to the highest bid-
der, reportedly selling for a price that was "in the millions" in
late 2015.

In October 2016, Cher announced that she would return to
the stage in February 2017, with *Classic Cher*, a residency
show containing her biggest hits, set to take place in Las Vegas and Washington, DC. The following month, it was revealed that Sonny & Cher's 1965 US#1 *I Got You Babe was*
among twenty-five songs to be inducted into the Grammy
Hall Of Fame in 2017.

Trivia: As of June 2018, Cher has over 3,600,000 followers
on Twitter, and has been nominated for the 'Must Follow
Artist on Twitter' MTV O Music Award (2011), as well as

Shorty Award nominations for 'Best Singer on Social Media' (2016) and 'Best Celebrity on Social Media' (2017).

Cries from Syria, a documentary film about the Syrian Civil War, premièred at the Sundance Festival in January 2017. For it, Cher recorded the Diane Warren-penned track *Prayers For This World*, which was nominated for Best Original Song at the Satellite Awards.

March saw the release of *Edith+Eddie*, a short film based on the true and tragic story of America's oldest interracial newlyweds, Edith Hill (96) and Eddie Harrison (95). Cher served as an executive producer of the film and led a successful awards campaign for it and its director Laura Checkoway, earning them no less than half-a-dozen film festival awards, as well as an Oscar nomination for Best Documentary Short Subject. On May 21, one day after her 71st Birthday, Cher performed two of her signature hits, *If I Could turn Back Time* and *Believe*, whilst accepting the Icon Award at the Billboard Music Awards.

Cher voiced the character Chercophonie in an August episode of Netflix original animation *Home: Adventures with Tip & Oh*, including the performance of solo song *Ooga Boo*. In October, Cher revealed her upcoming appearance in July 2018's *Mamma Mia: Here We Go Again*, in which she'll perform the Abba tracks *Super Trouper* and *Fernando* — the latter she performed for the first time at April 2018's CinemaCon in Las Vegas.

In May 2018, two months after receiving an overwhelming response to her performance at the 40th annual Mardi Gras in Sydney, Cher announced her first Australian tour for thirteen years: the September-October 2018 *Here We Go Again Tour*. In June, Cher revealed that she had recorded the majority of her 26th solo studio album.

After a small June run in Chicago, *The Cher Show*, a musical based on the life of Cher, is set to open on Broadway in December 2018 — its synopsis reads: "The Cher Show is 35 smash hits, six decades of stardom, two rock-star husbands, a Grammy, an Oscar, an Emmy, and enough Bob Mackie gowns to cause a sequins shortage in New York City, all in one unabashedly fabulous new musical."

"I feel like a bumper car. If I hit a wall, I'm backing up and going in another direction. And I've hit plenty of fucking walls in my career. But I'm not stopping. I think maybe that's my best quality: I just don't stop."

– Cher

The Cher Discography

Albums

Sonny & Cher released their début album *Look At Us* in 1965. It went all the way to #2 on the US Billboard 200 — a position that it held for a whopping eight weeks! Cher's solo debut studio album *All I Really Want To Do* followed it to the Top 20, and stayed on the charts for an impressive six months. Both folk-rock albums sold over a million copies, whilst reaching the UK Top 10. By the end of the 1960's, Cher had managed to place a total of eight studio albums on the US album chart.

Cher began the 1970's by once again releasing million-selling studio albums both solo (*Gypsys, Tramps & Thieves*) and with Sonny (*All I Ever Need Is You*). These two Gold-certified adult-contemporary releases were followed by seven more charting studio albums by decade's end — one with Sonny and six solo — including the Gold-certified *Half-Breed* and the predominantly-disco *Take Me Home*.

Whilst most of her 1960's contemporaries had completely fallen off the hit albums radar by the 1980's, 1987's pop-rock self-titled *Cher* became Cher's her first Platinum-certified release in the US and first Gold-certified release in the UK. 1989's follow-up *Heart of Stone* did even better and became her first #1 album ever, when it topped the Australian album charts. It also became her first US top 10 album and was certified 3-times-Platinum there for shifting 3-million copies.

1991's multi-million-selling *Love Hurts* spent a remarkable six weeks at #1 in the UK and was certified Triple-Platinum, and was the best-selling female studio album of that year there. A move to dance-pop saw *Believe* become her biggest-selling album of all-time when released in 1998, selling over 11-million copies and being certified at least Gold in almost forty countries — including Quadruple-Platinum in the US. 2001's US top ten *Living Proof* became Cher's 6th consecutive studio album to be certified at least Gold in the UK.

Of course Cher's strong back-catalogue has given her huge success with compilation albums. Her first of such was 1967's *The Best of Sonny & Chér*, which spent a notable sixty-seven weeks on the US chart. *Greatest Hits: 1965-1992* spent a grand seven weeks at #1 in the UK, going Triple-Platinum and becoming the top-selling female album of the year there. Altogether, 1999's European chart-topping *The Greatest Hits* and 2003's US Top 5 *The Very Best of Cher* have sold over 5.5 million copies worldwide.

Cher — who has spent over 950 weeks on the US album chart — has also seen success with live and soundtrack albums, including Gold-certified albums *Sonny & Chér Live* (1971) and 2010's *Burlesque: Original Motion Picture Soundtrack*.

2013 saw Cher release her first studio album in twelve years, *Closer To The Truth*. It gave Cher her highest chart début ever on the Billboard 200 (#3), her highest solo position on the chart (#3), and expanded her span of US Top 3 albums to an astounding 48 years! Cher revealed in June 2018 that she is working on her 26th solo studio album.

Studio Albums

Look At Us

(with Sonny)

August 1965

Side 1: *I Got You Babe; Unchained Melody; Then He Kissed Me; Sing C'est La Vie; It's Gonna Rain*

Side 2: *500 Miles; Just You; The Letter; Let It Be Me; You Don't Love Me; You've Really Got A Hold On Me; Why Don't They Let Us Fall In Love*

US#2; 44 weeks on chart; Gold certification

UK#7; 13 weeks on chart

All I Really Want To Do

September 1965

Side 1: *All I Really Want To Do; I Go To Sleep; Needles and Pins; Don't Think Twice; She Thinks I Still Care; Dream Baby*

Side 2: *The Bells Of Rhymney; Girl Don't Come; See See Rider; Come And Stay With Me; Cry Myself To Sleep; Blowin' In The Wind*

US#16; 24 weeks on chart

UK#7; 9 weeks on chart

The Wondrous World Of Sonny & Chér

(with Sonny)

April 1966

Side 1: *Summertime; Tell Him; I'm Leaving It All Up To You; But You're Mine; Bring It On Home To Me; Set Me Free*

Side 2: *What Now My Love; Leave Me be; I Look For You; Laugh At Me; Turn around; So Fine*

US#34; 20 weeks on chart

UK#17; 7 weeks on chart

The Sonny Side Of Chér

April 1966

Side 1: *Bang Bang (My Baby Shot Me Down); Elusive Butterfly; Where Do You Go; Our Day Will Come; The Girl From Ipanema; It's Not Unusual*

Side 2: *Like A Rolling Stone; Time; Come To Your Window; Old Man River; Milord; A Young Girl (Une Enfante)*

US#26; 19 weeks on chart

UK#11; 11 weeks on chart

Chér

September 1966

Side 1: *Sunny; Twelfth Of Never; You Don't Have To Say You Love Me; I Feel Something In The Air (Magic In The Air); Will You Love Me Tomorrow; Until Its Time For You To Go*

Side 2: *Cruel War; Catch The Wind; Pied Piper; Homeward Bound; I Want You; Alfie*

US#59; 16 weeks on chart

In Case You're In Love

(with Sonny)

March 1967

Side 1: *The Beat Goes On; Groovy Kind Of Love; You Baby; Monday; Love Don't Come; Podunk*

Side 2: *Little Man; We'll Sing In The Sunshine; Misty Roses; Stand By Me; Living For You; Cheryl's Goin' Home*

US#45; 29 weeks on chart

With Love, Chér

November 1967

Side 1: *You Better Sit Down Kids; But I Can't Love You More; Hey Joe; Mama (When My Dollies Have Babies); Behind The Door*

Side 2: *Sing For Your Supper; Look At Me; There But For Fortune; I Will wait For You; The Times They-Are-A-Changin'*

US#47; 14 weeks on chart

Backstage

July 1968

Side 1: *Go Now; Carnival; It All Adds Up Now; Reason To Believe; Masters Of War; Do You Believe In Magic*

Side 2: *I Wasn't Ready; A House Is Not A Home; Take Me For A Little While; The Impossible Dream (The Quest); The Click Song Number One; Song Called Children*

3614 Jackson Highway

August 1969

Side 1: *For What's It's Worth; (Just Enough To Keep Me) Hangin' On; (Sittin' On the Dock Of The Bay); Tonight I'll Be Staying Here With You; I Threw It All Away; Walk On Guilded Splinters*

Side 2: *Lay Baby Lay; Please Don't Tell Me; Cry Like A Baby; Do Right Woman, Do Right Man; Save The Children*

(2001 CD re-issue bonus tracks: *Easy To Be Hard; I Believe; Danny Boy; Momma Looks Sharp; It Gets Me Where I Want to Go; You've Made Me So Very Happy; Yours Until Tomorrow; The Thought Of loving You; The First Time; Chastity's Song (Band Of Thieves); Chastity's Song (Band Of Thieves) (Stereo Album Version); Superstar*)

US#160; 3 weeks on chart

Chér (renamed **Gypsys, Tramps & Thieves**)

September 1971

Side 1: *The Way Of Love; Gyspys, Tramps & Thieves; He'll Never Know; Fire And Rain; When You Find Out Where You're Goin' Let Me Know;* (UK Bonus track: *Classified 1A*)

Side 2: *He Ain't Heavy, He's My Brother; I Hate To Sleep Alone; I'm In The Middle; Touch And Go; One Honest Man;* (UK bonus track: *Don't Put It On Me*)

US#16; 45 weeks on chart; Gold certification

All I Ever Need Is You

(with Sonny)

February 1972

Side 1: *All I Ever Need Is You; Here Comes that Rainy Day Feeling; More Today Than yesterday; Crystal Clear/Muddy Waters; United We Stand*

Side 2: *A Cowboy's Work Is Never Done; I Love What You Did With The Love I Gave You; You Better Sit Down Kids; We'll Watch The Sun Coming Up; Somebody*

US#14; 29 weeks on chart; Gold certification

Foxy Lady

July 1972

Side 1: *Living In A House Divided; It Might As Well Stay Monday (From Now On); Song For You; Down, Down, Down; Don't Try To Close A Rose*

Side 2: *The First Time; Let Me Down Easy; If I Knew Then; Don't Hide Your Love; Never Been To Spain*

US#43; 22 weeks on chart

Bittersweet White Light

April 1973

Side 1: *By Myself; I Got It Bad And That Ain't Good; Am I Blue; How Long Has This Been Going On; The Man I Love*

Side 2: *Jolson Medley: Sonny Boy / My Mammy / Rock-A-Bye Your Baby With A Dixie Melody; More Than You Know; Why Was I Born; The Man That Got Away*

US#140; 8 weeks on chart

Mama Was A Rock and Roll Singer, Papa Used To Write All Her Songs

(with Sonny)

June 1973

Side 1: *It Never Rains In California; I Believe In You; I Can See Clearly Now; Rhythm Of Your Heartbeat; Mama Was A Rock and Roll Singer, Papa Used To Write All Her Songs*

Side 2: *By Love I Mean; Brother Love's Travelling Salvation Show; You Know Darn Well; The Greatest Show On Earth; Listen To The Music*

US#132; 6 weeks on chart

Half-Breed

September 1973

Side 1: *My Love; Two People Clinging To A Thread; Half-Breed; The Greatest Song I Ever Heard; How Can You Mend A Broken Heart?; Carousel Man*

Side 2: *David's Song; Melody; The Long And Winding Road; This God-Forsaken Day; Chastity Sun*

US#28; 25 weeks on chart; Gold certification

Dark Lady

May 1974

Side 1: *Train Of Thought; I Saw A Man And He Danced With His Wife; Make The Man Love Me; Just What I've Been Lookin' For; Dark Lady*

Side 2: *Miss Subway Of 1952; Dixie Girl; Rescue Me; What'll I Do; Apples Don't Fall Far From The Tree*

US#69; 14 weeks on chart

Stars

May 1975

Side 1: *Love Enough; Bell Bottom Blues; These Days; Mr. Soul; Just This One Time*

Side 2: *Geronimo's Cadillac; The Bigger They Come The Harder They Fall; Love Hurts; Rock And Roll Doctor; Stars*

US#153; 7 weeks on chart

I'd Rather Believe In you

October 1976

Side 1: *Long Distance Love Affair; I'd Rather Believe In You; I Know (You Don't Love Me); Silver Wings & Golden Rings; Flashback*

Side 2: *It's A Crying Shame; Early Morning Strangers; Knock On Wood; Spring; Borrowed Time*

Cherished

April 1977

Side 1: *Pirate; He Was Beautiful; War Paint And Soft Feathers; Love The Devil Out Of Ya; She Loves To Hear The Music*

Side 2: *L.A. Plane; Again; Dixie; Send The Man Over; Thunderstorm*

Two The Hard Way

(with Gregg Allman as "Allman & Woman")

November 1977

Side 1: *Move Me; I Found You Love; Can You Fool; You've Really Got A Hold On Me; We're Gonna Make It; Do What You Gotta Do*

Side 2: *In For The Night; Shadow Dream Song; Island; I Love Makin' Love To You; Love Me*

Take Me Home

February 1979

Side 1: *Take Me Home; Wasn't It Good; Say The Word; Happy Was The Day We Met*

Side 2: *Git Down (Guitar Groupie); Love & Pain; Let This Be A Lesson To You; It's Too Late To Love Me Now; My Song*

US#25; 21 weeks on chart; Gold certification

Prisoner

October 1979

Side 1: *Prisoner; Holdin' Out For Love; Shoppin'; Boys & Girls*

Side 2: *Mirror Image; Hell On Wheels; Holy Smoke!; Outrageous*

Black Rose

(as a member of Black Rose)

August 1980

Side 1: *Never Should've Started; Julie; Take It From The Boys; We All Fly Home*

Side 2: *88 Degrees; You Know It; Young And Pretty; Fast Company*

I Paralyze

May 1982

Side 1: *Rudy; Games; I Paralyze; When The Love Is Gone; Say What's On Your Mind*

Side 2: *Back On The Street Again; Walk With Me; The Book Of Love; Do I Ever Cross Your Mind?*

Cher

November 1987

Side 1: *I Found Someone; We All Sleep Alone; Bang-Bang; Main Man; Give Our Love A Fightin' Chance*

Side 2: *Perfection; Dangerous Times; Skin Deep; Working Girl; Hard Enough Getting Over You*

US#32; 41 weeks on chart; Platinum certification

UK#26; 22 weeks on chart; Gold certification

"I had a really good time with those songs. They were songs I wanted to do, you know? I mean, maybe all of them didn't come out perfectly, but they were songs I really loved, and it was what I wanted to do. I wanted to do that kind of music. It fit me well, and I felt it. I really felt that music. I wasn't a very good singer then... I'm a much better singer now. Before I did that album, I had just been doing movies and hadn't sung at all. I think I sang at Paul Newman's house one night, around the piano, but I just wasn't sure how this [album] was gonna go. Bernadette Peters told me about this fabulous teacher named Adrienne Angel. She really helped me with my voice and made it so much better. Gave me control, gave me higher notes. I mean, I sing a billion times higher than I was ever able to sing in the beginning."

– Cher

Heart Of Stone

July 1989

Side 1: *If I Could Turn Back Time; Just Like Jesse James; You Wouldn't Know Love; Heart Of Stone; Still In Love With You; Love On A Rooftop*

Side 2: *Emotional Fire; All Because Of You; Does Anybody Really Fall In Love Anymore?; Starting Over; Kiss To Kiss; After All (Love Theme From Chances Are)*

US#10; 53 weeks on chart; Triple-Platinum certification

UK#7; 82 weeks on chart; Platinum certification

Love Hurts

June 1991

Side 1: *Save Up All Your Tears; Love Hurts; Love And Understanding; Fires Of Eden; I'll Never Stop Loving You;* (Europe bonus track: *The Shoop Shoop Song (It's In His Kiss)*)

Side 2: *One Small Step; A World Without Heroes; Could've Been You; When Love Calls Your Name; When Lovers Become Strangers; Who You Gonna Believe*

US#48; 34 weeks on chart; Gold certification

UK#1 (6 weeks); 51 weeks on chart; Triple-Platinum certification

It's A Man's World

July 1995

Side 1: *Walking In Memphis; Not Enough Love In The World; One By One; I Wouldn't Treat A Dog; Angels Running; Paradise Is Here; I'm Blowin' Away*

Side 2: *Don't Come Around Tonite; What About The Moonlight; The Same Mistake; The Gunman; The Sun Ain't Gonna Shine Anymore; Shape Of things To Come; It's A Man's Man's Man's World*

(US release: Side 1: *One By One; Not Enough Love In The World; Angels Running; What About The Moonlight; Paradise Is Here; The Same Mistake*

Side 2: *I'm Blowin' Away; Walking In Memphis; The Sun Ain't Gonna Shine Anymore; The Gunman; It's A Man's Man's Man's World*)

US# 63; 10 weeks on chart

UK#10; 22 weeks on chart; Gold certification

Believe

November 1998

Side 1: *Believe; The Power; Runaway; All Or Nothing; Strong Enough*

Side 2: *Dov'è L'Amore; Takin' Back My Heart; Taxi Taxi; Love Is The Groove; We All Sleep Alone*

US#4; 76 weeks on chart; Quadruple-Platinum certification

UK#7; 45 weeks on chart; Double-Platinum certification

Not.com.mercial

November 2000

Still; Sisters Of Mercy; Runnin'; Born With The Hunger; The Fall (Kurt's Blues); With Or Without You; Fit To Fly; Disaster Cake; Our Lady Of San Francisco; Classified 1A

Living Proof

November 2001

Side 1: *The Music's No Good Without You; Alive Again; (This Is) A Song For The Lonely; A Different Kind Of Love Song; Rain, Rain; Love So High*

Side 2: *Body To Body, Heart To Heart; Love Is A Lonely Place Without You; Real Love; Love One Another; You Take It All; When The Money's Gone*

(US release: *Song For The Lonely; A Different Kind Of Love Song; Alive Again; The Music's No Good Without You; Rain, Rain; Real Love; Love So High; Body To Body, Heart To Heart; Love Is A Lonely Place Without You; Love One Another; When You Walk Away; When The Money's Gone*)

US#9; 21 weeks on chart; Gold certification

UK#46; 3 weeks on chart; Gold certification

Closer To The Truth

September 2013

Side 1: *Woman's World; Take It Like A Man; My Love; Dressed To Kill; Red; Lovers Forever*

Side 2: *I Walk Alone; Sirens; Favorite Scars; I Hope You Find It; Lie To Me*

(International Deluxe Edition Bonus Tracks: *I Don't Have To Sleep To Dream; Pride; You Haven't Seen The Last Of Me (Original Version); Woman's World (R3hab Remix); Woman's World (Jodie Harsh Remix); Will You Wait For Me*)

US#3; 24 weeks on chart

UK#4; 7 weeks on chart; Silver certification

"I didn't realize that I hadn't done anything in so long. Was it 11 years? I don't know. I didn't think about recording again. And then finally, one of my managers said, 'You really should do that.' And so I finally got in. The first song I did was *Woman's World*. The record company wasn't excited, truthfully, but they gave me the shot, so I have to give them credit. But then when I did that, and everyone heard it, they thought, 'OK, maybe she still has it.'"

- – **Cher**

Compilation Albums

Listed are Cher's US and UK hit compilation albums.

Baby Don't Go

(with Sonny, with various artists)

October 1965

Side 1: *Baby Don't Go; Love Is Strange; When* (by The Lettermen); *I Surrender (To Tour Touch)* (by Bill Medley); *Walkin' The Quetzal* (instrumental); *Leavin' Town* (by Bill Medley); *Do You Want To dance; La la la la la* (by The Blendells); *Their Hearts Were Full Of Spring* (by The lettermen); *Two Hearts* (by The Lettermen); *Wo Yeah!* (by Bill Medley); *Let The Good Times Roll*

US#69; 16 weeks on chart

The Best Of Sonny & Chér

(with Sonny)

August 1967

Side 1: *The Beat Goes On; What Now My Love; I Got You Babe; Little Man; Just You; Let It Be Me*

Side 2: *A Beautiful Story; It's The Little Things; But You're Mine; Sing C'est La Vie; Laugh At Me; Living For You*

US#23; 64 weeks on chart

Golden Greats

November 1968

Side 1: You Better Sit Down Kids; Sunny; Come and Stay with Me; Alfie; Take Me for a Little While; All I Really Want to Do

Side 2: Bang Bang (My Baby Shot Me Down); Needles and Pins; Dream Baby; Elusive Butterfly; Where Do You Go; Hey Joe

US#195; 3 weeks on chart

Superpak

December 1971

Side 1: *All I Really Want to Do; The Bells of Rhymney; Girl Don't Come; Come and Stay With Me; Blowin' in the Wind; Needles and Pins*

Side 2: *Bang Bang (My Baby Shot Me Down); Elusive Butterfly; Time; Where Do You Go?; Until It's Time for You to Go; Will You Love Me Tomorrow*

Side 3: *Alfie; Homeward Bound; Catch the Wind; Reason to Believe; House Is Not A Home; You Don't Have To Say You Love Me*

Side 4: *You Better Sit Down Kids; Sunny; There But For Fortune; Do You Believe In Magic; Mama (When My Dollies Have Babies); Click Song*

US#92; 10 weeks on chart

The Two Of Us

(with Sonny)

September 1972

Side 1: *I Got You Babe; Unchained Melody; Then He Kissed Me; Sing C'est La Vie; It's Gonna Rain; Baby Don't Go*

Side 2: *Just You; The Letter; Let It Be Me; You Don't Love Me; You've Really Got A Hold On Me; Why Don't They Let Us Fall In Love*

Side 3: *The Beat Goes On; Groovy Kind Of Love; You Baby; Monday; Love Don't Come; Podunk*

Side 4: *Little Man; We'll Sing In The Sunshine; Misty Roses; Stand By Me; Living For You; Cheryl's Goin' Home*

US#122; 12 weeks on chart

Superpak Vol. 2

September 1972

Side 1: *Our Day Will Come; The Times They Are A-Changin'; Come to Your Window; I Wasn't Ready; Hey Joe; Milord*

Side 2: *Don't Think Twice; She Thinks I Still Care; The Cruel War; A Young Girl (Une Enfante); Song Called Children; The Girl from Ipanema*

Side 3: *Ol' Man River; Impossible Dream; Cry Myself to Sleep; Carnival; The Twelfth of Never; Like a Rolling Stone*

Side 4: *It's Not Unusual; I Want You; I Will Wait For You; Take Me For A Little While; Sing for Your Supper; Go Now*

US#95; 9 weeks on chart

Greatest Hits

(with Sonny)

September 1974

Side 1: *All I Ever Need Is You; When You Say Love; You Better Sit Down Kids; Crystal Clear / Muddy Waters; I Got You Babe (live)*

Side 2: *A Cowboy's Work Is Never Done; United We Stand; The Beat Goes On (live); What Now My Love (live); Mama Was A Rock and Roll Singer, Papa Used To Write All Her Songs*

US#146; 6 weeks on chart

Greatest Hits

November 1974

Side 1: *Dark Lady; The Way of Love; Don't Hide Your Love; Half-Breed; Train Of Thought*

Side 2: *Gypsys, Tramps & Thieves; I Saw A Man And He Danced With His Wife; Carousel Man; Living in a House Divided; Melody*

US#152; 7 weeks on chart

Cher's Greatest Hits: 1965-1992

November 1992

Side 1: *Oh No Not My Baby; Whenever You're Near; Many Rivers To Cross (Live From The Mirage); Love And Understanding*

Side 2: *Save Up All Your Tears; The Shoop Shoop Song; If I Could Turn Back Time; Just Like Jesse James*

Side 3: *Heart Of Stone; I Found Someone; We All Sleep Alone; Bang-Bang*

Side 4: *Dead Ringer For Love* (with Meat Loaf)*; Dark Lady; Gypsys, Tramps & Thieves; I Got You Babe*

UK#1 (7 weeks); 41 weeks on chart; Triple-Platinum certification

Trivia: Cher's *Greatest Hits: 1965-1992* was the #1 female album of 1992 in the UK, and is Cher's best-selling album there (over 1,100,000 copies sold).

If I Could Turn Back Time – Cher's Greatest Hits

March 1999

Side 1: *Don't Come Cryin' To Me; Love And Understanding; Save Up All Your Tears; The Shoop Shoop Song (It's In His Kiss); After All (Love Theme From "Chances Are"); If I Could Turn Back Time; Just Like Jesse James; Heart Of Stone (Remix); I Found Someone*

Side 2: *We All Sleep Alone; Bang Bang; Take Me Home; Dark Lady; Half-Breed; The Way Of Love; Gypsys, Tramps & Thieves; I Got You Babe* (with Sonny)

US#57; 17 weeks on chart; Gold certification

Trivia: For two consecutive weeks, Cher's #1 album *Believe* prevented #2 album *If I Could Turn Back Time – Cher's Greatest Hits* from reaching the Danish top spot! Moreover, within 1999, Cher managed to achieve two Top 2 "Greatest Hits" compilation albums in Denmark!

The Greatest Hits

November 1999

Side 1: *Believe; The Shoop Shoop Song (It's In His Kiss); If I Could Turn Back Time; Heart Of Stone; Love And Under-standing; Love Hurts; Just Like Jesse James; I Found Someone; One By One*

Side 2: *Strong Enough: All Or Nothing: Walking In Mem-phis: Love Can Build A Bridge* (with Chrissie Hynde, Neneh Cherry & Eric Clapton); *All I Really Want To Do; Bang Bang; Gypsies, Tramps And Thieves; The Beat Goes On* (with Sonny); *I Got You Babe* (with Sonny); *Dov'è L'Amore (Emilio Estefan Jnr. Mix)*

UK#7; 32 weeks on chart; Double-Platinum certification

The Very Best Of Cher

April 2003

Believe; If I Could Turn Back Time; Heart Of Stone; Just Like Jesse James; Save Up All Your Tears; After All (with Peter Cetera); *I Found Someone; One By One (Junior Vasquez Vocal Edit); Strong Enough; All Or Nothing; Song For The Lonely; Take Me Home; The Shoop Shoop Song (It's In His Kiss); All I Really Want To Do; Bang Bang (My Baby Shot Me Down); Half-Breed; Gypsies, Tramps & Thieves; Dark Lady; The Beat Goes On;* (with Sonny)*; I Got You Babe* (with Sonny)*; A Different Kind Of Love Song (Rodney Jerkins Main Mix)*

(UK release: *Believe; If I Could Turn Back Time; Save Up All Your Tears; Walking in Memphis; The Shoop Shoop Song (It's in His Kiss); Love and Understanding; I Found Someone; Just Like Jesse James; One by One; Love Can Build a Bridge* (with Chrissie Hynde, Neneh Cherry & Eric Clapton)*; Strong Enough; All or Nothing; A Different Kind of Love Song; Heart of Stone; The Music's No Good Without You; Dov'è l'amore" (Emilio Estefan Jnr. Mix); Gypsys, Tramps & Thieves; The Beat Goes On"* (with Sonny)*; I Got You Babe* (with Sonny)*; All I Really Want to Do; Bang Bang (My Baby Shot Me Down)*)

US#4; 56 weeks on chart; Double-Platinum certification

UK#17; 18 weeks on chart; Gold certification

Live Albums

Sonny & Cher Live

(with Sonny)

September 1971

Side 1: *What Now My Love; The Beat Goes On; Once In A Lifetime; More Today Than Yesterday; Got To Get You Into My Life; Someday (You'll Want Me To Want You)*

Side 2: *Danny Boy; Laugh At Me; Something; Hey Jude; I Got You Babe*

Live In Las Vegas Vol.2

(with Sonny)

December 1973

Side 1: *All I Ever Need Is You / Music-Comedy Dialogue; I Can See Clearly Now / You've Got A Friend / Where You Lead / Reprise: You've Got A Friend*

Side 2: *Comedy Monologue / Gypsys, Tramps & Thieves; Brother Love's Travelling Salvation Show; You And I*

Side 3: *Superstar / Comedy Dialogue; Bang Bang (My Baby Sot Me Down)*

Side 4: *Introduction; You'd Better Sit Down Kids / A Cowboy's Work Is Never Done / Band Introduction; I Got You Babe*

VH-1 Divas Live/99

(with various artists)

November 1999

The Best (Tina Turner); *The Bitch Is Back* (Tina Turner & Elton John); *Proud Mary* (with Tina Turner & Elton John); *If I Could Turn Back Time; How Do I Live* (LeAnn Rimes); *I'm Still Standing* (Elton John); *Have You Ever / Almost Doesn't Count* (Brandy); *(Everything I Do) I Do It for You*; (Brandy & Faith Hill); *This Kiss (Faith Hill); Ain't No Way;* (Whitney Houston & Mary J. Blige); *I Will Always Love You* (Whitney Houston); *I'm Every Woman* (Whitney Houston & Chaka Khan); *I'm Every Woman (Reprise)* (Whitney Houston, Chaka Khan, Faith Hill, Brandy, Mary J. Blige & LeAnn Rimes)

Divas Las Vegas

(with various artists)

November 2002

You Shook Me All Night Long (Céline Dion With Anastacia); *Believe; (This Is) A Song For The Lonely; Underneath Your Clothes* (Shakira); *Landslide* (Dixie Chicks With Stevie Nicks); *One Day In Your Life* (Anastacia); *I'm Alive* (Céline Dion); *A New Day Has Come* (Céline Dion); *Elvis Medley Finale: Jailhouse Rock* (Anastacia) - *Always On My Mind* (Shakira) - *Heartbreak Hotel - Can't Help Falling In Love* (Céline Dion)

Live! The Farewell Tour

September 2003

I Still Haven't Found What I'm Looking For; Song For The Lonely; All Or Nothing; I Found Someone; Bang Bang (My Baby Shot Me Down); All I Really Want To Do / Half-Breed / Gypsies, Tramps & Thieves / Dark Lady; Take Me Home; The Way Of Love; After All; Just Like Jesse James; Heart Of Stone; The Shoop Shoop Song (It's In His Kiss); Strong Enough; If I Could Turn Back Time; Believe

UK#79; 1 week on chart

Soundtrack Albums

Listed are soundtrack albums that have two or more Cher songs and that feature her on the cover.

Good Times — Original Motion Picture Soundtrack

(with Sonny)

May 1967

Side 1: *I Got You Babe (Instrumental); It's The Little Things; Good Times; Trust Me*

Side 2: *Don't Talk To Strangers; I'm Gonna Love You; Just A Name; I Got You Babe (film version*

US#73; 18 weeks on chart

Mermaids — Original Motion Picture Soundtrack

(with various artists)

January 1990

Side 1: *The Shoop Shoop Song (It's In His Kiss); Big Girls Don't Cry* (by Frankie Valli And The Four Seasons); *You've Really Got A Hold On Me* (by Smokey Robinson & The Miracles); *It's My Party* (by Lesley Gore); *Johnny Angel* (by Shelley Fabares)

Side 2: *Baby I'm Yours; Just One Look* (by Doris Troy); *Love Is Strange* (by Mickey & Sylvia); *Sleepwalk* (by Santo & Johnny); *If You Wanna Be Happy* (by Jimmy Soul)

US#65; 24 weeks on chart

UK (Compilations Chart) #6; 15 weeks on chart; Silver certification

Burlesque — Original Motion Picture Soundtrack

(with Christina Aguilera)

November 2010

Something's Got A Hold On Me (by Christina Aguilera)*; Welcome To Burlesque; Tough Lover* (by Christina Aguilera)*; But I Am A Good Girl* (by Christina Aguilera)*; Guy What Takes His Time* (by Christina Aguilera); *Express* (Christina Aguilera)*; You Haven't Seen The Last Of Me; Bound To You* (by Christina Aguilera)*; Show Me How You Burlesque* (by Christina Aguilera)*; The Beautiful People (From Burlesque)* (by Christina Aguilera)

US#18; 53 weeks on chart; Gold certification

UK (Compilations Chart) #27; 61 weeks on chart; Silver certification

Singles

Cher's first hit single was 1965's solo UK Top 10 *All I Really Want To Do*. That and three Sonny & Cher hits, including eventual Top 10 *Baby Don't Go*, placed simultaneously on the US Top 50 in September 1965. One of the others was the US Gold-certified multi-million Sonny & Cher classic *I Got You Babe*, which spent three weeks at #1 in the US and two weeks at #1 in the UK (and was later dubbed the 444th greatest song of all-time by *Rolling Stone*). Simultaneously, the duo's *Sing C'est La Vie* hit #1 in Belgium.

Cher's million-selling solo tune *Bang bang (My Baby Shot Me Down)* peaked at #2 in 1966, and with it, Cher had scored 7 Top 10 hits (including 2 #1's) in Canada in less than 9 months. Sonny & Cher's late '66 *Little Man* became the duo's fourth #1 hit when it topped the charts in four European countries. In the second half of the sixties, Cher had scored 25 hit singles around the world, including 20 on the US Hot 100 — such as Top 10's *The Beat Goes On* and *You Better Sit Down Kids*.

Between 1971 and '74, Cher had three US#1 singles with *Gypsies, Tramps & Thieves*, *Half Breed* and *Dark Lady*. In that quartet of years alone, she sold over 11-million singles worldwide, with help from US Top 10 *A Cowboy's Work Is Never Done* and million-selling transatlantic Top 10 *All I Ever Need Is You* — both with Sonny. 1979's *Take Me Home* became her fourth US Gold-certified million-seller of the decade.

After a hiatus from music to concentrate on movies, Cher released four Top 10 million-sellers between 1987 and '89: the MTV Video Music Award-nominated *I Found Someone*; *After All* (with Peter Cetera); *Just Like Jesse James*; and *If I Could Turn Back Time* — which spent 7 weeks at #1 in Australia and became her third Billboard Adult Contemporary #1.

In the 1990's, Cher amassed an impressive 23 hits in the UK and was the only female artist of the decade to reach #1 three times. *The Shoop Shoop Song (It's In His Kiss)* topped the charts in five European countries, including five weeks at #1 in the UK — also the peak position of Charity single *Love Can Build A Bridge* with Chrissie Hynde, Neneh Cherry and Eric Clapton. The country also gave her Top Tens with *Love & Understanding* and *One By One*.

In 1998, at age fifty-two, Cher scored her biggest hit single ever with the Grammy Award-winning record-breaking *Believe* — Billboard Music Award's "Single of the Year". The dance-pop number topped the charts in 16 countries, and sold over 7 million copies worldwide. All four singles from its parent album *Believe* gained top 5 positions — including further million-seller *Strong Enough*.

In 2001 and '02, Cher released three Top 20 hits, including top 5 hit *The Music's No Good Without You*, which reached #8 in the UK — giving her UK Top 10 hits in five consecutive decades.

Cher, who has achieved a staggering 80 hit singles around the globe, returned with new one *Woman's World* in 2013, increasing her span of Billboard #1's to over 48 years as it became her 8th #1 on the publication's Hot Dance Club Songs Chart chart. Follow-up *I Hope You Find It* increased her span of Top 30 hits in the UK to a whopping six consecutive decades, whilst making her the oldest female singer to score a Top 30 single with a new release.

"The question I'm asked most is 'Do I believe in life after love?', and if no one ever asks me that again, I'd be a happy camper."

– Cher

The Letter

(with Sonny, as "Caesar & Cleo")

February 1965

US#75; 5 weeks on chart

Ringo I Love You

(as "Bonnie Jo Mason")

February 1964

Love Is Strange

(with Sonny, as "Caesar & Cleo")

September 1964

US#131

Baby Don't Go

(with Sonny)

September 1964

US#8; 12 weeks on chart

UK#11; 9 weeks on chart

Dream Baby

(as "Cherilyn")

December 1964

Just You

(with Sonny)

April 1965

US#20; 9 weeks on chart

All I Really Want To Do

June 1965

US#15; 12 weeks on chart

UK#9; 10 weeks on chart

I Got You Babe

(with Sonny)

June 1965

US#1 (3 weeks); 14 weeks on chart; Gold certification

UK#1 (2 weeks); 12 weeks on chart

"What happened was there were songs we made before, so when *I Got You Babe* became famous, they released the songs that we had done before *I Got You Babe*. So everything was just released at one time."

– Cher

Sing C'est La Vie

(with Sonny)

September 1965

But You're Mine

(with Sonny)

October 1965

US#15; 8 weeks on chart

UK#17; 8 weeks on chart

Where Do You Go

October 1965

US#25; 7 weeks on chart

What Now My Love

(with Sonny)

January 1966

US#14; 8 weeks on chart

UK#13; 11 weeks on chart

Let The Good Times Roll

(with Sonny, as "Caesar & Cleo")

February 1966

Bang Bang (My Baby Shot Me Down)

March 1966

US#2; 11 weeks on chart

UK#3; 12 weeks on chart

Have I Stayed Too Long

(with Sonny)

May 1966

US#49; 6 weeks on chart

UK#42; 3 weeks on chart

Alfie

July 1966

US#32; 6 weeks on chart

I Feel Something In The Air

July 1966

UK#43; 2 weeks on chart

Little Man

(with Sonny)

September 1966

US#21; 7 weeks on chart

UK#4; 10 weeks on chart

Sunny

September 1966

UK#32; 5 weeks on chart

Living For You

(with Sonny)

November1966

US#87; 2 weeks on chart

UK#44; 4 weeks on chart

Behind The Door

November 1966

US#97; 1 week on chart

Mama (When My Dollies Have Babies)

December 1966

US#124

The Beat Goes On

(with Sonny)

January 1967

US#6; 11 weeks on chart

UK#29; 8 weeks on chart

A Beautiful Story

(with Sonny)

April 1967

US#53; 5 weeks on chart

Plastic Man

(with Sonny)

May 1967

US#74; 3 weeks on chart

It's The Little Things

(with Sonny)

July 1967

US#50; 7 weeks on chart

Hey Joe

August 1967

US#94; 2 weeks on chart

You Better Sit Down Kids

October 1967

US#9; 13 weeks on chart

Good Combination

(with Sonny)

December 1967

US#56; 6 weeks on chart

Circus

(with Sonny)

February 1968

The Click Song Number One

February 1968

Take Me For A little While

June 1968

You Gotta Have A Thing of Your Own

(with Sonny)

September 1968

Yours Until Tomorrow

February 1969

Chastity's Song (Band of Thieves)

April 1969

You're A Friend of Mine

(with Sonny)

May 1969

I Walk On Guilded Splinters

June 1969

For What It's Worth

September 1969

US#125

You Made Me So very Happy

November 1969

Superstar

June 1970

Get It Together

(with Sonny)

July 1970

Lay, Baby, Lay

February 1971

Classified 1A

May 1971

"We put that song out in 1970 and no one would play it because they said it was un-American, because I'm singing the part of a soldier that's in Vietnam dying and those are his last words."

         – Cher, on *Classified 1A*

Real People

(with Sonny)

June 1971

Gypsies, Tramps & Thieves

September 1971

US#1 (2 weeks); 16 weeks on chart; Gold certification

UK#4; 13 weeks on chart

All I Ever Need Is You

(with Sonny)

October 1971

US#7; 15 weeks on chart

UK#8; 12 weeks on chart

The Way of Love

January 1972

US#7; 13 weeks on chart

A Cowboy's Work Is Never Done

(with Sonny)

February 1972

US#8; 13 weeks on chart

Living In A House Divided

May 1972

US#22; 8 weeks on chart

When You Say Love

(with Sonny)

July 1972

US#32; 10 weeks on chart

Don't Hide Your Love

September 1973

US#46; 8 weeks on chart

Mama Was A Rock & Roll Singer, Papa Used To Write All Her Songs

(with Sonny)

March 1973

US#77; 5 weeks on chart

Am I Blue

May 1973

US#111

The Greatest Show On Earth

(with Sonny)

July 1973

Half Breed

July 1973

US#1 (2 weeks); 20 weeks on chart; Gold certification

Dark Lady

January 1974

US#1 (1 week); 16 weeks on chart

UK#36; 4 weeks on chart

"I was doing these kind of poppy songs. I was not content, necessarily, to do them, but... Like, I never liked *Dark Lady*, and it was a big hit. I was like hanging around with Anjelica Huston and Jack Nicholson, Warren Beatty, and I was singing... They're making like fabulous art and I'm making *Dark Lady*. But then they were huge hits, and so, you know, somebody says, 'You can't argue with huge hits, Cher.'"

– Cher

Train of Thought

April 1974

US#27; 11 weeks on chart

I Saw A Man & He Danced With His Wife

August 1974

US#42; 9 weeks on chart

Carousel man

October 1974

A Woman's Story

December 1974

Rescue Me

April 1974

A Love Like Yours (Don't Come Knocking Every Day)

(with Harry Nilsson)

April 1975

Geronimo's Cadillac

June 1975

Long Distance Love Affair

October 1976

Pirate

January 1977

US#93; 2 weeks on chart

You're Not Right For Me

(with Sonny)

March 1977

War Paint and Soft Feathers

May 1977

Move Me

(with Gregg Allman)

December 1977

Take Me Home

February 1979

US#8; 19 weeks on chart

Wasn't It Good

May 1979

US#49; 5 weeks on chart

Hell On Wheels

September 1979

US#59; 5 weeks on chart

Holdin' Out For Love

November 1979

It's Too Late (To Love Me Now)

March 1980

Never Should've Started

(as a member of Black rose)

November 1980

Dead Ringer For Love

(with Meat Loaf)

November 1981

UK#5; 17 weeks on chart; Silver certification

Rudy

March 1982

I Paralyze

August 1982

I Found Someone

November 1987

US#10; 21 weeks on chart

UK#5; 13 weeks on chart

We All Sleep Alone

April 1988

US#14; 15 weeks on chart

UK#47; 5 weeks on chart

Skin Deep

July 1988

US#79; 4 weeks on chart

Main Man

December 1988

After All

(with Peter Cetera)

March 1989

US#6; 20 weeks on chart; Gold certification

UK#84; 3 weeks on chart

If I Could Turn Back Time

July 1989

US#3; 23 weeks on chart; Gold certification

UK#6; 15 weeks on chart

Just Like Jesse James

October 1989

US#8; 18 weeks on chart

US#11; 11 weeks on chart

Heart of Stone

February 1990

US#20; 14 weeks on chart

US#43; 5 weeks on chart

You Wouldn't Know Love

July 1990

UK#55; 4 weeks on chart

Baby I'm Yours

October 1990

UK#89; 1 week on chart

The Shoop Shoop Song (It's In His Kiss)

November 1990

US#33; 15 weeks on chart

UK#1 (5 weeks); 15 weeks on chart; Gold certification

Trivia: Cher had the #1 female single (*The Shoop Shoop Song (It's In His Kiss)*) and album (*Love Hurts*) of 1991 in the UK.

Love and Understanding

June 1991

US#17; 15 weeks on chart

UK#10; 8 weeks on chart

Save Up All Your Tears

October 1991

US#37; 15 weeks on chart

UK#37; 5 weeks on chart

Love Hurts

November 1991

UK#43; 5 weeks on chart

When Love Calls Your Name

March 1992

Could've Been You

April 1992

UK#31; 4 weeks on chart

Oh No Not My Baby

November 1992

UK#33; 4 weeks on chart

Many Rivers To Cross (Live From The Mirage)

January 1993

UK#37; 3 weeks on chart

Whenever You're Near

February 1993

UK#72; 1 week on chart

I Got You Babe (re-issue)

(with Sonny)

May 1993

UK#66; 1 week on chart

I Got You Babe

(with Beavis & Butt-head)

January 1994

UK#35; 3 weeks on chart

It Ain't Necessarily So

August 1994

Love Can Build A Bridge

(with Chrissie Hynde, Neneh Cherry & Eric Clapton)

March 1995

UK#1 (1 week); 15 weeks on chart; Silver certification

Walking In Memphis

October 1995

UK#11; 9 weeks on chart

One By One

January 1996

US#57; 14 weeks on chart

UK#7; 9 weeks on chart

Not Enough Love In The World

April 1996

UK#31; 2 weeks on chart

The Sun Ain't Gonna Shine Anymore

August 1996

UK#26; 3 weeks on chart

Paradise Is Here

December 1996

Trivia: In the UK, Cher's single *Believe* was #1 on the 1998 year-end chart, #5 on the 1990's decade-end chart and is #17 on the country's all-time chart. It is the best-selling single by a female solo artist in the U.K. (over 1,800,000 copies sold – being the only single to be certified Triple-Platinum in the UK).

Believe

October 1998

US#1 (4 weeks); 31 weeks on chart; Platinum certification

UK#1; (7 weeks); 31 weeks on chart; Triple-Platinum certification

"I honestly think that the most fun I ever had making a song was *Believe*. Because you didn't know it was me in the beginning, and I was so excited."

– Cher

Strong Enough

February 1999

US#57; 12 weeks on chart

UK#5; 10 weeks on chart; Silver certification

All or Nothing

June 1999

UK#12; 10 weeks on chart

Dov'è L'Amore

October 1999

UK#21; 8 weeks on chart

Più Che Puoi

(with Eros Ramazzotti)

May 2001

The Music's No Good Without You

November 2001

UK#8; 11 weeks on chart

> **Trivia**: Cher is the only female artist to have a UK top ten single in five consecutive decades (1960s, 1970s, 1980s, 1990s and 2000s).

Song For The Lonely

March 2002

US#85; 6 weeks on chart

Alive Again

April 2002

A Different Kind of Love Song

July 2002

When The Money's Gone

February 2003

You Haven't Seen The Last of Me

November 2010

"I can't get on radio because they're not playing women who are almost 100".

– Cher

Woman's World

June 2013

US#125

UK#129

Trivia: *Believe, Strong Enough, All Or Nothing, Song For The Lonely, A Different Kind Of Love Song, When The Money's Gone, You Haven't Seen The Last Of Me* and *Woman's World* have all hit #1 on Billboard's Dance Club Play chart; *Take Me Home, Take It Like A Man* and *I Walk Alone* all hit #2.

I Hope You Find It

October 2013

UK#25; 4 weeks on chart

Take It Like A Man

November 2013

"On *Take It Like A Man*, I wanted the autotune on the verses. It was like *Believe*. We couldn't make *Believe* right because the verses were so interminable and not very interesting. That's what I felt about *Take It Like A Man*. It took forever to get to the chorus. I'm the only one who wanted the autotune. I like it, I think it sounds cool."

– Cher

I Walk Alone

January 2014

Trivia: *The Click Song Number* One (#78), *Am I* Blue (#79); *A Woman's Story* (#66) and *Rescue Me* (#84) were all hits on the United States' Cashbox chart but not on the Billboard charts.

Songs Written By Cher

It was after her 1972 separation from first husband Sonny Bono — who had written a good number of the hits of Sonny & Cher, and Cher solo — that Cher began to get serious in the art of songwriting herself.

In 1973, Cher covered an album track called *Ruby Jean and Billie Lee* by Seals & Crofts. Taken from their US#4 hit album *Diamond Girl* that year, Cher kept the melody but largely adjusted the lyrics for her own 1973 album, *Half-Breed*. Cher's reworked version was a tribute to her daughter Chastity, aptly entitled *Chastity's Sun*. However, despite having changed most of the original composition's lyrics, Cher waived the opportunity to have a songwriting credit.

In 1979, Cher released the appropriately-titled self-penned ballad *My Song (Too Far Gone)* as the closing track to her Gold-certified 1979 album *Take Me Home*. Sharing a song writing credit with Mark Hudson who perhaps only contributed the music, the subject of the song was her failed marriage to second — and final — husband Gregg Allman. The song gained further exposure as the B-side of the album's lead single — the Gold-certified US top ten disco title-track *Take Me Home* - and with a performance on The Mike Douglas Show.

Cher branched her songwriting career further the next year by writing the lyrics to the song *Bad Love* - a song recorded for inclusion on the February 1980 soundtrack to the film *Foxes* of that same year. The Donna Summer-style disco song, which had music by none-other-than Summer's oft-collaborator Giorgio Moroder, garnered enough praise to be appointed as an track on the international 2-disc edition of *The Very Best of Cher* in 2003.

Cher also formed and fronted the band Black Rose in 1980. With the group's lead guitarist Les Dudek writing the music, she wrote the track *Don't Trust That Woman* — lyrically similar to Hall & Oates late-'82 US#1 *Maneater*. The song was rumoured to be written for the Black Rose's second album but as their eponymous first album failed to chart, the album — and therefore the song — were shelved. Dudek went on to record it in 1981 for his album *Gipsy Ride*. In 1986, the song was given a second lease of life, being partially rewritten by none other than global superstar Elton John for inclusion on his album *Leather Jackets* that year. Unfortunately, the album was one of John's least successful with the man himself ultimately declaring it as his least favourite album of his entire lengthy career. 30 years later, it remained the only Elton John album that had yet to be remastered.

Luckily, Cher was not put-off songwriting, although she waited all the way until 1994 for a major return to laying lyrics to paper. She wrote the lyrics to a number of songs at a writers' retreat in France that would ultimately end up on the internet-only acoustic-rock studio album *Not.com.mercial*, released in 2000. Cher's favourite song on the collection, *(The Fall) Kurt's Blues*, with additional lyrics by Bruce Roberts, was Cher's tribute to the late rock singer Kurt Cobain — lead singer of Nirvana — who had committed suicide earlier that year. Another song, *Fit To Fly*, was initially written for her Grandfather who was in the invasion of Normandy in WWII, but was finalised as a song for "All the men and women who have served their country and then somehow been 'kicked to the curb.'"

Pat MacDonald contributed additional lyrics and music to one of the album's tracks, *Sisters of Mercy* — which Cher wrote for her mother, who was forced to put Cher in a catholic orphanage for several months when she was a baby. MacDonald said about Cher, and the album, "When I worked with Cher, we were doing songs she wrote herself, including all the lyrics. They were poems she wanted to put to music. That was a challenge. Her lyrics were anything but commercial. She said "f**k" in practically every song, just like how she talks. It's her personality coming through."

Still, which Cher appointed as her "most revealing" lyric; the autobiographical *Runnin'*, with additional lyric by Bruce Roberts; *Disaster Cake* about an ex-girlfriend of son Chaz; and *Our Lady Of San Francisco*, about a homeless woman, were all included on the album. Finally, Cher solely provided both lyrics and music for the album's rock ballad *With or Without You*.

At the same time, Cher wrote the track *Lovers Forever* which singer-songwriter Shirley Eikhard recorded and released on her own 2005 album, *Pop*.

1995 saw Cher release her album *It's A Man's World* with its second single *One By One* arriving in January 1996. The single, written by Anthony Griffiths, plus most of the album were remixed for their US releases later on in June 1996. For the US releases, Griffiths was joined by Cher in the songwriting credits. The US version of the single would hit #52 on the US Hot 100, and appeared on the end credits of 1996 HBO television movie *If these Walls Could Talk*.

Unbeknownst to perhaps most — Cher's most recognisable lyrics came in 1998 on her biggest hit ever — *Believe*. The star admitted that she was responsible — at least partly — for the song's second verse: "I wrote part of 'Believe' - the second verse. The first verse was about this woman who was sad that this guy was going, and the second verse was saying the same thing, so I changed it on the spot!" However, with at least six songwriters already having credit for writing the soon-to-be worldwide number one smash hit, Cher wasn't given a songwriting credit on the song.

Cher did manage to score a songwriting credit on a 2000 duet with Italian singer/songwriter Eros Ramazzotti on the moderately successful *Più Che Puoi*. The song, written by Adelio Cogliato, Antonio Galbiati, Cher and Ramazzotti, was a hit in many European countries, gaining top 20 positions in Belgium, Switzerland and Ramazzotti's native Italy. The song — which saw Cher and Ramazzotti each sing in both English and Italian — was included on the latter singer's hugely successful album *Stilelibero* of that same year.

In 2001, Cher released *Living Proof*, a dance album much in the same vein as its predecessor *Believe*. Cher wrote additional lyrics for one of the album's tracks — in fact, it was the album's lead single throughout most of the globe, and the album's best-selling single: *The Music's No Good Without You*. Written by James Thomas, Paul Barry, Mark Taylor with additional lyrics by Cher, the single reached the top 30 in over a dozen national charts — including the UK where it reached number 8.

After a 12-year hiatus, Cher released her next studio album *Closer To The Truth* in 2013. The album included a dramatic dance-pop version of the aforementioned co-penned *Lovers Forever*. Also included was a track entitled *Dressed To Kill*. Written by Mark Taylor and Sam Preston, the song served as a flop single for its latter writer in 2009. The electro-pop song's lyrics were revamped by Cher — and perhaps Taylor — for Cher's album. Cher also earned herself a song-writing credit for the album's *Take It Like A Man*. Written with Tim Powell, Tebey Ottoh, Mary Leay and Cher, it served as a single in the US, reaching #2 on its Billboard's Dance Club Songs chart.

Chastity's Sun

Written by James Seals & Dash Crofts (Cher uncredited)

Recorded by Cher for *Half-Breed*, 1973, US#28

My Song (Too Far Gone)

Written by Cher & Mark Hudson

Recorded by Cher for *Take Me Home*, 1979, US#25

Bad Love

Written by Cher & Giorgio Moroder

Recorded by Cher for *Foxes Soundtrack*, 1980, Billboard's Dance Club Songs #30

Don't Trust That Woman

Written by Les Dudek & Cher

Recorded by Les Dudek for *Gipsy Ride*, 1981

Written by Cher & Lady Choc Ice (Elton John)

Recorded by Elton John for *Leather Jackets*, 1986, US#91, UK#24

One By One (US Version)

Written by Anthony Griffiths & Cher

Recorded by Cher for *It's A Man's World* (US Version), 1996, US#64

Released as a single by Cher, 1996, US#52

Still

Lyrics by Cher, music by Cher, Bruce Roberts & Bob Thiele

Recorded by Cher for *Not.com.mercial*, 2000

Sisters Of Mercy

Lyrics by Cher, additional lyrics by Pat MacDonald, music by Cher, Pat Macdonald & Bruce Roberts

Recorded by Cher for *Not.com.mercial*, 2000

Runnin'

Lyrics by Cher. Additional lyrics by Bruce Roberts, Music by Pat MacDonald & Bruce Roberts

Recorded by Cher for *Not.com.mercial*, 2000

The Fall (Kurt's Blues)

Lyrics by Cher. Additional lyrics by Bruce Roberts, Music by Pat MacDonald & Bruce Roberts

Recorded by Cher for *Not.com.mercial*, 2000

With Or Without You

Lyrics & music by Cher

Recorded by Cher for *Not.com.mercial*, 2000

Fit To Fly

Lyrics by Cher, music by Cher, Kevin Savigar & Doug Millett

Recorded by Cher for *Not.com.mercial*, 2000

Believe

Written by Brian Higgins, Paul Barry, Steven Torch, Matthew Gray, Stuart McLennen & Timothy Powell (Cher uncredited)

Recorded by Cher for *Believe*, 1998, US#4, UK#7

Released as a single by Cher, 2013, US#1, UK#1

Più Che Puoi

Lyrics by Eros Ramazzotti, Antonio Galbiati & Cher, music by Eros Ramazzotti & Antonio Galbiati

Recorded by Eros Ramazzotti & Cher for *Stilelibero*, 2000

Released as a single by Eros Ramazzotti & Cher, 2001

The Music's No Good Without You

Written by James Thomas, Paul Barry & Mark Taylor, with additional lyrics by Cher

Recorded by Cher for *Living Proof*, 2001, US#9, UK#46

Released as a single by Cher, 2013, Billboard's Dance Club Songs #19, UK#8

Lovers Forever

Written by Cher & Shirley Eikhard

Recorded by Shirley Eikhard on *Pop*, 2005

Recorded by Cher for *Closer To The Truth*, 2013, US#3, UK#4

Take It Like A Man

Written by Tim Powell, Tebey Ottoh, Mary Leay & Cher

Recorded by Cher for *Closer To The Truth*, 2013, US#3, UK#4

Released as a single by Cher, 2013, Billboard's Dance Club Songs #2

Dressed To Kill

Written by Mark Taylor, Sam Preston & Cher

Recorded by Cher for *Closer To The Truth*, 2013, US#3, UK#4

The Cher Filmography

Films

Cher's film career as a lead actress began with 1967's light-hearted Sonny & Cher-vehicle *Good Times* but her critically-acclaimed film career didn't start until she appeared alongside Sandy Dennis and Karen Black in the 1982 Robert Altman-directed *Come Back to the 5 & Dime, Jimmy Dean, Jimmy Dean* — for which she bagged herself a Golden Globe Award nomination for Best Supporting Actress.

Cher won a Golden Globe Award for Best supporting actress the next year for her depiction of Karen Silkwood's unglamorous lesbian friend Dolly Peliker in the critically-hailed US Box Office #1 biographical drama *Silkwood*, alongside Meryl Streep and Kurt Russell. It grossed $35-million in the US and Cher was nominated for her first Academy Award, for Best Supporting Actress.

1985 saw Cher receive rave reviews — and the Best Actress Award at the following year's Cannes Film Festival — for her portrayal of Rusty Dennis, the mother of facial disfigurement sufferer Rocky Dennis, in *Mask*. It established Cher as a bankable lead actress, grossing $48-million at the US Box Office.

Trivia: Cher's personal favorite movie role is *Mask*.

Cher starred in three hit films in 1987 — including her role alongside "devil" Jack Nicholson and fellow "witches" Susan Sarandon and Michelle Pheiffer in the US Box Office

#1 fantasy-comedy *The Witches of Eastwick*, which grossed $68-million in the US.

Cher's big screen pièce de résistance however was that year's Norman Jewison-directed romantic comedy *Moonstruck* alongside Nicholas Cage. It grossed $80-million at the US Box Office and ended up as the fifth highest-grossing film of the year. Cher's BAFTA-nominated performance as Italian-American Loretta Castorini was highly-praised: she won the Golden Globe Award for Best Actress and the prestigious Best Actress Award at the Academy Awards.

Cher starred in the 1990 drama-comedy *Mermaids* alongside Bob Hoskins and Winona Ryder. The film grossed $35-million in the US (having to battle huge-earners *Home Alone*, *Edward Scissorhands* and *Look Who's Talking 2* throughout it's run in theatres). Before decade's end, Cher starred alongside Judi Dench, Maggie Smith and Lily Tomlin in Franco Zeffirelli's semi-autobiographical *Tea With Mussolini*. It was met with a modest Box Office performance and positive reviews.

The 2000's saw just one film appearance by Cher, the Farrelly Brother's 2003 comedy *Stuck on You*, which starred Matt Damon and Greg Kinnear, and grossed $65-million worldwide. However, Cher made a surprising comeback to movies in 2010, playing character Tess in the musical *Burlesque* alongside Christina Aguilera. It grossed $89-million worldwide — and adjusted for ticket price inflation, it saw Cher's total US Box Office gross as a supporting and lead actress surpass $700-million. The movie has since sold over 1.5-million DVD copies in the US, grossing an additional $23-million there.

Based on the music of Abba, Cher will appear in July 2018's musical romantic comedy film *Mamma Mia! Here We Go Again* — the sequel to 2008's Mamma Mia!, which grossed over $615,000,000 worldwide.

Wild on the Beach

Starring: Sherry Jackson, Gayle Calwell & Jackie Miller

Directed by: Maury Dexter

Release date: 25 August 1965

Cher's type of role: cameo

Cher's character: Cher

Good Times

Starring: Sonny & Cher

Directed by: William Friedkin

Release date: 12 May 1967

US gross: $600,000

Worldwide gross: $800,000

Cher's type of role: lead

Cher's character: Cher

Chastity

Starring: Cher

Directed by: Alessio dePaola

Release date: 24 June 1969

Cher's type of role: lead

Cher's character: Chastity

Come Back to the 5 & Dime, Jimmy Dean, Jimmy Dean

Starring: Sandy Dennis, Cher & Karen Black

Directed by: Robert Altman

Release date: 12 November 1982

US gross: $840,958

Cher's type of role: supporting

Cher's character: Sissy

Awards for Cher: Golden Globe Award nomination for Best Supporting Actress - Motion Picture

Silkwood

Starring: Meryl Streep, Kurt Russell & Cher

Directed by: Mike Nichols

Release date: 16 December 1983

US Box Office peak position: #1

US gross: $35,615,609

Cher's type of role: supporting

Cher's character: Dolly Peliker

Awards for Cher: Golden Globe Award win for Best Supporting Actress - Motion Picture; Academy Award nomination for Best Supporting; BAFTA Film Award nomination for Best Supporting Actress

Mask

Starring: Cher, Sam Elliot & Eric Stolt

Directed by: Peter Bogdanovich

Release date: 8 March 1985

US Box Office peak position: #2

US gross: $48,230,162

Cher's type of role: lead

Cher's character: Florence "Rusty" Dennis

Awards for Cher: Best Actress win at Cannes Film Festival; Golden Globe Award nomination for Best Actress - Motion Picture Drama

The Witches Of Eastwick

Starring: Jack Nicholson, Cher, Susan Sarandon & Michelle Pfeiffer

Directed by: George Miller

Release date: 12 June 1987

US Box Office peak position: #1

US gross: $63,766,510

Cher's type of role: lead

Cher's character: Alexandra Medford

Suspect

Starring: Cher & Dennis Quaid

Directed by: Peter Yates

Release date: 23 October 1987

US Box Office peak position: #3

US gross: $18,782,400

Cher's type of role: lead

Cher's character: Kathleen Riley

Moonstruck

Starring: Cher & Nicholas Cage

Directed by: Norman Jewison

Release date: 18 December 1987

US Box Office peak position: #3

US gross: $80,640,528

Cher's type of role: lead

Cher's character: Loretta Castorini

Awards for Cher: Academy Award win for Best Actress; Golden Globe Award win for Best Actress; BAFTA Film Award nomination for Best Actress

Mermaids

Starring: Cher, Bob Hoskins & Winona Ryder

Directed by: Richard Benjamin

Release date: 14 December 1990

US Box Office peak position: #6

US gross: $35,419,397

Cher's type of role: lead

Cher's character: Rachel Flax

The Player

Starring: Tim Robbins

Directed by: Robert Altman

Release date: 10 April 1992

US Box Office peak position: #4

US gross: $21,706101

Worldwide gross: $28,876,702

Cher's type of role: cameo

Cher's character: Cher

Ready To Wear / **Prêt-à-Porter**

Starring: Sophia Loren & Marcello Mastroianni

Directed by: Robert Altman

Year of release: 25 December 1994

US Box Office peak position: #13

US gross: $11,300,653

Worldwide gross: $19,806,660

Cher's type of role: cameo

Cher's character: Cher

Faithful

Starring: Cher, Chazz Palminteri & Ryan O'Neal

Directed by: Paul Mazursky

Release date: 5 April 1996

US Box Office peak position: #15

US gross: $2,104,439

Worldwide gross: $2,500,000

Cher's type of role: lead

Cher's character: Margaret

Tea With Mussolini

Starring: Cher, Joan Plowright, Judi Dench, Maggie Smith & Lily Tomlin

Directed by: Franco Zeffirelli

Release date: 14 May 1999

US Box Office peak position: #9

US gross: $14,401,563

Worldwide gross: $17,500,000

Cher's type of role: supporting

Cher's character: Elsa Morganthal Strauss-Almerson

Stuck On You

Starring: Matt Damon & Greg Kinnear

Directed by: The Farrelly Bros.

Release date: 12 December 2003

US Box Office peak position: #3

US gross: $33,832,741

Worldwide gross: $65,784,503

Cher's type of role: supporting

Cher's character: Cher

Burlesque

Starring: Cher & Christina Aguiera

Directed by: Steve Antin

Release date: 24 November 2010

US Box Office peak position: #3

US gross: $39,440,655

Worldwide gross: $89,519,773

Cher's type of role: supporting

Cher's character: Tess

> "I don't get the scripts that I want at all. I don't get many coming my way. I was disappointed in *Burlesque* — it could have been such a better movie."

– Cher

Zookeeper

Starring: Kevin James

Directed by: Frank Coraci

Release date: 8 July 2011

US Box Office peak position: #3

US gross: $80,360,843

Worldwide gross: $169,852,759

Cher's type of role: voice

Cher's character: Janet

Mamma Mia! Here We Go Again

Starring: Christine Baranski; Pierce Brosnan; Dominic Cooper; Colin Firth; Andy García; Lily James; Amanda Seyfried; Stellan Skarsgård; Julie Walters; Cher & Meryl Streep

Directed by: Ol Parker

Release date: 20 July 2018

Cher's type of role: supporting

Cher's character: Ruby Sheridan

> "I didn't even look at the script. The reason I did *Mamma Mia! 2* is because my agent — my old agent, and my dear dear friend — Ronnie Meyer, who's the head of all of Universal, he called me up and said, 'Cher, you're doing *Mamma Mia*', and hung up. And I wouldn't take it from anybody in the world except him, so I said, 'No, okay, fine.'"
>
> **– Cher**

Television

Between 1971 and '77, Cher starred in three hit variety series. Running from 1971-1974, *The Sonny & Cher Comedy Hour* earned her a Golden Globe Award for Best Actress — Musical or Comedy Series and four Emmy Award nominations. She received another Emmy Award nomination for her solo 1975-'76 *Cher*, before reuniting with Sonny for 1976-1977's *The Sonny & Cher Show*. All three shows attracted huge guest stars such as Michael Jackson, Elton John, David Bowie, Tina Turner, Muhammed Ali, Bette Midler and Ronald Reagan.

Cher starred in a dozen TV specials from 1971 to 2013. 19.5-million households tuned into 1977's fittingly-titled variety special *Cher... Special*, for which she received her sixth Emmy Award nomination. Her 1983 *Cher: A Celebration at Caesars* earned her a CableACE Award, 1991's CBS concert special *Cher... At The Mirage* was watched in 17.5-million homes and 9.9-million tuned into watch timeslot-winning documentary *Sonny & Me: Cher Remembers* in 1998.

As well as being one of the stars of fundraising concert special *VH-1 Divas Live/99*, which gave the network its highest viewership ever, 1999 saw *Cher: Live in Concert — From the MGM Grand in Las Vegas* become the highest-rated original HBO programme of 1998-99. She won an Emmy Award for Outstanding Variety, Music or Comedy Special for her 2003 concert special *Cher - the Farewell Tour*, which was watched by 16.6 million viewers.

Cher starred in and directed a third of highly-acclaimed television movie *If These Walls Could Talk* — HBO's highest-rated movie ever. For it, she was nominated for a Golden Globe Award and Satellite Award, before winning a Women in Film Lucy Award. In 2013, she produced and starred in *Dear Mom, Love Cher* on cable channel Lifetime, for which she won a Women's Image Network Award for Outstanding Show Produced by a Woman.

Since 1965, Cher has: acted in *The Man From U.N.C.L.E.* and *Love, American Style*; performed twice on *The Ed Sullivan Show*; guest starred in two episodes of *Will & Grace* that were both watched by over 22 million households; and performed *The Star Spangled Banner* at *Super Bowl XXXIII*, which was watched by 83.7 million viewers. She performed a dozen times — from 1965 to 2001 — on UK's legendary *Top of The Pops* and performed in front of Queen Elizabeth II on *The Royal Variety Performance* in 2001. She was the subject of: 1999 Emmy Award-nominated TV movie *And The Beat Goes On: The Sonny & Cher Story*; an episode of *Behind The Music* in 2000; BBC documentary *Still Cher* in 2001; and a lengthy A&E Biography documentary in 2003.

Cher's 1988 on-screen reunion with Sonny on *Late Show with David Letterman* won a TV Land Award almost 20 years later for TV's Greatest Music Moment. For their work in television, Sonny & Cher received a star on the Hollywood Walk of Fame in 1998. More recently, in November

2013, she was a guest judge and two-time performer on a Cher-themed *Dancing With The Stars* episode, watched by 13.7-million viewers.

Sonny & Cher: Nitty Gritty Hour

Starring: Sonny & Cher

Programme type: variety special

Original air date: 1971

The Sonny & Cher Comedy Hour

Starring: Sonny & Cher

Programme type: variety series

Original air date: August 1971-March 1974

Original network: CBS

Original viewership: 15.4-million (1973-1974 season) (#7 Top-rated primetime television series of the 1973-74 season as measured by Nielsen Media Research); 14.5-million (1974-75 season) (#27 Top-rated primetime television series of the 1971-72 season as measured by Nielsen Media Research)

Awards for Cher: Golden Globe win for Best Actress Musical or Comedy series (1974); Emmy Award nomination for Outstanding Music — Variety Series (1974); Emmy award nomination for Outstanding Variety Musical Series (1973); Emmy Award nomination for Outstanding Variety Series — Musical (1972); Emmy Award nomination for Outstanding Single Program — Variety or Musical (1972)

Cher

Starring: Cher

Programme type: variety series

Original air date: February 1975-January 1976

Original network: CBS

Original viewership: 14.5-million (1974-75 season) (#22 Top-rated primetime television series of the 1974-75 season as measured by Nielsen Media Research);

Awards for Cher: Emmy Award nomination for Outstanding Comedy, Variety or Music Series

The Sonny & Cher Show

Starring: Sonny & Cher

Programme type: variety series

Air date: February 1976-March 1977

Original network: CBS

Original viewership: 14.7-million (1975-1976 season) (#23 top-rated primetime television series of the 1975-76 season as measured by Nielsen Media Research)

Cher... Special

Starring: Cher

Programme type: variety special

Original air date: April 1978

Original network: ABC

Original viewership: 19.5-million

Awards for Cher: Emmy Award nomination for Outstanding Continuing or Single Performance By a Supporting Actress in Variety or Music

Cher ...And Other Fantasies

Starring: Cher

Programme type: variety special

Original air date: March 1979

Original network: NBC

Standing Room Only: Cher in Concert

Starring: Cher

Programme type: concert special

Original air date: February 1981

Original network: HBO

Cher: A Celebration at Caesars

Starring: Cher

Programme type: concert special

Original air date: April 1983

Original network: Showtime

Awards for Cher: CableACE Award win for Actress in a Variety Program

Cher... At The Mirage

Starring: Cher

Programme type: concert special

Original air date: February 1991

Original network: CBS

Original viewership: 17.5-million

An Evening With... Friends of the Environment

Starring: Bette Midler, Cher, Goldie Hawn, Meryl Streep, Olivia Newton-John & Robin Williams

Programme type: concert special

Original air date: 1990

Original network: ABC

If These Walls Could Talk

Starring: Demi Moore, Sissy Spacek & Cher

Programme type: television movie

Original air date: September 1996

Original network: HBO

Original viewership: 6.9-million

Awards for Cher: Golden Globe Award nomination for Best Supporting Actress in a Series, Mini-Series or Motion Picture Made for TV; Satellite Award nomination for Best Supporting Actress in a Series, Mini-Series or Motion Picture Made for TV; Women in Film Lucy Award win for Innovation in Television

Sonny & Me: Cher Remembers

Starring: Cher

Programme type: documentary

Original air date: May 1998

Original network: CBS

Original viewership: 9.8-million

VH-1 Divas Live/99

Starring: Whitney Houston, Cher, Tina Turner & Brandy

Programme type: concert special

Original air date: April 1999

Original network: VH-1

Original viewership: 9-million

Awards for Cher: none

Cher: Live in Concert — From the MGM Grand in Las Vegas

Starring: Cher

Programme type: concert special

Air date: August 1999

Original network: HBO

Original viewership: 6-million

Awards for Cher: Emmy Award nomination for Outstanding Individual Performance in a Variety or Music Program

Divas Las Vegas

Starring: Celine Dion, Cher, Dixie Chicks & Shakira

Programme type: concert special

Original air date: May 2002

Original network VH-1

Cher – The Farewell Tour

Starring: Cher

Programme type: concert special

Original air date: April 2003

Original network: NBC

Original viewership: 16.6-million

Awards for Cher: Emmy Award win for Outstanding Variety, Music or Comedy Special

Dear Mom, Love Cher

Starring: Cher & Georgia Holt

Programme type: documentary

Original air date: May 2013

Original network: Lifetime

Original viewership: 1.2-million

Awards for Cher: Women's Image Network Award win for Outstanding Show Produced by a Woman; Women's Image Network Award nomination for Outstanding Documentary Film

Music Videos

Long before the phrase "music video" was regularly used, or used in the way that we know it today, or before the medium became the norm, Cher began to make pre-recorded promotional video clips in the 1960's for singles such as *Sunny* and Sonny & Cher's *I Got You Babe* for them to be featured on television shows. The couple also produced such a thing for single *It's the Little Things* to be featured in their 1967 movie *Good Times*.

The majority of music performed on the 1971-1974 *The Sonny & Cher Comedy Hour* was live performances, however, Cher's 1973 performance of US#1 Half Breed — pre-recorded vocals, no microphone whilst sitting on a horse — was not a far cry from what would become "music videos", alas a simple one. The video was selected to be on Cher's *The Very Best of Cher: The Video Hits Collection*. The same could perhaps be said for the 1974 animated video made for her US#1 *Dark Lady*.

Cher's 1979 television special *Cher... and Other Fantasies was a* great platform for Cher to experiment with music video ideas, producing somewhat complex promotional videos for a number of pre-recorded songs: namely a multi-genre cover of 1920's blues number *Ain't Nobody's Business*, *Take Me Home* ballad album track *Love & Pain* and a upbeat cover of Bob Seger's *Feel Like A Number*.

Later in 1979, Cher released what everybody can agree on is a bona fide music video — for single *Hell On Wheels.*

Showing off her impressive roller-skating skills, the MTV-style video, though notable pre-MTV, was shown on multiple television shows.

> CHER, on *Hell On Wheels*: "Well, it was really fun. You know, it wasn't a great song, but it was fun to do."

Cher appeared alongside Meat loaf in the 1981 music video for their duet *Dead Ringer For Love*, showcasing the pair and their friends facing off in a bar.

In 1987, Cher filmed and directed the music video for *I Found Someone*, co-starring her then-boyfriend Rob Camilletti. The video showcased a mini-storyline reflecting the single's lyrics, intercut with scenes of Cher performing the song on stage in a black body-stocking and leather jacket. A second music video exists of footage solely from the stage performance. The video received an MTV Video Music Award nomination for Best Female Video.

A sultry video set predominantly on a bed co-starring Camilletti was shot for next single, 1988's *We All Sleep Alone*. A second video was shot that added scenes of Cher performing with a group of dancers in a street scene, with further shots of Cher singing in a concert setting donning a bra and a leather jacket. A music video was then produced for that same year's *Main Man*, showing Cher singing at home, once again with Camilletti, interspersed with footage of Cher performing the ballad at the 1988 MTV Video Music Awards.

Cher's next video is arguably her most famous – or perhaps infamous. *If I Could Turn Back Time* saw Cher perform the pop-rock belter on the USS Missouri battleship, whilst donning a barely-there black body-stocking in front of a group of sailors, with some scenes having her perform whilst straddling the ship's cannon. It was listed on VH1's "100 Greatest Videos" and "50 Sexiest Video Moments" lists.

Next video, *Heart Of Stone*, had her singing alone in a room with two large screens that display footage of her younger self, her children and former loves before moving onto scenes of world-famous heart-rending events, great injustice, people of power, war, peace, drugs and poverty.

The Shoop Shoop Song (It's In His Kiss) had Cher miming along to her lead vocals, and Winona Ryder and Cristina Ricci miming to the song's backing vocals, in a playful video that also featured scenes from their film *Mermaids*. An early version exists that does not show the movie clips, however. *Love & Understanding* had Cher performing on stage with a collection of dancers around her, and *Save Up All Your Tears* showed Cher in sexy outfits — including a very risqué dominatrix one – in a gothic and fiery surrounding.

The video for *Many Rivers To Cross (Live From The Mirage)* was a full live performance of the song lifted from Cher's *Heart Of Stone Tour*. *I Got You Babe* with Beavis & Butthead is a live-action animated video with real-life Cher in a black biker outfit duet with the cartoon characters in a humorous mostly-animated colourful video. Cher is seen holding hands with the animated Butt-head, as well as riding a motorbike.

Cher's next two music videos were black and white: charity song *Love Can Build A Bridge* had Cher perform with Chrissie Hynde and Neneh Cherry in a sisterly performance bookended with brief footage of the Ethiopian famine, and the Elvis Presley tribute *Walking In Memphis* saw Cher singing on the steps of a bus, whilst spending much of the video dressed as, and performing as, Elvis. *One By One* was a sepia video focusing on a couple's relationship issues, whilst Cher is seen singing the song on their television. The US version of the video is altered, with more shots of Cher.

Believe was supported by a pulsating music video with a seemingly-supernatural Cher performing the song inside a glass booth in a club with the club-goers surrounding it, before she teleports to a stage half-way through the clip with a costume change. The clip was nominated for Best Dance Video at the 1999 MTV Video Music Awards, Best Dance Clip Of The Year at the Billboard Awards plus Best Dance Video at the MVPA Awards

A residential building is struck by lightning, broadcasting a silver-haired Cher onto a fighting couple's computer monitor and other residents' television sets in the form of a virus in *Strong Enough*. *All Or Nothing* had Cher perform the song on stage in a red wig whilst borrowing footage from her then-current *Do You Believe? Tour*. And *Dov'è L'Amore* saw Cher wear a big red flamenco dress whilst singing and petting a chihuahua dog.

Più Che Puoi was a predominantly Eros Ramazzotti video, but had clips of Cher singing her parts in a recording studio alongside Ramazzotti. *The Music's No Good Without You* features Cher as a blonde outer-space queen missing a lover.

Alive Again was formed from footage actually shot for advertisements for her album *Living Proof*, thus only a small portion of it sees her singing that song. It included Cher in many costume changes in a blue room, having fun with the set and camera. Cher appears in the 9/11-dedicated *Song For The Lonely* video walking around New York City streets in the black-and-white 1800's in modern-day clothing before moving onto sepia and eventually colour as it travels through the decades. Other shots show Cher in all-white against a black background, singing.

2013's *Woman's World* stars Cher in three different outfits singing the song alongside other women of different ages, races and appearances. The single saw Cher enter the world of lyric videos — the one for this song featured bygone pin-ups with bold animated lyrics whilst the one for *I Hope You Find It* follows the songs lyrics on a wooden surface with them being written on items such as postcards, letters and maps.

Hell On Wheels

1979, Directed by Art Fisher

Dead Ringer For Love (with Meat Loaf)

1981

Appears on

I Found Someone

1987, Directed by Cher

We All Sleep Alone

1988, Directed by Cher

Main Man

1988, Directed by Cher

If I Could Turn Back Time

1989, Directed by Marty Callner

"On the *If I Could Turn Back Time* video, we shot for days. There was a whole story — I climbed up stuff, I was running away from a lover, I was in a cage, in a speedboat... And when the director got to the edit, he just said, "F*ck this, here's the money [shot]"... me on the battleship with the sailors. They were real sailors, too. They were funny. They kept calling me 'ma'am'."

– Cher

Heart Of Stone

1989, Directed by Art Fisher

The Shoop Shoop Song (It's In His Kiss)

1990, Directed by Marty Callner

Love & Understanding

1991

Save Up All Your Tears

1991, Directed by Cher

Many Rivers To Cross (Live From The Mirage)

1992, Directed by Cher

I Got You Babe (with Beavis & Butt-head)

1994

Love Can Build A Bridge (with Chrissie Hynde, Neneh Cherry & Eric Clapton)

1995

Walking In Memphis

1995, Directed by Marcus Nispel

One By One

1996, Directed by Marcus Nispel

Believe

1998, Directed by Nigel Dick

Strong Enough

1999, Directed by Nigel Dick

All Or Nothing

1999

Dov'è L'Amore

1999, Directed by Marcus Nispel

Più Che Puoi

2000

The Music's No Good Without You

2001, Directed by Nigel Dick

Song For The Lonely

2002, Directed by Stu Maschwitz

Alive Again

2002

You Haven't Seen The Last Of Me

2010, Directed by Steve Antin

Woman's World

2013, Directed by Ray Kay

Music Video Collections

The Video Collection

March 1993

The Shoop Shoop Song; If I Could Turn Back Time; Save Up All Your Tears; Love and Understanding; Heart of Stone; Main Man; We All Sleep Alone; I Found Someone; Dead Ringer for Love; Many Rivers to Cross (Live From The Mirage); I Got You Babe (with Sonny on *Top of The Pops*)

The Very Best of Cher: The Video Hits Collection

June 2004

Believe; If I Could Turn Back Time; Save Up All Your Tears; Walking in Memphis; One by One (US version)*; Main Man; I Found Someone; Strong Enough; Song for the Lonely; Half Breed; We All Sleep Alone; Heart of Stone; The Shoop Shoop Song (It's in His Kiss); Dov'è L'Amore; Love Can Build a Bridge* (with Chrissie Hynde, Neneh Cherry & Eric Clapton)

US: Platinum

Cher's Tours

"I've had like five farewell tours and every one of them was honest — it didn't occur to me that anyone would want me to come back."

– Cher

Cher's International tours and Las Vegas residencies — which are famed for her outlandish outfits and countless costume changes (usually Bob Mackie concoctions) — have grossed well over $650-million.

Together, her *Take Me Home Tour* and her following residency *A Celebration at Caesar's Palace* grossed over $40,000,000 during 1979-1983. She once again grossed over $40,000,000 during her 76-date 1989-1990 *Heart of Stone Tour* and another $20,000,000 during her much shorter *Love Hurts Tour* in 1992.

Her 1999-2000 *Do You Believe? Tour* grossed over $160,000,000 to become one of the highest-grossing female tours of all-time. Then 2002-2005's mighty 325-date *Living Proof: The Farewell Tour* did one better — *actually* becoming the highest-grossing tour by a female act ($250,000,000).

Her 2008-2011 Las Vegas residency, *Cher at the Colosseum*, grossed over $97,000,000 and won her "Best All-Around Performer", "Best Resident Show" and "Best Singer" awards from Las Vegas publications.

Cher's concerts have gave her Top 40 albums, award-winning television broadcasts, Multi-Platinum DVD releases and have included: a mechanical bull; a giant shoe; Diana Ross, Bette Midler and Cher impersonators; an on-stage closet; a pool table; aerialists; a stilt-walker; a life-size elephant puppet; and full-on choreography to showcase Cher as a triple-threat entertainer.

On 22 March 2014, Cher began her 76-date North American *Dressed To Kill Tour*. Its first leg grossed over $55,000,000 during its 49 shows. In 2017, Cher returned to the concert stage with new residency show 'Classic Cher', which, as of February 2018, has already grossed over $29,000,000. She will embark on her first Australian tour in thirteen years, the *Here We Go Again Tour*, in September 2018.

Here We Go Again Tour

Duration: 2018

Number of concerts: 8 (announced, as of June 2018)

Classic Cher

Duration: 2017-2018

Number of concerts: 87 (announced, as of June 2018)

Number of tickets sold: 190,198 (as of February 2018)

Gross amount: $29,316,863 (as of February 2018)

Songs performed: *Woman's World; Strong Enough; Gayatri Mantra; All or Nothing; The Beat Goes On; All I Really Want to Do; I Got You Babe; Gypsys, Tramps & Thieves; Dark Lady; Half-Breed; Welcome to Burlesque; Take Me Home; After All; Walking in Memphis; The Shoop Shoop Song (It's in His Kiss); I Found Someone; If I Could Turn Back Time; Believe*

Dressed To Kill Tour

Duration: 2014

Number of concerts: 49

Number of tickets sold: 609,519

Gross amount: $55,112,056

Associated album: *Closer To The Truth*

Songs performed: *Woman's World; Strong Enough; Dressed To Kill; The Beat Goes On; I Got You Babe; Gypsy's Tramps & Thieves; Dark Lady; Half Breed; Welcome To Burlesque; You Haven't Seen The Last Of Me; Take It Like A Man; Walking In Memphis; Just Like Jesse James; Heart Of Stone; The Shoop Shoop Song (It's In His Kiss); Bang Bang; I Found Someone; If I Could Turn Back Time; Believe; I Hope You Find It*

Cher At The Colosseum

Duration: 2008-2011

Number of concerts: 192

Number of tickets sold: 697,765

Gross amount: $97,421,298

Songs performed: *I Still Haven't Found What I'm Looking For; Song For The Lonely; Love Is A Battlefield; The Beat Goes On; The Fire Down Below; Old Time Rock & Roll; All Or Nothing; I Found Someone; The Best Goes On; All I Really Want To Do; Half Breed; Gypsies, Tramps & Thieves; Dark lady; Don't Leave Me This Way; Take Me Home; Love Hurts; The Way of Love; After All; Walking In Memphis; Let The Good Times Roll; Help Me Make It Through The Night; The Shoop Shoop Song (It's In His Kiss); Strong Enough; If I Could Turn Back Time; Believe*

"I should have filmed the Las Vegas show it was really good. I'll never do another show without filming."

– Cher

Living proof: The Farewell Tour

Duration: 2002-2005

Number of concerts: 325

Number of tickets sold: 3,000,000

Gross amount: $250,000,000

Associated albums: *Living Proof; The Very Best of Cher*

US TV airings: *Cher: The Farewell Tour*, 2003

Video release: *The Farewell Tour*, 2003

Songs performed: *I Still Haven't Found What I'm Looking For; Song For The Lonely; A Different Kind of Love Song; One By One; Taxi Taxi; Love Is The Groove; Love One Another; All Or Nothing; We All Sleep Alone; I Found Someone; Bang Bang; All I Really want To Do; Half Breed; Gypsies, Tramps & Thieves; Dark lady; Take Me Home; The Way of Love; Love Hurts; The Power; After All; Just Like Jesse James; Heart of Stone; Walking In Memphis; The Shoop Shoop Song (It's In His Kiss); Strong Enough; Save Up All Your Tears; If I Could Turn Back Time; Believe*

Do You Believe? Tour

Duration: 1999-2000

Number of concerts: 121

Gross amount: $160,000,000

Associated album: *Believe*

US TV airing: *Cher: Live in Concert - From the MGM Grand in Las Vegas*, 1999

Video release: *Live In Concert*, 1999

Songs performed: *I Still Haven't Found What I'm Looking For; All Or Nothing; The Power; We All Sleep Alone; I Found Someone; The Way of Love; Half Breed; Gypsies, Tramps & Thieves; Dark lady; Take Me Home; After All; Walking In Memphis; Just Like Jesse James; Heart of Stone; The Shoop Shoop Song (It's In His Kiss); Dov'è L'Amore; Strong Enough; If I Could Turn Back Time; Believe*

Love Hurts Tour

Duration: 1992

Number of concerts: 24

Gross amount: $20,000,000

Associated album: *Love Hurts*

Songs performed: *I Still Haven't Found What I'm Looking For; Love On A Rooftop; Bye Bye Baby; One Night; Fires of Eden; Could've Been You; We All Sleep Alone; I Found Someone; Love & Understanding; Save Up All Your Tears; After All; Many Rivers To Cross; The Way of Love; Fire; Just Like Jesse James; Who Make My Dreams Come True; Love Is A Battlefield; If I Could Turn Back Time; The Shoop Shoop Song (It's In His Kiss); Fire Down Below*

Heart of Stone Tour

Duration: 1989-1990

Number of concerts: 76

Gross amount: $40,000,000

Associated album: *Heart of Stone*

US TV airing: *Cher ...At The Mirage*, 1992

Video releases: *Extravaganza: Live At The Mirage*, 1992; *Live At The Mirage*, 2005

Songs performed: *I'm No Angel; Hold On; We All Sleep Alone; Bang Bang; I Found Someone; Perfection; Tougher Than The Rest; After All; Take It To The Limit; If I Could Turn Back Time; I'll Be There For You; Desperado; Love Hurts; Many Rivers To Cross; Heart of Stone; Fire Down Below; Takin' It To The Streets*

A Celebration At Caesars Palace

Duration: unknown-1983

US TV airing: *Cher: A Celebration At Caesar's Palace*, 1983

Songs performed: *Could I Be Dreaming; Signed, Sealed, Delivered I'm Yours; You Make My Dreams; Da Ya Think I'm Sexy?; Those Shoes; Out Here On My Own; Take It To The Limit; Friends; Lookin' For Love; When Will I Be Loved; More Than You know; Fame*

Black Rose Tour

Duration: 1980

Associated album: *Black Rose*

Songs performed: *Never Should've Started; Julie; You Know It; Ain't Got No Money; Dirty Old Man*

Take Me Home Tour

Duration: 1979-unknown

Associated album: *Take Me Home*

US TV airings: *The Monte Carlo Show*, 1980; *Standing Room only: Cher in Concert*, 1981

Songs performed: *Ain't Nobody's Business; Signed, Sealed, Delivered I'm Yours; Fire; Easy To Be Hard; Ain't No Mountain High Enough; Friends; Jailhouse Rock; Dream Lover; Great Balls of Fire; Rockin' Robin; Johnny B. Goode; Dedicated To The One I Love; Hand Jive; Honky Tonk Woman; Old Time Rock & Roll; Take It To The Limit; Take Me Home; Takin' It To The Streets; Ain't Got No Money*

Two The Hard Way Tour

Duration: 1977

Associated album: *Two The Hard Way*

Songs performed: *Move Me; Do What You Gotta Do; You've Really Got A Hold On Me; Love The One You're With; Love Me; Half Breed*

Sonny & Cher Tour, 1977

Duration: 1977

Songs performed: *All I Ever Need Is You; I Can See Clearly Now; United We Stand; Without You; The Way of Love; Love Will Keep Us Together; Baby Don't Go; All I Really Want To Do; You Better Sit Down Kids; Send In The Clowns; The Beat Goes On; Half Breed; Gypsies, Tramps & Thieves; Dark Lady; A Cowboy's Work Is Never Done; I Got You Babe*

Tour Releases

Extravaganza: Live At The Mirage

June 1992

I'm No Angel; Hold On; We All Sleep Alone; Bang Bang; I Found Someone; Perfection; Tougher Than The Rest; After All; Take It to the Limit; If I Could Turn Back Time; Many Rivers to Cross; The Fire Down Below; Takin' It to the Streets

Live In Concert

December 1999

I Still Haven't Found What I'm Looking For; All or Nothing; The Power; We All Sleep Alone; I Found Someone; The Way of Love; Half-Breed; Gypsies, Tramps and Thieves; Dark Lady; Take Me Home; After All; Walking in Memphis; Just Like Jesse James; The Shoop Shoop Song (It's in His Kiss); Dov'è L'Amore; Strong Enough; If I Could Turn Back Time; Believe

UK: Platinum

The Farewell Tour

August 2003

I Still Haven't Found What I'm Looking For; Song for the Lonely; Gayatri Mantra; All or Nothing; I Found Someone; Bang Bang (My Baby Shot Me Down); The Beat Goes On; Baby Don't Go; I Got You Babe; All I Really Want to Do; Half-Breed; Gypsies, Tramps & Thieves; Dark Lady; Take

Me Home; The Way of Love; After All; Just Like Jesse James; Heart of Stone; The Shoop Shoop Song (It's in His Kiss); Strong Enough; If I Could Turn Back Time; Believe

(Bonus songs: *Save Up All Your Tears; We All Sleep Alone; A Different Kind Of Love Song*)

US: Triple-Platinum

UK: Platinum

Live At The Mirage

November 2005

I'm No Angel; We All Sleep Alone; Bang Bang (My Baby Shot Me Down); I Found Someone; Take It to the Limit; If I Could Turn Back Time; Perfection; The Fire Down Below; Takin' It to the Streets; After All

(Bonus songs: *Hold On; Many Rivers To Cross; Tougher Than The Rest*)

Cher's Awards

Cher has won hundreds of awards from around the world for her dedication to music, film, television, fashion and philanthropy.

Perhaps her most treasured is her 1988 Academy Award for Best Actress for *Moonstruck*. That, and her 2000 Grammy Award and her 2003 Emmy Award make her just a Tony Award-win away from becoming an EGOT (Emmy-, Grammy-, Oscar- and Tony-winner) — a feat that only 12 individuals have ever achieved.

Cher has also achieved three Golden Globe Awards for her TV and Film acting, whilst achieving the prestigious 'Best Actress' title at the Cannes Film Festival.

1965

Billboard Award

First Hot 100 #1 single

Disc Magazine Award — Silver Disc Award

I Got You Babe

1968

WLS Radio Hit Parade Award

Best Female

WLS Radio Hit Parade Award

Best Duet

Sonny & Cher

1971

Disc Magazine Award — Silver Disc Award

Gypsies, Tramps & Thieves

1972

AGVA Entertainer of the Year Award

Musical Group of the Year

Sonny & Cher

MOA JukeBox Award

Artists of the Year

Sonny & Cher

Special Dallas Times Award

1973

AGVA Entertainer of the Year Award

Vocal Act of the Year

Sonny & Cher

Millicent Waldron Award

Spectacular Costumes Award

Sonny & Cher

1974

AGVA Entertainer of the Year Award

Vocal Act of the Year

Sonny & Cher

Golden Globe Award

Best Actress, Television Series Musical or Comedy

The Sonny & Cher Comedy Hour

1975

Shidurei Israel Radio Award

Best Female Singer

1981

Vegas Magazine Award

Female Performer of the Year

1983

CableACE Award

Best Actress in a Variety Program

Cher: A Celebration at Caesars

1984

Golden Globe Award

Best Supporting Actress, Motion Picture

Silkwood

1985

Cannes Film Festival Award

Best Actress

Mask

Hasty Pudding Woman of the Year Award

1987

Kansas City Critics Film Circle Award

Best Actress

Moonstruck

1988

Academy Award

Best Actress

Moonstruck

David di Donatello Award

Best Foreign Actress

Moonstruck

Golden Globe Award

Best Actress, Motion Picture Musical or Comedy

Moonstruck

Italian National Syndicate of Film Journalists — Silver Ribbon Award

Best Foreign Actress

Moonstruck

Utah Film Critics Association Award

Best Actress

Moonstruck

1989

BMI Pop Award

After All

People's Choice Award

Favourite All-Around Female Star

1991

Bravo Otto Award

Favorite Female Singer - Pop: Silver Award

1992

ECHO Award

International Female Artist

IRMA Music Award

International Female Artist

Pro Set L.A. Music Award

Best Female Pop Vocalist

VSDA Award

Health and Fitness Homer Award

CherFitness: A New Attitude

1998

GLAAD Media Award

Vanguard Award

Hollywood Walk of Fame star

Sonny & Cher

IFPI Platinum Europe Award

Believe

IFPI Platinum Europe Award

The Greatest Hits

Rockbjörnen Award

Foreign Song of the Year

Believe

1999

Anděl Awards

Best Foreign Female Singer

Billboard Music Award

Single of the Year

Believe

CFDA Fashion Award

Special Award

Danish Music Award

Best International Hit

Believe

International Dance Music Award

Best Hi NRG 12"

Believe

International Dance Music Award

Best Pop 12" Dance Record

Believe

Ivor Novello Award

Best Selling UK Single

Believe

Ivor Novello Award

Best Song Musically and Lyrically

Believe

Ivor Novello Award

International Hit of the Year

Believe

Midem's Dance d'Or Award

Best International Single

Believe

Music Control Airplay Award

Most Played International Artist

Believe

Premios Amigo Award

Best International Album

Believe

Premios Amigo Award

Best International Female Solo Artist

PRS Award

Club Play Award

Believe

World Music Award

Legend Award for Outstanding Contribution to the Music Industry

US International Film and Video Festival Award

Gold Camera Award

Believe

2000

ASCAP Pop Music Award

Song of the Year

Believe

ASCAP Pop Music Award

Pop Award

Believe

Blockbuster Entertainment Award

Favorite Female Artist (Pop)

ECHO Award

International Female Artist

Grammy Award

Best Dance Recording

Believe

Hungarian Music Award

Foreign Pop Album of the Year

Believe

Online Film & Television Association Award

Best Host or Performer of a Variety, Musical, or Comedy
Special

Cher — Live in Concert

Women in Film Lucy Award

If These Walls Could Talk

2001

Bambi Award

International Pop Artist

Premios Ondas

Lifetime Achievement Award

2002

Billboard Music Award

Artist Achievement Award

Billboard Music Award

Dance/Club Play Artist of the Year

Guinness Book of British Hit Singles

Oldest Solo Female Artist to Top the Charts

Guinness Book of British Hit Singles

Best-Selling Single by a Female Artist

Believe

2003

Emmy Award

Outstanding Variety, Music or Comedy Special

Cher: The Farewell Tour

2004

Women's World Award

World Arts Award

2005

MTV Australia Award

VH1 Music First Award

XM Nation Music Award

Most Likely to Have Another "Final" Tour Award

2007

Guinness World Record

Highest Grossing Tour by a Female Artist of All Time

Guinness World Record

Oldest Female Solo Artist to Top the Billboard Hot 100 Chart

TV Land Award

TV's Greatest Music Moment

"Sonny & Cher on *Late Night with David Letterman*"

2008

Tashir Armenia Music Award

Legend Award

2010

Annual Las Vegas Review Journal's "Best of Las Vegas"

Best All-Around Performer

Cher at the Colosseum

Grauman's Chinese Theatre

Handprints and Footprints Ceremony

Glamour Award

Woman of the Year, Lifetime Achievement Award

Los Premios 40 Principales

Lifetime Achievement Award

Satellite Award

Best Original Song

You Haven't Seen the Last of Me

2011

Annual Las Vegas Review Journal's "Best of Las Vegas"

Best Singer

Cher at the Colosseum

Broadway World Las Vegas Award

Best Resident Show

Cher at the Colosseum

iVillage Entertainment Award

The Most Welcome Celebrity Comeback

2013

Attitude Award

Legend Award

BMI London Award

4 Million Performance Award

Believe

Women's Image Award

Best TV Show Produced by a Woman

Dear Mom, Love Cher

2014

White Party Palm Springs Icon Award

2015

amfAR Award

Inspiration Award

2017

Grammy Hall of Fame

I Got You Babe — Sonny & Cher

Billboard Music Award

Icon Award

Polls and Lists

1965

#9 on NME's "World Female Singer"

#12 on NME's "World Vocal Group"

1966

#5 on NME's "World Female Singer"

#20 on NME's "World Vocal Group"

1967

#18 on NME's "World Female Singer"

1971

#5 on NME's "World Female Singer"

1975

#9 on People Magazine's "25 Most Intriguing People"

1977

#8 on Ladies' Home Journal's "10 Celebrities Girls Want To Be"

1987

#10 on People Magazine's "25 Most Intriguing People"

1990

#7 on Gallup's "Today's Most Admired Women"

1991

#2 on Madame Tussaud's Wax Museum's "5 Most Beautiful
Women of History"

1996

#23 on Celebrity Sleuth's "50 Best Butts"

1997

#58 on Entertainment Weekly's "100 Greatest Entertainers
of All Time"

1998

#9 on Billboard's "Most #1 Hits by Female Artist"

#5 on Billboard's "Most Top 40 Hits by Female Artist"

#5 on Billboard's "Most Charted Hits by Female Artist"

1999

#1 on Billboard's "Oldest Female Artist to Top the Hot 100
Chart" — 52 Years, 297 Days"

#1 on Billboard's "Record of Largest Gap Between #1 Hits
on Billboard's Hot 100 Singles Chart" — 25 Years"

#1 on Billboard's "Record of Largest Span of #1 Hits on
Billboard's Hot 100 Singles Chart" — 34 Years.

#43 on VH1's "100 Greatest Women Of Rock and Roll"

2000

#60 on VH1's "100 Greatest Dance Songs" — *Believe*

#9 on Forbes' "Celebrity 100 Power Ranking"

2001

#49 on VH1's "100 Greatest Videos" — *If I Could Turn Back Time*

2002

#26 on VH1's "100 Sexiest Artists of All Time"

#13 on TV Guide's "50 Sexiest TV Stars Of All-Time"

#58 on Q Magazine's "100 Women Who Rock the World"

#56 on Entertainment Weekly's "100 Greatest Performances that Should Have Won an Oscar but Didn't" — *Mask*

2003

#17 on VH1's "50 Greatest Women Of The Video Era"

#41 on VH1's "200 Greatest Pop Culture Icons"

#40 on VH1's "50 Sexiest Video Moments" — *If I Could Turn Back Time*

#2 on VH1's "25 Greatest Rock Star Cameos" — *Will & Grace*

#34 on Blender Magazine's "50 Hottest Rock & Roll Couples of All Time"

#28 on Forbes' "Celebrity 100 Power Ranking"

#10 on Rolling Stone's "50 Richest Rockers"

#6 on Time's "Ultimate Top 10 List of Pop's Moneymakers"

#19 on USA Today's "Pop Candy's 100 People of the Year"

2004

#40 on Forbes' "Celebrity 100 Power Ranking"

#63 on Forbes' "Celebrity 100 Power Ranking by Press"

#42 on Forbes' "Celebrity 100 Power Ranking by Salary"

#49 on Forbes' "Celebrity 100 Power Ranking by TV"

#14 on Forbes' "Celebrity 100 Power Ranking by Web Hits"

#9 on MuchMoreMusic's "Top 20 Divine Divas"

#43 on Rolling Stone's "50 Richest Rockers"

#444 on Rolling Stone's list of the "500 Greatest Songs of All Time" — *I Got You Babe*

2007

#74 on VH1's "100 Greatest Songs of the 90's" — *Believe*

#20 on VH1's "100 Greatest Love Songs" — *I Got You Babe*

#72 on "Entertainment Weekly's Top 100 TV Icons"

#2 on MuchMoreMusic's "Top 20 Richest Rockers"

2008

#36 on Zimbio's "The 50 Sexiest Women Over 50"

#12 on MuchMoreMusic's "Top 20 Most Distinctive Voices"

2009

#1 on MuchMoreMusic's "Top 20 Artists With the Wildest Hair"

#12 on MuchMoreMusic's "Top 20 Women Who Work the Video"

#55 on PPL's "Top 75 Songs Most Played in Public in Britain in the Last 75 Years" — *Believe*

2011

#1 on Billboard's "Record of Having #1 Singles in Six Consecutive Decades"

#35 on Billboard's "The 40 Biggest Duets Of All Time" — *I Got You Babe*

#42 on Billboard's "Top 50 Adult Contemporary Artists Ever"

#17 on Billboard's "25 Greatest Pop Hooks of All Time" — *Believe*

#9 on Rolling Stone's "The 10 Greatest Duets of All Time" — *I Got You Babe*

2012

#7 on Rolling Stone's "The Most Memorable Super Bowl National Anthems"

#31 on VH1's "100 Greatest Women in Music"

#67 on Complex's "The 100 Hottest Female Singers of All Time"

2013

#1 on Billboard's "Female Artist with Longest Span of Top 5 Albums on Billboard's Top 200 Albums Chart" — Over 48 Years"

#37 on Yahoo!'s "Top 250 Female Singers of the 20th Century".

#16 on Fabriah's "The Top 50 Iconic Hairstyles of the Last 50 Years"

#2 on MTV's "The Top 40 Musicians-Turned-Actors"

2014

#23 on Billboard's "Top 25 Live Artists Since 1990"

#1 on Billboard's "Record of Having Top 20 Singles in Five Consecutive Decades on Billboard's Adult Contemporary Chart"

#1 on VH1's "10 Times When Auto-Tuning Totally Worked" — *Believe*

#12 on VH1's "15 Greatest Legs in The Music Biz"

#18 on Rolling Stone's "20 Greatest Duos of All Time"

2015

#17 on Billboard's "25 Greatest Pop Hooks of All Time" — *Believe*

2016

#35 on Billboard's "The 40 Biggest Duets Of All Time" — *I Got You Babe*

#43 on Billboard's "Hot 100 All-Time Top Artists"

#44 on Esquire's "The 75 Greatest Women of All Time"

2017

#18 on Billboard's "Greatest of All Time Hot 100 Women Artists"

#23 on Billboard's "Greatest of All Time Top Dance Club Artists"

#99 on Billboard's "Greatest of All Time Hot 100 Songs by Women" — *Half Breed*

Cher's Relationships

"The trouble with some women is they get all excited about nothing — and then marry him".

– Cher

Before meeting first husband Sonny Bono, a 16-year-old Cher had a brief romance with 25-year-old actor Warren Beatty. It fizzled out before Cher met Sonny, with whom she began a serious relationship. They had one child, daughter Chastity Sun Bono, born 4 March 1969, shortly before getting married (despite the pair telling the public that they were already wed when rising to super-stardom in 1965.)

Sonny and Cher separated in 1972 but remained married until 1974. In the meantime, Cher dated music mogul David Geffen. In the mid 1970's, Cher almost went for a date with King of Rock 'n' Roll Elvis Presley, but her nerves got the better of her and she backed out: "Almost, I got nervous, I didn't get there [to the date], I was that nervous. I wish I had."

Cher started a much-publicised relationship with The Allman Brothers Band's Gregg Allman in 1974. Cher and Allman married in 1975, before having one child together, son Elijah Blue Allman, born 10 July 1976. The pair separated in 1977, and divorced in 1978.

She began a three-year-long relationship in 1977 with Gene Simmons, whom declared Cher as his first love. This was in the days before Simmons' rock band Kiss — whom always sported face paint during public appearances — had revealed their bare faces to the world. Thus, the majority of the many photographs of Cher and Simmons at the time show him with his face half-covered.

Cher met guitarist Les Dudek when she created rock project Black Rose in 1980. The pair became romantically-involved, which lasted until 1982. Cher was introduced to 22-year-old actor Val Kilmer during a party for her 36th Birthday and the two began a near-two-year relationship.

Joshua Donen, the American film producer and son of Stanley Donen — director of such films as *Singin' in the Rain* and *Charade* — was Cher's next boyfriend, beginning in late 1984 and ending in 1986. However, midway through, the pair seemingly had a break as Cher briefly dated actor Tom Cruise in 1985.

On the eve of Cher's 40th Birthday, Cher met bagel shop worker Rob Camilletti, and later asked him for a date. The pair were an item for three years, until 1989. Cher rebound with Bon Jovi guitarist Richie Sambora for a matter of months. Cher was once again photographed with Camilletti at multiple events in 1991. However, her usual dates for events for the rest of the decade were her son Elijah and daughter Chastity.

Cher was openly on the dating scene again in 2008 and 2009, this time with former Hells Angel Tim Medvetz. In 2010, Cher was regularly snapped with new beau, television writer Ron Zimmerman whom she met on Facebook. The pair were photographed together as late as 2012.

Warren Beatty, b. 1937

Dated in 1962

Cher: "I did it because my girlfriends were crazy about him and so was my mother. What a disappointment!"

Sonny Bono, b. 1935

Dated 1962-1969, married 1969-1975 (separated in 1972)

Cher: "I was the kid, I was 16 and he was 28, and so he just knew a lot more than I did so that I got used to him being right about things that I kind of stopped trying. You know, I just thought, *well, you know, whatever, Sonny knows what he's doing so I'll just let him do it,* and I just got a little bit lazy too."

David Geffen, b. 1943

Dated 1973-1974

Cher: "I was the first person to share his bed and to share his life. People don't believe that, or they don't want to believe it, or they don't understand how it could be."

Gregg Allman, b. 1947

Dated 1974-1975, married 1975-1978 (separated in 1977)

Cher: "I loved him and he is a very gentle spirit that just isn't strong enough to deal with fame and fortune and he just should have stayed down home... I loved him that makes you weak right there but I was the pillar, I was the strong woman who was going to change him and all that."

Gene Simmons, b.1949

Dated 1977-1980

Cher, in 1979: "We just had a wonderful suite at Chicago's Ritz-Carlton overlooking the lake, and Gene said at breakfast that it never ceases to amaze him how comfortable he is with me. He has never had a steady girlfriend, never had a relationship with anybody. That's pretty heavy stuff. He's a very strange, complicated and honest person"

Les Dudek, b. 1952

Dated 1980-1982

Ron Duguay, b.1957

Dated 1982

Cher: "That lasted for about a minute and a half."

Val Kilmer, b.1959

Dated 1982-1984

Cher: "[We spent] a week just talking before we kissed. We had a friendship first. I was wondering if something was wrong with him. I don't know what he thought of me. But when we did kiss, I thought my head would shoot right off my body. I had to catch my breath."

CHER: "I could write what I know about men on the head of a pin — and still have room for the Yellow Pages."

Josh Donen, b. 1955

Dated 1984-1986

Cher, 1985: "[He] has the best strengths of all the men I've been with."

Tom Cruise, b.1962

Dated 1985

Cher: "He was shy and sweet and just the most adorable man you can imagine. I was crazy about him."

Rob Camilletti, b. 1964

Dated 1986-1989

Cher, 1998: "The hardest thing for me to understand was that he simply seemed to love me as I was. We are best friends to this day. And I will never not love him."

Richie Sambora, b. 1959

Dated 1989

"I only dated younger men because they were the ones to ask. Older men don't ask me out. Are they frightened of me? I don't know. Older men never find me that attractive. It seems strange that a young man isn't intimidated, but an older man is."

– Cher

Tim Medvetz, b. 1970

Dated 2008-2009

Ron Zimmerman, b. 1958

Dated 2010-2012

Cher: "Ron is short, a bit scraggly, like an absent-minded professor. He's the funniest person I have ever met, and the most eccentric — so bizarre and kind and very special."

"I've had many loves in my life. I've had one love in my life that was fabulous. I've had a couple of loves in my life actually. I've had three..."

- **– Cher**

Cher Q&A

Q: What is your earliest memory?

A: Being lost in the woods. I was four.

Q: You always credit Sonny with "creating" the persona of Cher. Where do you think you would be now if he hadn't come into your life?

A: When I met Sonny, I was a sixteen year old girl. Totally scattered energy. I've been Cher since I was three. But he focused the energy, but I have no idea. I might be a bank robber. Or editor of French *Vogue*.

Q: Do you miss Sonny?

A: I think about him a lot sometimes. There are things about him that I miss.

Q: Did you ever work with Elvis?

A: I never worked with him, but he was a huge influence. Elvis and James Dean were two big influences on my art. Listen we kind of sound a like! Not so much on my later albums, but my middle albums. It's kind of hard for me because I didn't have any really female entertainer role models. I had actresses that I love but I wasn't like any of them. It was hard for me and it wasn't that easy.

Q: Who is the most inspiring artist you've worked with?

A: Oh, Meryl Streep. Also, Val Kilmer. I once did an audition with Val for a playhouse we wanted to be a part of, and while we were doing this scene I forgot what I was doing and just stopped and watched him.

Q: What happened when you and Meryl Streep saved a girl from being mugged?

A: Well — Meryl had just had Mimi and wanted to get some ice cream, she was just telling me what a safe neighborhood it is. It's Little Italy bordering on Chinatown. We walked around the corner, there was this huge guy ripping this girl's clothes and trying to get her purse. Meryl just took off and starting yelling running towards them. Then I did too. The guy got frightened and started running towards us!

I thought, *Great, we saved the girl and now we're going to get killed*. When we got to the girl, she was completely shaken up. Her dress was ripped and she was crying. We kind of patted her, and we started talking to her, and we asked her if she needed help going anywhere or doing anything. She said she was a singing waitress. Then she started screaming "Oh my god I was just saved by Meryl Streep and Cher!". Then we looked over and there were two men standing there and they didn't do anything. These two big asshole men just watched her.

Q: What was one of the most memorable moments of your career?

A: Oh gosh. The scene in *Mask* when I find out that Rocky is dead. That was a particularly, I don't know. It was horrible, but I felt really proud of it afterwards.

Q: Did you enjoy making *Mask*?

A: I did enjoy making the movie with the actors, I did not enjoy working with the director. Until about the last third he was really mean to me.

Q: How was working with Jack Nicholson?

A: Oh, it's wonderful, he's a love. I've known him my whole adult life. He is more amazing then people think he is, and so kind, and he loves women. Actually he loves hanging out with women. He painted a little bull for me for my birthday because we are both Taurus'. Taurus people rule!

Q: Which movie did you enjoy making the most?

A: Maybe *Moonstruck* because we never felt like we were working. We were a family and we weren't acting. I never felt like I was acting.

Q: Will you ever do another romantic comedy?

A: I'd like to!

Q: Who would you love to star with in a movie?

A: Val Kilmer.

Q: What is your favorite movie?

A: That's an almost impossible question. The thing that popped into my mind is the *Godfather*. And maybe *Godfather II* might be better. Actually, Francis gave me as a present the two of them cut together, which is amazing. I think that's what I think is a perfect film, the two of them cut together.

Q: What's your most fondest memory of you and Michael Jackson's friendship?

A: I guess him teaching me the routine we did together on TV, all of us, because he was so complicated for me. You can see it on YouTube.

Q: What is your favorite color?

A: Black. If black is not a color and I love white and if I have a color, turquoise or anything neon. This is why I'd never be good one of those dating things, and I had multiple answers and questions.

Q: Do you still think Letterman is an asshole?

A: Yeah but that's what I love about him.

Q: What is your favorite holiday?

A: Groundhog Day.

Q: What was your most memorable Halloween moment?

A: I was doing the *Cher* show and I had all of the stage crew come set up my house like a cemetery. I was a vampire. We had dead bodies bouncing out of coffins and we had ghosts flying around the trees and this huge sound system it was amazing. We had vultures and trees and Elijah was not even a year old and he was in a devil costume.

Q. Are you afraid of ghosts?

A: Absolutely not! I love ghosts. I actually think that Sonny makes a light go on. I have a beautiful chandelier that he makes the light go on when it is impossible, there is no power on. I love ghosts, I prefer ghosts to some people.

Q: What is your favorite flower?

A: I like — it's a toss up — gardenias, oh, the kind of jasmine you get in Tahiti but I don't know what it's called and Casablanca lilies.

Q: What's your favorite ice cream flavor?

A: Rocky road and chocolate chip. And I also like pistachio. Those are my three favorites. And Häagen-Dazs strawberry ice cream. I could eat a whole pint of it — and I have. I once ate a dozen Entenmann's donuts, and four chocolate dove bars and I didn't even offer my assistant Jen a bit. I'd been in court for a week, and I couldn't eat because it was so traumatic for me, and 9/11 happened in the middle of it, and I almost lost the case; after I won the case I went to the market and got all of it and I didn't even get sick. We lost one juror because he was working for Satan!

Q: What would be your ideal birthday present?

A: A Balinese house in Tahitii. Or a frozen hot chocolate from Serendipity in New York.

Q: What is the best and worst part about being Cher?

A: The worst part is no privacy. I don't know what the best part is. I'm not sure if this is the best part, but I don't give up. I don't give up and I have a really good sense of humor.

You know what else is really great, is I get to go everywhere and meet different kinds of people. Like I just woke up one morning and decided I was going to Katmandu. That opened up a completely new life with great new friends.

Q: Is there a particular picture or photoshoot that really captures the essence of who you are?

A: Richard Avedon. Well I've had so many, come on. Norman Seeff. I really liked the Argentinian boys Estudio Machado Cicala Morassut.

Q: What is your favorite costume that Bob Mackie has made for you?

A: Oh the outfit that I wore on the Academy Awards when I gave the best performing actor award to Don Ameche, ...*Turn Back Time* outfit and the cover of *Time* magazine.

Q: What is something that you would absolutely not wear on stage?

A: Orange.

Q: What is your most memorable moment from being on Tour?

A: The time I got my hair stuck in my costume at the Astrodome. I got my hair stuck in my zipper!

Q: What advice do you have for young women in abusive relationships?

A: You have to get out of it immediately. Life is too short. Also, no one can love you if they are abusing you. Those two things can't happen at the same time. Also if you are young you can't see the future. That's dead end, sometimes literally.

Q: What skin products do you use on your face?

A: Well, I use Jan Marini and sometimes proactive.

Q: What do you do to keep yourself in shape and healthy?

A: I don't smoke, drink or do drugs. Maybe twice a year I have a shot of Papi. Don't eat meat and choose wisely in the gene department. I literally work my ass off. Thank god I like exercising!

Q: Do you like to be a brunette or blonde better?

A: I don't care I'm going to be one one day, another the next day. Kinda keeps going round in a circle!

Q: What is your real hair like?

A: Black and long. But I cut it recently but I'm going to let it grow really long. It's not too short but it's not long enough, I'm used to it being really long. It's about 6 or 8 inches below my shoulders.

Q: I've always been curious about the pink toned eyeshadow, why?

A: I don't know. It used to start with blue. I used to make my own eye shadow when I was younger, because I couldn't get what I wanted, I would make it an a double boiler. I don't know it just kind of started that way. And now it's kind of pink and purple with colored stones, I like doing that. And glitter, for anyone that hasn't figured that out already.

Q: Do you enjoy meet-and-greets with fans?

A: I actually do. But I don't usually do them on the road because I come in at the last minute, because if I wait around too long I get too nervous, and then I would just do a runner off the stage. If you don't, you don't get out of the parking lot. You have to get to the next city in time to sleep. After all, 100 years old, you need your beauty sleep. Usually I meet people in the town that I am playing in by accident. I do meet cranio-facial kids, or Make-A-Wish or kids with special problems I find out about it. I can't put on a show, and do hair and makeup, and do meet-and-greets all the time.

Q: What was your reaction, as a parent, to having a transgender child? What can other parents do to support their children who identify as transgender or as members of the LGBT community in general?

A: Well, I'm not sure if it's scary to all parents. What I've realized, just lately, in the beginning I think I was afraid of losing a child before I got the new one. Of losing the old one before I got the new one. But we have such a great time now, and I realize that there is no loss. In the beginning, you're just not sure. As parents, it's a little bit scary. Maybe, what people need to do is just *chill* and not be frightened. It's not all about you, or it wasn't about me.

Q: Did you know you were a diva before anyone knew the meaning?

A: Absolutely. The first thing I said to the doctor: "Make sure you cut me a nice belly button, I'm going to be showing it to the world".

Q: Does music still feed your soul?

A: It's such a strange relationship, but I do love singing. I like just like the feeling of it. I actually like the physical feeling of it.

Q: What happened to *The Greatest Thing* with you and Lady Gaga?

A: She didn't like it. Actually, we should have been in the same room. It could have been better, if we'd worked on it more, it could have been good enough to put out. I think it's a really great song, I love the song, and I'm extremely sorry that it didn't come out. I'm sorry that the idiot who leaked it leaked the wrong version. I'd never even heard that version.

Q: If you had to pick one other artist to do a duet with, who would it be?

A: Bruno Mars. Or P!nk. Or Merle Haggard. I can't forget Merle Haggard. Or if he was really, really good, Blake Shelton!

Q: Who is your favorite singer of this generation?

A: Oh my god that's so hard. Adele. I think Adele.

Q: How do you keep your voice so strong, and clear?

A: I practice.

Q: What is your favorite and least favorite song on *Closer to the Truth*?

A: If you'd asked me this about any other album, I'd have an answer immediately. This album is different. I love *Favorite Scars* and *Red*. I don't have a least favorite one. They are like children. Depends on what time of day.

Q: How does it feel to be one of the most famous people in world?

A: I don't know. I don't ever go around thinking it, it's actually never entered my mind once in my life.

Q: Do you have any regrets?

A: Of course I do. You can't really dwell them on them because you just become paralyzed. You have to go on and resolve to do better. Just beating up on yourself doesn't do you any good or I'd be black and blue. It's not a Buddhist way to do things. You have to be kind to yourself in order to be a better person for everyone else.

Q: Have you ever wished you had a quiet life, instead of being a star?

A: Yes

Q: What do you love the most about your fans?

A: Just that they are so supportive of me and have been since the beginning and they are so supportive of each other which I really appreciate.

Q: What is the number one wish that most fans ask you to grant?

A: "Follow me"

Q: What would be the core message that you want all your fans to keep in mind?

A: My imperfections are boundless.

Q: What's the most important thing you've learned in life?

A: Don't sweat the small stuff. And my mother's advice: "If it doesn't matter in five years, it doesn't matter." Try to do better tomorrow. Those are the things I know.

What Other Stars Say About Cher

"Let's call it what it is, before Britney, before Madonna, there was *only* Cher."

– KISS bassist **Gene Simmons**

"The kind of fame that Cher has, and the audience base that she has, is very unique and sort-of once-in-a-lifetime, that kind of celebrity."

– US comedienne **Rosie O'Donnell**

"She's been in our lives every decade. She kind of grew up with us."

– US singer/songwriter **Cyndi Lauper**

"She comes in the room and owns the place, puts everybody at ease. She's good news."

– Movie legend **Meryl Streep**

"I think she's aged very gracefully."

– Queen of Pop **Madonna**

"She is undeniably one of the most fascinating and charismatic performers of all-time."

– Chat show queen **Oprah Winfrey**

"I remember seeing *Moonstruck* and loving it so much. Then I learned more about Cher as a singer. She's actually my favorite karaoke choice and also one my top people to follow on Twitter. Cher is very entertaining. I connect with her history of her major ups and major downs. Not only is she stunning, she's very inspiring."

– *Crazy Ex-Girlfriend* star **Gabrielle Ruiz**

"She's a good friend and she's really a great girl."

– The Righteous Brothers' **Bill Medley**

"She's a mother, she's talent, she's beauty, she's style, she's puella eternis all in one delicious package. In fact, she's reinvented herself so many times, she's got nineteen patents on her ass."

– Aerosmith vocalist **Steven Tyler**

"Cher is one of my greatest heroines."

– *Absolutely Fabulous* star **Jennifer Saunders**

"She's a bright and truly funny gal. It goes without saying she is talented and will be doing her thing for as long as she wants to."

– Music legend **Dionne Warwick**

"Cher was a stunning presence with her beautiful, flowing hair and her floor-length gowns. She was pure showbiz."

– US actress **Teri Garr**

"The most remarkable thing about Cher is that she constantly reinvents herself but maintains a strong sense of identity."

– US actor **Stanley Tucci**

"When the industry has labelled Cher as being 'too this' or 'too that', she's come out and shown everyone that the individual can overcome those labels."

– The Supremes' **Mary Wilson**

"When I was growing up, like my biggest dream was to maybe have sex with Cher. And it's because she always wears stuff like that. You know, it's the stuff. You know, it's just provocative."

– US actor & rapper **Will Smith**

"Somebody who I always really admired and still do, because of her very being and her beauty... But I've always admired her. I love her acting, and I love her self-transformation."

– Dead or Alive vocalist **Pete Burns**

"She's inventive, she's outspoken, I think it always makes good press, she's fascinating, you don't know everything about her but she's candid."

– US actress & comedienne **Lily Tomlin**

"She's a Goddess!"

– The Black Eyed Peas' **Fergie**

"She's been there and done everything, before any of us. How could you not learn from Cher with her work ethic and the way she commands attention when she walks into a room, but exudes such peaceful tranquillity and love for everyone."

– US singer/songwriter **Christina Aguilera**

"I think she's a magical woman; she's up there with Cleopatra."

– US songwriter & producer **Desmond Child**

"I love Cher, her voice is magical."

– *Got To Be Real* singer **Cheryl Lynn**

"She was everything I wanted her to be and more. She really was. You never know what to expect when there is someone so otherworldly in the same room as you. You treat her differently no matter how much you try not to because she's so iconic. But she's also so grounded and so surprisingly honest and sarcastic and funny. It made me feel so special that I was getting to know the human being behind this gigantic icon."

– US actress **Kristen Bell**

"I have so much respect for Cher and I love Cher so much."

– US singer/songwriter **Lady Gaga**

"Love her, eternally cool."

- The Go-Go's & solo singer **Belinda Carlisle**

"Her artistry, her commitment to her craft and her willingness to take on new creative challenges have served as an inspiration to me in my career. And she continues to inspire."

- Solo and No Doubt singer **Gwen Stefani**

"If you never give up,

and no matter what anyone says about you,

no matter what happens to you,

if you just never give up,

not only will you get you to the thing that you love,

but you might end up having the last giggle."

– Cher

Introduction

Cher started her career as a backing vocalist for Phil Spector's iconic Wall of Sound, before shooting to superstardom herself with the sixties anthem *I Got You Babe*. Cher mastered folk-rock, achieved three US #1's during the singer-songwriter era of the 1970's, whilst having a glittering television career. She made her mark on disco, Broadway and the 1980's hair metal scene and earned the highest acting honor available. Cher absolutely conquered the 1990's dance scene whilst in her 50's, and was given the Goddess Of Pop title in her 60's.

Along the way, Cher has knocked The Beatles off #1, had five US Hot 100 hits simultaneously, appeared on the Live Aid stage, had US#1 movies with Meryl Streep and Jack Nicholson, attended Madonna's wedding in a purple wig, called David Letterman an "asshole", inaugurated Disneyland, had the highest-grossing female tour of all-time, had hits in six decades and held Lady Gaga's meat purse.

She's done it all. She's Cher – The Goddess of Pop...

1963-1964

Sonny and Cher On Spector's Wall Of Sound

July, 1963: Sonny and Cher record backing vocals on The Ronette's *Be My Baby* and The Crystal's *Then He Kissed Me* at Gold Star Studios in Los Angeles, California.

September 08, 1963: Sonny and Cher record backing vocals for Darlene Love's *A Fine, Fine Boy* at Gold Star Studios.

September 1963: Phil Spector completes his multi-artist Christmas LP – many of its tracks have Sonny and Cher on backing vocals, notably Darlene Love's *Christmas (Baby Please Come Home)*, on which Cher is clearly audible.

November, 1963: Sonny and Cher record backing vocals on The Ronette's *Baby I Love You* and The Crystal's *I Wonder* and *Little Boy* at Gold Star Studios.

February, 1964: Sonny and Cher record backing vocals on The Ronettes' *(The Best Of) Breakin' Up* at Gold Star Studios.

February 18, 1964: Sonny and Cher record their first song *The Letter*, to be released under the guise "Caesar & Cleo".

March 04, 1964: Cher releases her debut solo single *Ringo I Love You* under the pseudonym "Bonnie Jo Mason".

March 11, 1964: Billboard magazine features Caesar & Cleo's *The Letter* as a "Pop Spotlight": "Unrelenting is the term for this driver. Side has fat, pushing sound and pours along on droning, highly danceable rock sound."

April, 1964: Sonny and Cher record a host of covers: *Love Is Strange* by Mickey & Sylvia; *Do You Want To Dance?* by Bobby Freeman; and *Let The Good Times Roll* by Louis Jordan and His Tympany Five.

August, 1964: Sonny and Cher record backing vocals on The Ronette's *You Baby*.

September 1964: Sonny and Cher record backing vocals for The Ronette's *Walking In The Rain* at Gold Star Studios.

October, 1964: Sonny and Cher record backing vocals for The Righteous Brothers' *You've Lost That Lovin' Feeling'*. Sonny and Cher record Sonny's latest composition *Baby Don't Go*.

December 1964: Cher records her second solo single *Dream Baby*, to be released under the name "Cherilyn".

December 26, 1964: Sonny & Cher's *Baby Don't Go* enters Billboard's Bubbling Under chart at #34.

January-May, 1965

Sonny & Cher: Regional Stars

January 20, 1965: Sonny & Cher record *Sing C'est La Vie*, written by Sonny and their managers Charles Greene and Brian Stone.

January 28, 1965: Sonny & Cher record Phil Spector sound-a-like *Just You*, written by Sonny, plus a further track, which is scrapped.

January 30, 1965: Billboard lists *Baby Don't Go* as a "Regional Breakout" hit in Washington, for "getting strong sales action by dealers" within the region without yet reaching the Hot 100.

February 17, 1965: Sonny & Cher perform *Baby Don't Go* on *Shindig!*

March 1965: Cher records her version of Bob Dylan's *All I Really Want To Do*.

April 03, 1965: Sonny & Cher make appearances performing *Sing C'est La Vie* and *Just You* on *Shivaree,* and *Just You* and *Baby Don't Go* on *Hollywood-A-Go-Go*.

April 10, 1965: Billboard magazine lists Sonny & Cher's *Just You* as a "Pop Spotlight": "Well-written teen ballad pitted against a strong, slow, solid dance beat. Good vocal work."

May 05, 1965: Sonny & Cher perform *Treat Me Nice, (Let Me Be Your) Teddy Bear*, *All Shook Up* and *Wooden Heart* on *Shindig!*.

May 15, 1965: Billboard lists *Just You* as a "Regional Breakout" hit in Los Angeles.

May 22, 1965: Cher performs *All I Really Want To Do* and *Dream Baby* on *Shivaree*.

May 26, 1965: Sonny & Cher perform *Just You*, *I Got You Babe* and *All I Really want To Do* on *Hollywood-A-Go-Go*, and *We're Gonna Make It* on *Shindig!*.

June-July, 1965

Sonny & Cher To Record *I Got You Babe*

June 07, 1965: Sonny & Cher record two of Sonny's compositions: *I Got You Babe* and *It's Gonna Rain*.

June 17, 1965: Sonny & Cher head into the studio to record songs for their debut album: covers *500 Miles*, *Why Don't They Let Us Fall In Love*, *Then He Kissed Me* and Cher's solo *Unchained Melody*.

June 23, 1965: Sonny & Cher record the remainder of their debut album: *Let It Be Me*, *You Don't Love Me*, *You've Really Got A Hold On Me* and Chris Kenner's *Something You Got*. However, the latter song is scrapped.

July, 1965: Two Bob Dylan songs, *Don't Think Twice, It's Alright* and *Blowin' In The Wind*, along with further covers *Girl Don't Come* and *The Bells of Rhymney*, are recorded by Cher for her debut solo LP.

July 02, 1965: Cher records *I Go To Sleep*.

July, 03, 1965: Cher débuts on the Hot 100 for the first time ever, with *All I Really Want To Do* entering at #86. Meanwhile, The Byrd's version débuts at #83. Commence a chart battle.

July 07, 1965: Sonny & Cher perform *I Got You Babe*, *It's Gonna Rain* and *Dream Baby* on *Shindig!*.

July 09, 1965: Cher records five songs for her debut solo album: *Come and Stay With Me*, *Cry Myself To Sleep*, *He Thinks I Still Care*, *Needles & Pins* and *See See Rider*.

July 10, 1965: Sonny & Cher's *I Got You Babe* débuts on the Hot 100 at #88. The pair perform the single and its B-Side *It's Gonna Rain* on *Shivaree*.

July 21, 1965: Sonny & Cher perform *I Got You Babe*, *Do You Love Me* and *All I Really Want To Do* on *Shindig!*.

July 30, 1965: Sonny & Cher perform *Baby Don't Go* and *All I Really Want To Do* on *Where The Action Is*.

August, 1965

I Got You Babe Heading Up The Charts

06: Sonny & Cher perform *I Got You Babe* on the UK's *Ready Steady Go*.

07: Sonny & Cher appear on *Thank Your Lucky Stars* in the UK.

12: Sonny & Cher make their debut appearance on the UK's *Top Of The Pops*, performing *I Got You Babe*.

I Got You Babe enters the UK Official Singles Chart Top 50 at #30.

14: *I Got You Babe* jumps from #5 to #1 on the Hot 100, replacing Herman's Hermits' *I'm Henry The VIII, I Am*. Billboard predict that Sonny & Cher's *Baby Don't Go* will reach the Top 100:

August 14, 1965 US Hot 100

1. *I Got You Babe*; Sonny & Cher

2. *(I Can't Get No) Satisfaction*; The Rolling Stones

3. *Save Your Heart For Me*; Gary Lewis And The Playboys

19: *I Got You Babe* makes a big leap from #30 to #4 on the UK Official Singles Chart Top 50, whilst Cher's *All I Really Want To Do* enters at #40, and Sonny's *Laugh At Me* enters at #45.

21: Cher's *All I Really Want To Do* rises to #15 on the Hot 100, whilst The Byrd's version is at #40. Sonny & Cher's *Baby Don't Go* also débuts on the chart at #70, whilst *I Got You Babe* is still at #1. Sonny's solo *Laugh At Me* enters at #83.

Excitingly, Sonny & Cher's debut album *Look At Us* makes its debut on Billboard's Top LP's, at #142. The album is marked as a "Pop Spotlight" by Billboard, whom list album track *You Don't Love Me* as a "standout" track.

26: *I Got You Babe* reaches #1 during its third week on the UK Official Singles Chart Top 50, knocking The Beatles' *Help!* From the top spot:

August 26, 1965 UK Official Singles Chart

1. *I Got You Babe*; Sonny & Cher

2. *Help!*; The Beatles

3. *Walk In The Black Forest*; Horst Jankowski

28th: *I Got You Babe* spends a third week at #1 on the US Hot 100. *Just You* débuts at #72, meaning that between them, Sonny and Cher now have five singles sitting within the Top 75 of the Hot 100: *Babe*, #1; *All I Really Want To Do*, a second week at #15; *Laugh At Me*, #52; *Baby Don't Go*, #60; and *Just You*, #72.

Meanwhile, *I Got You Babe* is at #19 over on the Billboard Hot R&B Songs chart.

September, 1965

Sonny & Cher To Hit Gold

02: Cher – with a cameo by Sonny – performs *All I Really Want To Do* on *Where The Action Is*.

04: Sonny & Cher's debut LP *Look At Us* makes a huge leap from #59 to #5 on Billboard's Top LP's.

07: Sonny & Cher perform *I Got You Babe* on *Where The Action Is*.

09: Cher and Sonny both earn their first solo UK Top Tens as *All I Really Want To Do* moves from #13 to #9 and *Laugh At Me* jumps from #19 to #10. Meanwhile, the duo's *I Got You Babe* is still at #2. Thus, between them, Sonny & Cher have three hits within the UK Top 10.

11: Sonny & Cher's *Look At Us* rises to #2 on Billboard's Top LP's:

September 11, 1965 US Billboard 200

1. *Help!*; The Beatles

2. *Look At Us;* Sonny & Cher

3. *Out Of Our Heads*; The Rolling Stones

Sonny and Cher have a total of five hit singles currently sitting within the Top 50 of the Hot 100! – *I Got You Babe* at

#7; Sonny's *Laugh At Me* at #19; Cher's *All I Really Want To Do* at #24; *Baby Don't Go* at #32; and *Just You* at #50.

13: Sonny & Cher make an appearance on *Shivaree*, performing *All I Really Want To Do*, and on *Hullabaloo*, performing *I Got You Babe* and *(I Can't Get No) Satisfaction*.

16: Sonny & Cher record their next single *But You're Mine*, written by Sonny, and its spoken B-Side *Hello*.

Sonny & Cher now have a combined total of four singles on the UK Official Singles Chart Top 50: *Babe*, #2; *Laugh At Me*, #9; *All I Really Want To Do*, #11; and new entry *Baby Don't Go* at #24, which is the highest new entry on the UK Official Singles Chart Top 50 this week.

Atlantic Records release a statement that Sonny & Cher have cancelled their upcoming appearances as the support act for Gene Pitney's 10-city tour, claiming that Sonny has a throat infection and physical exhaustion.

17: Sonny & Cher's *I Got You Babe* is certified Gold by the RIAA for shifting 1,000,000 copies across the US.

18: Cher's debut solo album *All I Really Want To Do* débuts on the Billboard's Top LPs at #119.

26: Sonny & Cher appear on *The Ed Sullivan Show*, performing a medley of *I Got You Babe*, Cher's upcoming single *Where Do You Go* and the duo's upcoming single *But You're Mine*.

30: Sonny & Cher's debut album *Look At Us* is certified Gold by the RIAA for racking up over $1,000,000 in sales in the US.

October, 1965

Sonny & Cher Taking Over Transatlantic Charts

"Setting A New Trend In Today's Pop World"

– Rave, October 1965

02: *Baby Don't Go* becomes Sonny & Cher's second US Top 10, by climbing to #9. *Laugh At Me* gives Sonny two simultaneous self-written Top 10's whilst sitting one place lower at #10.

Billboard magazine features a full-page ad for Cher's next solo single *Where Do You Go*, whilst predicting an eventual Top 20 placement for Sonny & Cher's next single *But You're Mine*.

Cher's album *All I Really Want To Do* becomes her first ever UK hit album by entering the Official Albums Chart Top 20 at #20.

09: There are four hits by "Sonny & Cher" on the US Hot 100, as *But You're Mine* enters at #68. *Baby Don't Go* enjoys a new peak of #8 whilst *Just You* experiences the same at #20.

Billboard predicts that Cher's next single *Where Do You Go*, with its "tremendous vocal performance", will become another Top 20 hit for her.

16: *Where Do You Go* becomes Cher's second solo US hit, by entering the Hot 100 at #83, whilst Sonny & Cher's *Baby Don't Go* enjoys a second week at #8.

Cher's album *All I Really Want To* enters the UK Top 10 at #10, whilst the duo's *Look At Us* makes its debut at #16.

21: Sonny & Cher, between them, now have five singles on the UK Official Singles Chart Top 50: *Baby Don't Go*, #13; *Babe*, #20; *Laugh At Me*, #30; *All I Really Want To Do*, #41; and new entry *But You're Mine* at #47.

23: Despite *Babe* having left the charts, Sonny and Cher, between them, now have a whopping six singles on the US Hot 100 this week, as a re-issue of *The Letter* joins in at #100. The duo appear on *Hollywood Palace*, lipsynching *Baby Don't Go*, with Cher then doing the same for *Where Do You Go*, before singing a live version of *But You're Mine* with host Milton Berle.

A new album *Baby Don't Go* by "Sonny & Cher & Friends" débuts on Billboard's Top LP's at #133, meaning that between them, Sonny and Cher now have three albums on the US album chart, joining Cher's solo LP at #23 and the duo's *Look At Us* at #2.

Cher's *All I Really Want To* climbs to #7 on the UK Official Albums Chart Top 20,

29: Sonny & Cher record the Sonny-penned *I Looked For You, Look For Me Baby* but it's left unreleased.

30: Cher's All I Really Want To Do album climbs into the Top 20 of the US Albums chart, from #23 to #17. Sonny & Cher's Look At Us is still #2.

November-December, 1965

November, 1965

06: Sonny & Cher's *Look At Us* finally slips down Billboard's Top LP's chart to #5 after spending a whopping 8 consecutive weeks at #2. Cher's solo *All I Really Want To Do* album reaches a new peak of #16 on the same chart.

08: Sonny & Cher record *Je m'en balance car je t'aime* – the French version of *But You're Mine*.

12: Sonny & Cher begin a 15-date US tour.

13: Cher's *Where Do You Go* reaches a new US peak of 25 whilst *All I Really Want to Do* remains at #16 on the Top LP's chart. Sonny & Cher's single *But You're Mine* is riding high at #15. Cher's LP *All I Really Want To Do* spends a second week at #16.

27: Sonny & Cher's *Look At Us* spends its sixth consecutive week within the UK Top 10, at #9.

December, 1965

04: Sonny & Cher's *Look At Us* spends its fourteenth week inside of the Top 10 of the US Billboard 200, at #8. Sonny and Cher's 1964 recording of *Love Is Strange* enters Billboard's Bubbling Under chart at #31.

07: Spotted: Sonny & Cher board a Pan American Flight from LA to Hawaii.

14: Sonny & Cher record *We Need Eachother* and *Love Don't Come*. However, both are scrapped.

15: Sonny & Cher record *What Now My Love* and further track *Just A Room*. However, both LA recordings are deemed unfit for release.

18: Sonny & Cher compilation album *Baby Don't Go* reaches a new peak of #69 on the Billboard 200.

20: Sonny & Cher record his new composition *Sing With The Music* and The Impression's recent hit *People Get Ready*, in LA. However, both recordings are scrapped.

January, 1966

Sonny & Cher Work On LP#2

01: Sonny & Cher make an appearance on *Hollywood palace*, with a live rendition of *What Now My Love*, plus a live performance of a New Year song with Bing Crosby.

05: In LA, Sonny & Cher rerecord *What Now My Love* and *I Looked For You, Look For Me Baby,* retitled *I Look For You*.

21: In LA, Sonny and Cher perform during at taping of *The Danny Thomas Special*, to be aired 06 February.

Sonny & Cher record four new songs for their second studio album: *Summertime, Crying Time, But I Really Don't Mind* and an untitled one with the Bat Band. However the latter three tracks are deemed unfit for the album. Cher also records *A Young Girl (Une Efante)* for her second solo studio album.

22: Billboard predict that Sonny & Cher's *What Now My Love* will be another Top 20 hit for duo: "This is the one to put the duo back at the top again".

26: Cher records *Ol' Man River* and *Come To Your Window* for her second solo LP.

27: Cher heads back into the studio to record a large portion of her second solo LP: *Elusive Butterfly*; *It's Not Unusual*; *Like A Rolling Stone*; *Our Day Will Come*; *The Girl From Ipanema*.

29: *What Now My Love* enters the US Hot 100 at #68.

February, 1966

07: Cher records *Time* for her second solo album.

08: *Bring It On Home To Me*, *Tell Him* and *Leave Me Be* are recorded in LA by Sonny & Cher for their second album.

11: Cher records Sonny's newly-written song *Bang Bang (My Baby Shot Me Down)* as a late addition to her upcoming second solo LP.

14: Sonny & Cher record Unit 4 + 2's 1965 UK#1 *Concrete & Clay* in LA. However, they scrap it. They also record *Set Me Free*, *So Fine* and *Turn Around* for their second LP.

March-April, 1966

Cher Releases *Bang Bang*

March, 1966

01: Sonny & Cher record *I'm Leavin' It All Up To You* at Gold Star studio for their second LP.

03: Sonny & Cher perform *What Now My Love* and *Bang Bang (My Baby Shot Me Down)* on *Where The Action Is*.

05: Sonny & Cher's *What Now My Love* has a new peak of #14 on the Hot 100.

12: Cher scores her third US Hot 100 solo hit as *Bang Bang (My Baby Shots Me Down)* enters at #75.

15: Sonny & Cher are nominated at the 8th Annual Grammy Awards for Best New Artist. Bob Hope opens the show, in Beverly Hills, coyly referring to generational divisions in show business, noting that the special features "just about every great artist in the musical world with the exception of Sonny & Cher. We hoped to have them but Sonny didn't have a tuxedo and Cher wouldn't loan him hers." The award is won by Tom Jones.

31: Sonny & Cher's *What Now My Love* spends its second consecutive week at #13 on the UK charts whilst Cher's solo *Bang Bang (My Baby Shot Me Down)* enters at #39.

April, 1966

"Sonny & Cher – In Pop Music, They're What's Happening"

– Post, April 1966

02: Sonny & Cher play at The Hollywood Bowl. Cher's *Bang Bang (My Baby Shot Me Down)* becomes her biggest solo US hit as it jumps from #17 to #9, becoming her first solo Top 10.

07: Between them, Sonny & Cher once again have two singles within the UK Top 20 as the duo's *What Now My Love* falls to #17 and Cher's solo *Bang bang (My Baby Shot Me Down)* rises to #18.

16: Sonny & Cher's second studio album *The Wondrous World Of Sonny & Cher* débuts at #134 on the US Billboard 200, whilst its predecessor *Look At Us* is still riding high at #54 during its 44th week on the chart.

21: Sonny & Cher record stand-alone single *Have I Stayed Too Long* in LA. *Bang Bang (My Baby Shot Me Down)* becomes Cher's second solo UK Top 10 as it jumps from #13 to 6 this week.

23: Cher's second solo LP *The Sonny Side of Cher* débuts on the US Billboard 200 at #134. Her *Bang Bang (My Baby Shot Me Down)* rises from #3 to #2 on the US Hot 100:

April 23, 1966 US HOT 100

1. *(You're My) Soul And Inspiration*; The Righteous Brothers

2. *Bang Bang (My Baby Shot Me Down)*; Cher

3. *Secret Agent Man*; Johnny Rivers

May-July, 1966

May 05, 1966: Cher's solo *Bang Bang (My Baby Shot Me Down)* is riding high on the UK Official Singles Chart Top 50 at #3 – her biggest solo hit yet:

May 05, 1966 UK Official Singles Chart

1. *Pretty Flamingo*; Manfred Mann

2. *Daydream;* Lovin' Spoonful

3. *Bang Bang (My Baby Shot Me Down)*; Cher

May 08, 1966: Sonny & Cher's second LP *The Wondrous World of Sonny & Cher* enters the UK Official Albums Chart Top 30 at #27.

May 28, 1966: Billboard predicts that *Have I Stayed Too Long* will become a Top 60 hit for Sonny & Cher.

June 04, 1966: *Have I Stayed Too Long* enters the Hot 100 at #82

June 05, 1966: *The Wondrous World of Sonny & Cher* spends its second consecutive week at #15 on the UK Official Albums Chart Top 30, whilst Cher's solo *The Sonny Side of Cher* is at #13, having peaked so far at #11.

June 10, 1966: Sonny & Cher record *What's Wrong With Me* at Gold Star studios, but it is scrapped.

June, 1966: Cher records *Alfie* and its B-Side *She's No Better Than Me*.

July 09, 1966: *The Wondrous World of Sonny & Cher* reaches a new peak of #34 on the Billboard 200, whilst *The Sonny Side of Cher* is one place higher at #33.

After peaking at #49 for two weeks, *Have I Stayed Too Long* drops down the US Hot 100.

July 16, 1966: *The Sonny Side of Cher* spends a second week at #26 on the US Hot 100.

Sonny & Cher perform *What Now My Love* on Germany's *Beat-Club*.

July 29, 1966: Sonny & Cher record *Monday* at Gold Star studio in LA.

July 30, 1966: Cher's *Alfie* enters the US Hot 100 at #62 – Cher's highest debut yet, solo or otherwise.

August-September, 1966

Sonny & Cher Unleash *Little Man*

August 04, 1966: Cher's solo *I Feel Something In The Air* becomes her third solo UK hit, entering the Official Singles Chart Top 50 at #43.

August 25, 1966: Sonny & Cher record vocals for *Little Man* at EMI Studios in London. The duo perform the song on UK's *Top Of The Pops*.

August 26, 1966: *Little Man* is released in the UK. And Sonny & Cher perform it on the UK's *Ready Steady Go*.

August 27, 1966: *Alfie* comes close to becoming Cher's fourth solo consecutive US Top 30 hit as reaches #32 on the US Hot 100.

August 30, 1966: Spotted: Sonny & Cher arriving at Amsterdam Schiphol Airport.

September 01, 1966: Sonny & Cher leave the Netherlands from Schiphol Airport.

September 14, 1966: Sonny & Cher's *Little Man* enters the UK Official Singles Chart Top 50 at #35.

September 24, 1966: Sonny & Cher perform *Then He Kissed Me*, *Little Man*, *I Feel Something In The Air* and *Laugh At Me* on Germany's *Beat-Club*.

September 29, 1966: *Little Man* becomes Sonny & Cher's second UK Top 5 hit as it reaches #4 on the UK Official Singles Chart Top 50. Meanwhile, Cher's solo *Sunny* enters the Top 40, jumping from #47 to #37.

October-December, 1966

Sonny & Cher Begin LP#3.

October 01, 1966: Sonny & Cher's *Little Man* enters the US Hot 100 at #72, whilst Cher's solo third album *Cher* enters the Billboard 200 at #116.

October 04, 1966: Sonny & Cher record *A Groovy Kind Of Love* and *You Baby* for their third studio album.

October 07, 1966: Sonny & Cher cover *Stand By Me* and *We'll Sing In The Sunshine* for their third studio album.

October 12, 1966: Cher records *Behind The Door*.

October 19, 1966: Sonny & Cher record *Living For You* and *Love Don't Come*.

October 22, 1966: *The Hits Of Cher*, featuring *Bang Bang (My Baby Shot Me Down)*, *Where Do You Go*, *All I Really Want To Do* and *I Feel Something In The Air*, enters the UK EP Charts at #10.

Sonny & Cher appear on *Beat-Club* in Germany, performing *Little Man* and its B-Side *Monday*.

October 29, 1966: The UK's Record Mirror announce that the public have voted Cher as their #2 World Female Vocalist, with Dusty Springfield taking first place. The publication also reports that Cher's next UK single will be *Behind The Door*, "expected to be released by Liberty in about three weeks' time." *Little Man* climbs to a new peak of #21 on the US Hot 100.

November 17, 1966: Sonny & Cher's *Living For You* enters the UK Official Singles Chart Top 50 at #49. Cher's solo *Mama (When My Dollies Have Babies)* enters the US Bubbling Under chart at #33.

November 19, 1966: *Living For You* enters the US Hot 100 at #97.

November 26, 1966: Cher's *Behind The Door* enters Hot 100 at #97, whilst *Living For You* has risen ten places to #87.

December 15 1966: Sonny & Cher record *The Beat Goes On.*

January-April, 1967

The Beat Goes On For Sonny & Cher

January 14, 1967: Sonny & Cher record *Il cammino di ogni speranza,* Sonny's solo *L'umanita* and Cher's solo Ma *piano (per non svegliarmi).* The duo's *The Beat Goes On* enters the US Hot 100 at #72.

January 23, 1967: Sonny & Cher record *Podunk.*

January 26, 1967: Sonny & Cher take part in Italy's Sanremo Festival. The duo enter with *Il cammino di ogni speranza* whilst Cher enters solo with *Ma piano (Per non svegliarmi).* However, both entries fail to make it to the finals.

February 02, 1967: *The Beat Goes On* becomes Sonny & Cher's ninth UK hit as it enters the Official Singles Chart Top 50 at #49.

February 11, 1967:: *The Beat Goes On* becomes Sonny & Cher's first US Top 10 since 1965, as it enters the US Hot Top 10 at #10.

March 02, 1967: Sonny & Cher attend the 9th Annual Grammy Awards at Los Angeles.

March 04, 1967: *The Beat Goes On* spends its second week at its current peak of #6 during its fifth week within the Top 10.

March, 05, 1967: Sonny & Cher appear on The Andy Williams Show to perform *The Beat Goes On* and *Podunk.*

March 10, 1967: Sonny & Cher appear on The Man From *U.N.C.L.E.*.

March 17, 1967: Sonny & Cher record the majority of the songs of the soundtrack to their new film *Good Times*: *It's The little Things*; *Good Times*; *Trust Me*; *Don't Talk To Strangers*; *Just A Name*; and a new slow version of *I Got You Babe*.

March 25, 1967: Sonny & Cher's third studio album *In Case You're In Love* débuts at #144 on the US Billboard 200.

April 04, 1967: Sonny & Cher record Sonny's *A Beautiful Story*.

April 22, 1967: Billboard predict another US Top 60 chart entry for Sonny & Cher with *A Beautiful Story*.

April 30, 1967: Sonny & Cher host a party at the home of talent agent Irving Paul "Swifty" Lazar to welcome British model Twiggy to Los Angeles.

May-October, 1967

May 01, 1967: Sonny & Cher record *Plastic Man* at Gold Star studios.

May 13, 1967: Sonny & Cher's *In Case You're In Love* becomes their third consecutive US Top 50 studio album as it climbs to #45 on the Billboard 200 this week.

May 21, 1967: Sonny & Cher appear on *The Smothers Brothers Comedy Hour* to perform *It's The Little Things*, *Plastic Man* and *Alfie*.

May 27, 1967: *A Beautiful Story* seemingly peaked at #53 on the US Hot 100 last week as it heads back down to #65 this week. Meanwhile, Sonny & Cher's *Good Times* Soundtrack album débuts on the Billboard 200 at #170.

August 12, 1967: Compilation album *The Best Of Sonny & Cher* débuts at #140 on the Billboard 200. Studio album *In Case You're In Love* is at #123 in its 29th week on the chart whilst the duo's soundtrack album *Good Times* is at #73.

September 02, 1967: Sonny & Cher's sixth charting album in the US, *The Best of Sonny & Cher*, becomes their second-highest-charting LP there as it climbs to #31 on the Billboard 200. *It's The Little Things* becomes Sonny & Cher's ninth US Top 50 hit single by rising from #60 to #50.

September 09, 1967: *It's The Little Things* by Sonny & Cher spends its second week at #50 on the US Hot 100, as Cher's solo *Hey Joe* débuts at #94.

September 23, 1967: *The Best Of Sonny & Cher* comes close to becoming the duo's second US Top 20 LP as it climbs to #23 on the Billboard 200. Their *Good Times* soundtrack is still on the Billboard 200 at #135 in its 18th week on the chart.

October 18, 1967: Sonny & Cher attend the world première of *The Jungle Book* at Grauman's Chinese Theatre in Los Angeles.

October 28, 1967: Cher's solo Sonny-penned *You Better Sit Down Kids* enters the US Hot 100 at #79.

November-December, 1967

Cher Hits With *You Better Sit Down Kids*

November, 1967

04: *The Best of Sonny & Cher* spends its tenth week inside the US Top 40, at #38.

06: Sonny & Cher appear on The Carol Burnett Show to perform *Living For You* and *You Better Sit Down Kids*.

18: Cher's fourth solo album *With Love, Cher* enters the US Billboard 200 at #191.

20: Sonny & Cher record *Good Combination* and *You And Me*.

25: *You Better Sit Down Kids* becomes Cher's third solo US Top 20 hit as it jumps from #31 to #17 on the Hot 100.

27: Cher begins recording for her next solo studio album, with *Song called Children*.

29: Sonny & Cher step into the studio to record next song *I Can't Keep My Eyes Off Of You*, however, it is scrapped.

December, 1967

09: Billboard predict that Sonny & Cher's next single *Good Combination* ought to be another Top 60 hit for them: "Top vocal performance and groovy rhythm material should carry the duo to a high spot on the Hot 100".

12: Sonny & Cher attend the première party for *The President's Analyst* in Los Angeles, hosted by its star James Coburn.

13: Cher records *Reason To Believe*.

15: Cher records *Take Me For A Little While*.

16: Cher is back within the US Hot 100 Top 10, for the second time solo, as *You Better Sit Down Kids* climbs from #12 to #10.

23: Cher's *You Better Sit Down Kids* rises to #9 on the US Hot 100.

27: Cher records *The Click Song Number One*.

1968

January 13, 1968: Billboard reports that Sonny & Cher's 1965 hit *Just You* is currently spending its second week at #2 on the charts in Philippines.

January 16, 1968: Sonny writes in his diary: "Today is my 33rd birthday. I am never sans Cher. She lives inside my body. Cher is truly a star, from the top of her head to the bottom of her feet. Thank God I have Cher. She's my stabilizer. She's my generator too. She's my reason."

January 22, 1968: Sonny & Cher record stand-alone single *Circus*, plus Sonny's solo *I Would Marry You Today*.

February 01, 1968: Cher records the final song, *It All Adds Up Now*, for her forthcoming studio album.

February 10, 1968: Sonny & Cher attend the 40th Annual Academy Awards in California.

March 11, 1968: Sonny & Cher appear on *Rowan & Martin's Laugh-In*.

June 28, 1968: Sonny & Cher perform at the *Soul Together* Martin Luther King benefit concert at Madison Square Garden in New York.

July 04, 1968: Sonny & Cher record stand-alone single *You Gotta Have A Thing Of Your Own*.

August 03, 1968: Sonny & Cher perform at The Newport Pop Festival in Costa Mesa, California. The pair arrive by helicopter and are reportedly booed by the audience.

November 22, 1968: Cher writes in Sonny's diary: "In my whole life I never thought there was happiness like we have. Every morning when I wake up, I say to myself, 'Wow, you're going to have a real-live baby of your own.' I love him with all my heart and respect him more than any other human in the world."

November 30, 1968: Cher's first solo compilation album *Golden Greats* enters the US Billboard 200 at #198.

January-March, 1969

January 07, 1969: Cher records *The Thought Of Loving You* and *Yours Until Tomorrow*.

January 25, 1969: Cher records *You've Made Me So Very Happy*.

February 01, 1969: Cash Box reports that Cher has jumped labels: "Atlantic Records has inked Cher. Ahmet Ertegun announced the pact at the company's sales confab. Until now, Cher recorded as a single for Liberty, with Sonny & Cher cutting for Atlantic. New albums by Cher and Sonny & Cher will be released shortly."

"**Atco Records Proudly Presents Cher With Her New Hit Single *Yours Until Tomorrow***"

– Billboard and Cash Box, March 1969

March 04, 1969: Cher gives birth to daughter Chastity Sun Bono.

March 08, 1969: Billboard reviews Cher's new single *Yours until Tomorrow*: "Her move to the Atco label proves a powerful hot chart contender with an updating of the Goffin - King ballad material. Loaded with sales appeal, this should prove a big one."

March 24, 1969: Sonny & Cher record *Born To Be With You*, made famous by The Chordettes in 1956 and revived into a #1 Country single by Sonny James last year. Sonny & Cher scrap their version.

March 26, 1969: Sonny & Cher record The Beau Brummels' 1965 US#8 *Just A Little* but it is shelved.

April, 1969

Cher Records At 3614 Jackson Highway

April, 1969

21: Cher begins recording her next album at Muscle Shoals Sound Studio, 3614 Jackson Highway, Muscle Shoals, Alabama. Today, she records *Save The Children* – the first session ever held at Muscle Shoals. She then records *I Threw It All Away*.

22: Cher records Bob Dylan's *Tonight I'll Be Staying Here With You* at Muscle Shoals studio.

23: Cher records *Do Right Woman Do Right Man*, *For What It's Worth*, *(Just Enough To Keep Me) Hangin' On* and *Wedding Bell Blues* at Muscle Shoals studio.

24: Cher records *(Sitting On) The Dock Of The Bay* and *I Walk On Guilded Splinters*.

25: Cher records a track entitled *Always David* at Muscle Shoals Studio, but it is shelved.

30: Cher records *Cry Like A Baby* and *Please Don't Tell Me* at Muscle Shoals studio.

May, 1969

02: Sonny & Cher appear on ABC-TV's *This Is Tom Jones*, in London.

09: Sonny & Cher are in New York for a spot on ABC-TV's *Joey Bishop Show*.

14: Cher records *Lay Baby Lay* at Muscle Shoals studio. Sonny & Cher also record *You're A Friend of Mine*, *Honey Lamb* and a further track. The latter two are scrapped.

21: Cher records the sole vocal track of the soundtrack to her new film *Chastity*. The track is entitled *Chastity's Song (Band Of Thieves)*.

June-August, 1969

Chastity and *3614 Jackson Highway* Are Released

14: The UK's NME reviews Cher's new single *I Walk On Guilded Splinters*: "An excellent styling, in which the effect is heightened by voodoo-like chanting, crashing cymbals and shrieking brass."

The UK's Melody maker states: "Cher's version of the Dr. John song is excellent - evil and rocking. The band are funky and the whole production makes it a better bet than Marsha Hunt's version, if the tune is going to take off here at all."

The United State's Billboard review new single *Chastity's Song (Band Of Thieves)*: "Sensitive treatment of the Elyse Weinberg ballad from the forthcoming film *Chastity* has both play and sales potential."

The same country's Cash Box states: "Getting funkier than she's sounded in a long time, Cher delivers a powerhouse side that should set her in the programming spotlight with top forty and underground stations."

20: Cher's *3614 Jackson Highway* is released in the United States.

July, 1969

26: Cash Box review Cher's 3614 Jackson highway: "Plenty of sales potential in this highly polished set by songstress Cher. Selection of tunes is especially impressive, as included here are Stephen Stills' Buffalo Springfield classic *For What It's Worth*, Bob Dylan's current single *Lay Lady Lay*, and Otis Redding's great *Dock Of The Bay*, in addition to Cher's own latest single, *I Walk On Guilded Splinters*. Pay Attention to this one."

August, 1969

02: Billboard review Cher's *3614 Jackson Highway*: "Her emotional vocal work gives new meaning to these gems. This is Cher's most interesting and therefore her most commercial package in some time."

13: *Chastity* is positioned as Variety's #14 film showing in thirty-one theatres in three cities.

16: Cher's *3614 Jackson Highway* enters the Billboard 200 at #161.

Billboard predicts that Cher's next single *For What It's Worth* will become a Top 20 hit for her: "The past hit of the Buffalo Springfield is updated in what will prove to be one of Cher's biggest hits. Penned by Stephen Stills and produced by Jerry Wexler, she's in top vocal form in this infectious entry."

20: *Chastity* ranks as the #49th film showing in two theatres in two cities.

September-December, 1969

04: Sonny & Cher appear on The David Frost Show in the US.

06: The UK's Melody Maker review Cher's *3614 Jackson Highway*: "Songs from Dylan and Steve Stills, superb backings and Cher's voice combine to produce a tremendous album."

11: Cher records her next single *The First Time*, written by Sonny.

13: *For What It's Worth* enters Billboard's Bubbling Under The Hot 100 chart at #25.

The UK's NME review 3614 Jackson Highway: "She's in fine voice throughout, switching moods easily, as witness two of Dylan's numbers *Tonight I'll Be Staying Here With You* and *I Threw It All Away* - on the former she takes it easily, on the latter she's morose and wistful."

29: Sonny & Cher appear on *Rowan & Martin's Laugh-In*.

October, 1969

15: Cher performs *Cry Like A Baby* and *The First Time* on *The Mike Douglas Show*.

November, 1969

16: Sonny & Cher appear on the UK's *This Is Tom Jones*, to perform *Just A Little* and *Yours Until Tomorrow*.

28: Cher begins cracking on with her next solo studio album, beginning with a cover of Three Dog Night's recent US#4 smash *Easy To Be Hard* at Gold Star Studios.

29: Billboard reviews Cher's new single *The First Time*: "Strong, commercial ballad and one of Cher's top vocal workouts to date. Could easily prove a left field smash."

December, 1969

01: Cher records covers of *I Believe* and *It Gets Me Where I Want To Go* at Gold Star Studios.

03: Cher records *Danny Boy* at Gold Star Studios.

04: Sonny & Cher record *Play Me Some Music* and Cher records *Momma Look Sharp*. Both are at Gold Star Studios but both recordings are shelved, as are all of Cher's recent ones.

17: Sonny & Cher appear on *The Kraft Hall Music*, performing *You and Me*, *Let The Good Times Roll* with Phyllis Diller, Bob Hope and Mike Douglas, with Cher performing *Ol' Man River* solo.

1970

January, 1970: Hungarian-American actress Zsa Zsa Gabor opens at the Flamingo Hotel in Las Vegas. Sonny & Cher are guests at the opening.

January 27, 1970: Sonny & Cher appear on *Playboy After Dark*, performing *Can't Take My Eyes Off You* and *For Once In My Life*.

February 15, 1970: Sonny & Cher appear on *The Barbara McNair Show*, performing *What Now My Love*, a medley of *The Beat Goes On*, *I Got You Babe*, *Sing C'est La Vie*, *All I Really Want To Do* and *Little Man*. Cher performs *Danny Boy*.

February 19, 1970: Sonny & Cher appear on *The Merv Griffin Show*.

April 04, 1970: In Los Angeles, The Century Plaza host the opening of their new act Sonny & Cher.

April 29, 1970: Sonny & Cher record stand-alone single *Get It Together* and its B-side *Hold You Tighter*.

May 01, 1970: Sonny & Cher appear on *The Best On Record*.

May 27, 1970: Sonny & Cher record the song *It Gets Me Where I Want To Go* but it is scrapped.

June 03, 1970: Sonny & Cher appear on *The Dick Cavett Show*.

June 17, 1970: Sonny & Cher appear o*n The David Frost Show*.

October, 1970: Cher records next single *Superstar,* written by Bonnie Bramlett, Delaney Bramlett and Leon Russell, at Allegro Studios, New York City

November 07, 1970: Billboard reviews Cher's new single Superstar: "This super, driving ballad serves as powerful material for Cher. Will bring her back to the Hot 100 with sales impact. Her first solo release for the year gets a heavy producing job by Stan Vincent."

January-October, 1971

January 15, 1971: Sonny & Cher appear on *Love, American Style*.

May 28, 1971: Sonny & Cher record Sonny's composition *Somebody*.

June 09, 1971: Cher returns to the recording studio as a solo act to record a bunch of songs for her next studio album: James Taylor's *Fire & Rain*, The Hollies' *He Ain't Heavy, He's My Brother* and originals *I Hate To Sleep Alone* and *Gypsies, Tramps & Thieves*.

August 01, 1971: The first episode of the duo's Summer replacement show *The Sonny & Cher Show* airs.

September 05, 1991: The sixth and final episode of *The Sonny & Cher Show* airs.

September, 1971: Sonny & Cher record *All I Ever Need Is You* – written by Jimmy Holiday and Eddie Reeves, it was recorded by Ray Charles for his April 1971 album *The Volcanic Action of My Soul*.

September 10, 1971: Sonny & Cher appear on *Dinah's Place*.

September 18, 1971: Cher's *Gypsy's Tramps & Thieves* enters the Hot 100 at #88 to become her first hit since 1967's You Better Sit Down Kids.

September 25, 1971: Cher's sixth solo album *Chér* enters the US Billboard 200 at #194.

October 02, 1971: *Sonny & Cher Live* enters the Billboard 200 at #174.

October 16, 1971: *Gypsies, Tramps & Thieves* enters the US Top 10 to become Cher's third solo Top 10 on the US Hot 100. Sonny & Cher's *All I Ever Need Is You* enters the same chart at #89.

October 30, 1971: *Gyspies, Tramps & Thieves* matches Cher's previous highest solo position of #2 on the US Hot 100.

October 31: *Cher's Gyspies, Tramps & Thieves* enters the UK Official Singles Chart Top 50, becoming her first solo hit in the country for five years.

November, 1971

Cher Going Gold With *Gyspies*

01: Sonny & Cher record over half of their next studio album, with cuts *Here Comes That Rainy Day Feeling*, *Crystal Clear/Muddy Waters*, *United We Stand*, *A Cowboy's Work Is Never Done*, *I Love What You Did With The Love I Gave You*, *We'll Watch The Sun Coming Up (Shining Down On Your Love)* and *More Today Than Yesterday*.

06: *Gypsies Tramps & Thieves* becomes Cher's first solo #1 on the US Hot 100, and 2nd overall after 1965's *I Got You Babe* with Sonny:

November 06, 1971, US HOT 100

1. *Gypsys, Tramps & Thieves*; Cher

2. *Theme From Shaft*; Isaac Hayes

3. *Maggie May/Reason To Believe*; Rod Stewart

13: *Gypsies, Tramps & Thieves* spends a second week at #1 on the US Hot 100.

14: By rising to #7 in just its third week on the UK Official Singles Chart Top 50, *Gypsies Tramps & Thieves* becomes Cher's third solo Top 10 in the country.

19: Cher scores her first ever solo certification as the RIAA announce that *Gypsies, Tramps & Thieves* has shipped 1,000,000 copies in the US and has thus earned Gold status.

20: *Gypsies, Tramps & Thieves* slips down to #2 on the US Hot 100.

23: Cher records solo ballad *Living In A House Divided*.

21: *All I Ever Need Is You* rises from #2 to #1 on Billboard's Adult Contemporary Chart.

27: *The Best of Sonny & Cher* re-enters the US Billboard 200 at #182. *Gypsies, Tramps & Thieves* remains in the Top 2 of the US Hot 100 for the fifth consecutive week.

28: Cher's *Gypsies, Tramps & Thieves* spends its second week at #4 in the UK.

December 1971-February, 1972

The Sonny & Cher Comedy Hour

December, 1971

04: *Sonny & Cher Live* becomes the duo's fourth US Top 40 LP as it rises to #37 on the Billboard 200. Cher's solo LP *Chér*, having been re-branded as "*Gypsys, Tramps & Thieves*", is at #16, matching the peak position of her debut solo album.

11: Sonny & Cher's single *All I Ever Need Is You* enters the Top 10 of the US Hot 100, from #11 to #8. Cher's solo *Gypsies, Tramps & Thieves* is one place higher at #7, enjoying its ninth week inside the Top 10 – beating the seven week stay inside the Top 10 by 1965's *I Got You Babe*.

25: *All I Ever Need Is You* rises from #8 to #7 on the US Hot 100.

26: *Gypsies Tramps & Thieves* spends its seventh week within the UK Top 10.

27: *The Sonny & Cher Show* returns as *The Sonny & Cher Comedy Hour* for a full series on CBS.

January, 1972

"Sonny & Cher – Their New Variety Hour Arrives On Monday On CBS"

– TV Times, January 1972

267

"Sonny and Cher Launch Weekly Variety Show"

– Chicago Tribune TV Week, January 1972

09: Sonny & Cher score their first UK hit single in almost five years as *All I Ever Need Is You* enters the country's Top 50 at #42. It is their 10th hit single together in the UK.

15: *Cher Superpak*, a compilation LP of 1960's material, climbs into the top half of the Billboard 200, at #99.

23: Sonny & Cher attend a tribute To Jack Warner at the Beverly Hilton Hotel in California.

29: Cher's ballad *The Way Of Love* enters the US Hot 100 at #88.

February, 1972

06: *All I Ever Need Is You* climbs into the UK Top 10, becoming Sonny & Cher's third Top 10 single in the country, and their first since 1966.

26: Sonny & Cher's fourth studio album *All I Ever Need Is You* enters the Billboard 200 at #96. Between them, Sonny and Cher have five albums on the chart: Cher's *Gypsys, Tramps & Thieves* is also at #59; *Sonny & Cher Live* at #107; *The Best of Sonny& Cher* at #141; and *Cher Superpak* at #167.

March-June, 1972

Continued Chart Success

March, 1972

04: *The Way Of Love* enjoys a second week at #2 on Billboard's Adult Contemporary Chart.

11: *The Way Of Love* becomes Cher's fourth solo Top 10 hit single as it climbs from #11 to #9 on the US Hot 100.

20: The series finale of *The Sonny & Cher Comedy Hour* airs on CBS

25th: Sonny & Cher have two US Top 20 hits between them again as Cher's *The Way Of Love* is at #7 and the duo's *A Cowboy's Work Is never Done* is at #19.

April, 1972

01: *All I Ever Need Is You* becomes Sonny & Cher's second ever US Top 20 LP as it climbs to #19 on the Billboard 200.

13: Cher's self-titled 1971 album, also known as *Gypsy's Tramps & Thieves*, is certified Gold by the RIAA for shifting 500,000 copies in the US.

15: Sonny & Cher's *A Cowboy's Work Is Never Done* enters the US Hot 100 Top 10.

May, 1972

06: *All I Ever Need Is You* becomes Sonny & Cher's second ever Gold-certified album in the US, as RIAA announce that it has shipped 500,000 copies across the country.

A Cowboy's Work Is Never Done enjoys its third week in the US Top 10 at a peak of #8.

15: Cher records *Let Me Down Easy*.

18: Cher records *Don't Hide Your Love*, written by Neil Sedaka.

23: Sonny & Cher record *When You Say Love, Someone To Give My Love To* and *Louisiana Man*. However, the last two tracks are scrapped.

June-October, 1972

Living In A House Divided

June 03, 1972: Album *All I Ever Need Is You* spends its tenth week inside the Top 20 of the Billboard 200, at #17, after peaking at #14 for two weeks.

June 24, 1972: *Living In A House Divided* comes close to giving Cher her third solo – and fifth overall – consecutive Top 20 hit as it reaches #22.

July 01, 1972: *Living In A House Divided* is at #2 on Billboard's Adult Contemporary Chart this week.

July 27, 1972: *Sonny & Cher Live* is certified Gold by the RIAA for shifting 500,000 copies in the US.

August 26, 1972: *When You Say Love* spends its second week at #32 on the US Hot 100, giving Sonny & Cher their third consecutive Top 40 hit, whilst its Cher's sixth overall consecutive Top 40 hit in less than a year. The song spends its third week at #2 on Billboard's Adult Contemporary Chart.

September 09, 1972: *Don't Hide Your Love* by Cher enters the US Hot 100 at #94, whilst its parent album *Foxy Lady* spends its second week at #45 over on the US Billboard 200. Sonny & Cher compilation album *The Two Of Us* enters the Billboard 200 at #180.

September 10, 1972: Sonny & Cher attend a CBS party in LA.

September 15, 1972: *The Sonny & Cher Comedy Hour* begins its next season on CBS.

October 21, 1972: Cher's LP *Foxy Lady* exits the Top 50 of the Billboard 200, after spending eight weeks within it, with a peak of #43. *Cher Superpak, Vol. II* is at #99.

October 28, 1972: Sonny & Cher appear in voice roles and animated form on *The New Scooby-Doo Movies*. *Don't Hide Your Love* leaves the Top 50 of the Hot 100 after peaking at #46.

November-December, 1972

Sonny & Cher Marriage Troubles

November 04, 1972: Sonny writes in his diary: "The whole world has changed since the last time I wrote. We are now the stars of our TV show. We have a million-dollar house, and I guess you could call us rich. We have a lot of money in the bank. Now for the bad news: Everything exploded between Cher and myself. Chas is 3½ now, and she's fantastic. She doesn't know Mom and Dad are on the ropes. For the past five years I've been worried about our career, and I never worried about us."

November 15, 1972: Cher dresses in a floor length sequined red dress at a party for Merle Oberon at The Merle Oberon Playhouse.

"The Sexy Beat Of Sonny and Cher... Her Looks... Her Fashion... His Style"

– Vogue, December 1972

December, 1972

09: Sonny writes in his diary: "We finished our Christmas show tonight. When it's put together, I'm sure it will look very warm and loving. [But] Cher and I can only talk to each other at certain times."

18: Cher begins recording for her next solo album – a set of standards. The first to be recorded is *The Man I Love*.

20: Cher records *I Got It Bad (And That Ain't Good)* and *The Man That Got Away*.

21: Cher records *Am I Blue*.

26th: Sonny writes in his personal diary: "[Cher] is a changed person. Her wants and reasons have changed. I don't understand them. I don't know if she does either. I thought I was teaching. She thought I was intimidating. It's no longer our house. It's half mine, half Cher's. The same with our money, daughter, everything else."

January, 1973

Sonny & Cher Work On Studio LP#5

"The Whispers About Sonny & Cher's Marriage"

– Screen and TV Album, January 1973

January, 1973

27: Sonny, Cher and her her half-sister Georganne LaPiere attend the US première of director Bernardo Bertolucci's film *Last Tango in Paris* in New York City. Cher is wearing a Native American-inspired poncho, beaded necklaces, and feathers in her hair.

28: Sonny & Cher attend the 30th Golden Globe Awards in LA, at which *The Sonny & Cher Comedy Hour* is nominated for Best Series - Musical or Comedy. However, the award is won by *All In The Family*.

31: Sonny & Cher record lengthy Sonny composition *Mama Was A Rock & Roll Singer, Papa Used To Write All Her Songs*.

February, 1973

13: Sonny & Cher record half-a-dozen covers for their next album: *Listen To The Music, I Believe In You, Brother Love's Traveling Salvation Show, By Love I Mean, Rhythm Of My Heart Beat* and *It Never Rains In Southern California*.

15: Sonny & Cher record a further three tracks for their upcoming studio album: *The Greatest Show On Earth*, *I Can See Clearly Now* and *You Know Darn Well I Do*.

March-May, 1973

March 18: The season finale of *The Sonny & Cher Comedy Hour* airs on CBS.

March 24, 1973: Sonny & Cher's *Mama Was A Rock And Roll Singer, Papa Used To Write All Her Songs Part 1* enters the US Hot 100 at #90.

March 23, 1973: Sonny & Cher present Best Original Song at the 45th Academy Awards in LA.

April 14, 1973: Cher's solo studio album *Bittersweet White Light* enters the US Billboard 200 at #174.

May 07, 1973: Spotted: Sonny & Cher at the St. Regis Hotel in New York City.

May 12, 1973: *Am I Blue* enters the US Bubbling Under chart at #11.

May 19, 1973: *Bittersweet White Light* spends a second week at #140 on the US Billboard 200.

May 21, 1973: Cher records solo track *Half Breed*.

June-September, 1973

June 30, 1973: Sonny & Cher's fifth studio album *Mama Was A Rock And Roll Singer Papa Used To Write All Her Songs* enters the Billboard 200 at #165 to become their tenth charting album together.

July 1973: Cher records tracks for next solo studio album: *How Can You Mend A Broken Heart*, *My Love*, *The Long And Winding Road*, *Carousel Man*, *Chastity's Sun*, *David's Song*, *Melody*, *This God Forsaken Day*, *The Greatest Song I Ever Heard* and *Two People Clinging To A Thread*.

August 04, 1973: Cher's *Half Breed* enters the Hot 100 at #89 to become her first solo hit of the year.

August 21, 1973: Sonny writes in his diary: "The last time I wrote, I wanted Cher to come back to me. That's no longer my desire. The best I can do is be Cher's friend. We still have a TV show, and the public still thinks we are married, so we are both very involved in our careers. Connie and I live together as husband and wife. But my public wife is still Cher in order to maintain all the things I want right now. That's the way it has to be."

September 12, 1973: The Sonny & Cher Comedy begins its next season on CBS.

September 22, 1973: *Half Breed* enters the Top 10 of the Hot 100, climbing from #11 to #7. Its parent album *Half-Breed* enters the Billboard 200 at #171.

September 24, 1973: Cher records *Dark Lady.*

October 1973-February, 1974

Half Breed Heads To #1

October 06, 1973: *Half Breed* climbs from #3 to #1 to become Cher's second solo – and third overall – #1 in the States:

October 06, 1973 US HOT 100

1. *Half Breed*; Cher

2. *Loves Me Like A Rock;* Paul Simon (with The Dixie Hummingbirds)

3. *Let's Get It On*; Marvin Gaye

October 12, 1973: Cher's single *Half Breed* is certified gold by the RIAA for shifting 1,000,000 copies in the US.

October 13, 1973: *Half Breed* spends a second week atop the US Hot 100.

October 20, 1973: *Half Breed* slips down to #2 on the US Hot 100.

November 11, 1973: *Half Breed* spends its eighth week inside the US Top 10, at #8. Its parent album Half-Breed is at #28 on the US Billboard 200.

December 22, 1973: *Sonny & Cher Live In Las Vegas, Vol. 2* enters the US Billboard 200 at #193.

January 19, 1974: Cher scores another US Hot 100 solo hit as *Dark Lady* débuts at #82. Cher performs as ringmaster at the opening day of the Ringling Brothers Circus as part of a celebrity event with her daughter Chastity Bono in Inglewood, California.

"Cher – Is She Over-Exposed?"

– Rona Barrett's Gossip, February 1974

February 24, 1974: Cher scores her fifth solo and thirteenth overall UK Top 40 hit as *Dark Lady* jumps from #45 to #36.

March-May, 1974

Dark Lady Darts Up The Charts

March, 1974

01: David Geffen and Cher are photographed attending the American première production of *The Rocky Horror Picture Show* at Hollywood's Roxy Theatre.

02: Cher and Geffen attend the 16th Annual Grammy Awards at the Hollywood Palladium, Los Angeles, California. Cher co-presents the award of Album of The Year with Telly Savalas to winner Stevie Wonder.

Cher's single *Dark Lady* becomes her sixth solo Top 10 – and eleventh Top 10 overall – as it leaps from #16 to #9 on the US Hot 100.

04: Cher's *Half-Breed* album is certified Gold by the RIAA for shifting 500,000 copies in the US.

06: The final episode of *The Sonny & Cher Comedy Hour* airs.

22: Single *Dark Lady* is certified Gold by the RIAA for shifting 1,000,000 copies across the United States.

23: David Geffen and Cher attend the Jim Stacey Benefit at Century Plaza Hotel in Los Angeles, California, United States.

Dark lady moves from #3 to #1 on the US Hot 100, to become Cher's third solo chart-topper in less than two-and-a-half-years.

March 23, 1974, US HOT 100

1. *Dark Lady*; Cher

2. *Seasons In The Sun*; Terry Jacks

3. *Sunshine On My Shoulders*; John Denver

April 02, 1974: Cher attends the 46th Academy Awards in LA, co-presenting the award for Best Original Dramatic Score with Henry Mancini.

April 18, 1974: Cher records *Train Of Thought* and *What'll I Do* for her next studio album.

"Sonny & Cher – Will "Living Apart" Really Solve Their Problem?

– Rona Barrett's Hollywood, May 1974

May 25, 1974: Cher's *Train Of Thought* enters the US Hot 100 at #75.

June-December, 1974

"The Day It All Ended For Sonny and Cher"

– TV Guide, June 1974

June 01, 1974: Cher attends an American Civil Liberties Union tribute to Henry Fonda at the Beverly Wilshire Hotel, Beverly Hills, California.

Studio album *Dark Lady* arrives on the US Billboard 200 at #191.

June 29, 1974: *Train Of Thought* becomes Cher's tenth US Top 30 hit as it rises to #27 on the US Hot 100. Its parent album *Dark Lady* is at #69 on the Billboard 200.

August 10, 1974: Cher's *I Saw A Man And He Danced With His Wife* enters the US Hot 100 at #87.

August 31, 1974: Spotted: Cher at JFK Airport in New York City.

September 14, 1974: Sitting at #42 on the US Hot 100, *I Saw A Man And He Danced With His Wife* comes close to becoming another Top 40 solo hit for Cher.

September 21, 1974: *I Saw A Man And He Danced With His Wife* rises to #3 on the US Adult Contemporary chart.

September 28, 1974: Sonny & Cher's *Greatest Hits* enters the Billboard 200 at #189.

November 16, 1974: Solo Cher compilation album *Greatest Hits* enters the Billboard 200 at 176.

November 20, 1974: At the Metropolitan Museum of Art in New York City, Cher and Bob Mackie attends Diana Vreeland's exhibition 'Romantic and Glamorous Hollywood Design – the first blockbuster exhibition of Hollywood costume held in a major museum.

December 07, 1974: Cher's solo *Greatest Hits* spends a second week at #152 on the Billboard 200.

December 28, 1974: Cher, along with sister Georganne and daughter Chastity, attends the opening of her mother's new quilt-and-bed boutique in Brentwood, Granny's Cabbage Patch.

January-November, 1975

Cher Gets Her Own TV Show

January 06, 1975: Cher begins recording her solo television show *Cher*.

"Who's Man Enough For This Woman?"

– Esquire, February 1975

February 12, 1975: *Cher* débuts on TV.

March 04, 1975: Cher presents the Favourite Television Comedy Program Award at The 1st Annual People's Choice Awards.

March 23, 1975: Cher performs a medley of her three solo US#1 singles on her *Cher* show.

March 24, 1975: Paul McCartney hosts a party to celebrate the completion of his new solo album *Venus and Mars*. It takes place on board the Queen Mary ocean liner in Long Beach, California. The 200 guests include George Harrison, Cher, Bob Dylan, Joni Mitchell, Carole King, Marvin Gaye, The Faces, Phil Everly, The Jackson Five, Dean Martin, Tony Curtis, Derek Taylor and Mal Evans. The event is the first time Paul McCartney and Harrison have been seen in public since The Beatles' break-up.

April 27, 1975: The season one finale of the *Cher* show airs.

May 10, 1975: Cher's solo studio album *Stars* arrives on the US Billboard 200 at #178.

May 20, 1975: Cher holds her 29th birthday bash at Pips in Los Angeles with Gregg Allman.

May 28, 1975: Cher talks to Rona Barrett during the one-hour TV special *Rona Looks at Raquel, Liza, Cher and Ann-Margret*.

June 07, 1975: Cher's studio album *Stars* spends a second week at #153 on the Billboard 200.

June 30, 1975: Cher marries Greg Allman.

July 14, 1975: Sonny and Cher appear on *The Tonight Show*.

"**Cher & Gregg Allman – Can He Outlast David Geffen?**"

– Rona Barrett's Gossip, July 1975

August 09, 1975: The First Annual Rock Awards program is produced in 1975 in Los Angeles by Don Kirshner and features Elton John and Diana Ross as hosts and presenters. Cher presents Outstanding Rock Personality Of The Year.

September 07, 1975: The second season of *Cher* begins.

September 12, 1975: Cher appears on *Dinah!*.

September 27, 1975: Cher performs *Just This One Time*, from *Stars*, on *The Carol Burnett Show*.

"Exclusive Interview With Cher: 'I Made A Big Mistake Marrying Gregg Allman'!"

– Rona Barrett's Gossip, October 1975

November 20, 1975: Spotted: Cher and Chastity shopping on Madison Avenue in New York city.

November 21, 1975: Spotted: Cher shopping on Madison Avenue in NYC.

November 23, 1975: Spotted: Cher and Chastity at The Pierre Hotel in NYC, and later on a Los Angeles-bound airplane.

December 1975-September, 1976

Sonny & Cher To return To TV

December 04, 1975: In a press conference punctuated by quips, Sonny and Cher announce their joint return to television starting next year. For business purposes only they say. They add that they had no plans for a remarriage.

December 14, 1975: Cher arrives with husband Gregg Allman backstage at the Mid-South Coliseum prior to The Allman Brothers Band's set.

January 04, 1976: the final episode of *Cher* airs.

February 01, 1976: Sonny & Cher's reunion show *The Sonny & Cher Show* airs. Spotted: Cher at the Palm Restaurant in Beverly Hills.

February 23, 1976: Spotted: Cher at La Scala Restaurant in New York City.

April 11, 1976: The season one finale of the *The Sonny & Cher Show* airs.

May 21, 1976: Cher appears on *Dinah!*.

July 1976: Cher records the entirety of her next solo studio album: *Borrowed Time*; *Early Morning Strangers*; *Flashback*; *I Know (You Don't Love me No More)*; *I'd Rather Believe In You*; *It's A Cryin' Shame*; *Knock On Wood*; *Long Distance Love Affair*; *Silver Wings & Golden Rings*; *Spring*.

July 10, 1976: Cher gives birth to son Elijah Blue Allman.

September 26, 1976: Season two of *The Sonny & Cher Show* begins.

October 15, 1976: Sonny and Cher appear on *Donny and Marie*.

1977

January 19, 1977: Spotted: Cher and Gregg Allman at Dulles International Airport.

January 15, 1977: Cher enters the Hot 100 for the first time since 1974, as *Pirate* débuts at #96.

January 21, 1977: Spotted: Cher shopping in Washington, then later, Cher and Gregg Allman on Wisconsin Avenue in Georgetown heading towards Jimmy Carter's Inauguration.

March 06, 1977: Spotted: Cher visits the Beverly Hills Hotel for brunch.

March 09, 1977: Cher attends Filmex '77 Film Festival at Century Plaza in Los Angeles.

March 11, 1977: The final episode of The Sonny & Cher Show airs.

March 13, 1977: Spotted: Cher at the Los Angeles International Airport.

March 20, 1977: Cher returns to Los Angeles from a performance in Hawaii with Sonny.

April, 1977: Cher records the entirety of her next album: *Again*; *Dixie*; *He Was Beautiful*; *L.A. Plane*; *Love The Devil Out Of Ya*; *Send The Man Over*; *She Loves To Hear The Music*; *Thunderstorm*; and *War paint and Soft Feathers*.

April 05, 1977: Spotted: Sonny & Cher at Los Angeles International Airport.

April 15, 1977: Cher attending a Dolly Parton Concert.

April 21, 1977: Spotted: Cher at On The Rox Nightclub in Los Angeles.

May 05, 1977: Cher attends Peter Allen's opening show at The Roxy in Hollywood, California.

June, 1977: Spotted: at the El Privado Club in Los Angeles.

June 12, 1977: Spotted: Cher with Sonny at the Los Angeles International Airport.

July 20, 1977: Spotted: Sonny, Cher, Elijah and Chastity arrive at JFK Airport.

September 21, 1977: Spotted: Cher and son Elijah Blue at The Pierre Hotel.

September 23, 1977: Cher and Elijah appear on The Stanley Siegel Show.

November 11, 1977: Spotted: Cher And Gregg Allman at JFK Airport.

November 1977: Gregg Allman & Cher play a concert in Brussels, Belgium.

1978

January 12, 1978: Spotted: Cher, and her children Chastity and Elijah, in Aspen.

February 01, 1978: Spotted: Cher and her sister Georganne at Cher's Beverly Hills home.

February 04, 1978: Cher performs *Danny's Song* and *The Long and Winding Road* during *The 1978 Cerebral Palsy Telethon Benefit*.

March 26, 1978: Cher tapes a one-hour variety ABC television special, *Cher...Special*, in Los Angeles.

April 04, 1978: *Cher...Special* airs on ABC.

"Cher & Her New Flame – 'I'm Starting To Live Again,' She Says – And Gene Simmons of KISS Is One Reason."

– People Weekly, April 1978

September 20, 1978: Cher attends the Opium perfume launch at Studio 54.

October 1978: Cher begins recording her next solo studio album: *Happy Was The Day We Met*; *Love & Pain*; *My Song (Too Far Gone)*; *Take Me Home*; and *If He'd Take Me Back Again*. However, the latter song is scrapped.

1979

Take Me Home To The Charts

February 07, 1979: Cher performs *Take me Home*, *Love & Pain* and *My Song (Too Far Gone)* on *The Merv Griffin Show*.

February 10, 1979: Cher returns to the US Hot 100 after two years with *Take Me Home*, entering at #75.

February 24, 1979: Cher returns to the Billboard 200 with studio album *Take Me Home*, entering at #103 – her highest solo debut position on the chart so far.

February 26, 1979: Cher begins a week of co-hosting *The Mike Douglas Show*. Sonny is a guest, and the duo perform a medley of *United We Stand* and *Without You*. Cher sings *Take Me Home*.

February 27, 1979: Cher co-hosts *The Mike Douglas Show*, and performs *Happy Was The Day We Met*.

February 28, 1979: Cher co-hosts *The Mike Douglas Show* for a third day, and performs *Love & Pain*.

February 01, 1979: Cher answers the studio audience's questions as she co-hosts *The Mike Douglas Show*.

Ferbruary 02, 1979: Cher performs *My Song (Too Far Gone)* as she co-hosts *The Mike Douglas Show*.

March 06, 1979: Cher appears on *The Tonight Show*.

March 07, 1979: *Cher... and Other Fantasies* airs on TV.

March 17, 1979: *Take Me Home* rises to the US Hot 100 Top 40.

May 03, 1979: Cher's single *Take Me Home* is certified Gold by the RIAA for shifting 1,000,000 copies in the US.

May 05, 1979: *Take Me Home* becomes Cher's seventh US Top 10 hit as it climbs from #12 to #9 on the US Hot 100. By rising from #29 to #27, Cher's album *Take Me Home* becomes her third highest-charting solo LP ever.

May 17, 1979: Cher's album *Take Me Home* is certified Gold by the RIAA for shifting 500,000 copies in the US.

May 19, 1979: Cher's *Take Me Home* single spends a second consecutive week at #8 on the US Hot 100 whilst its identically-titled parent album spends a second consecutive week at #25.

"Cher – The Doll With The Ubiquitous Body"

– Celebrity Monthly, July 1979

June 02, 1979: *Wasn't It Good* enters the US Hot 100 at #88.

July 07, 1979: *Wasn't It Good* becomes Cher's fifteenth solo US Top 50 hit as it rises to #49 on the US Hot 100.

July 09, 1979: Cher begins five dates of concerts at Atlantic City.

August 16, 1979: Cher begins a residency at the Circus Maximus Showroom at Caesars Palace in Las Vegas.

September 15, 1979: Cher's *Hell On Wheels* enters the US Hot 100 at #81.

October 12, 1979: Cher appears on The Tonight Show Starring Johnny Carson.

October 19, 1979: Cher's *Hell On Wheels* music video is shown on NBC's *The Midnight Special*.

October 20, 1979: *Hell On Wheels* exits the US Hot 100, after peaking at #59.

December 17, 1979: Cher attends the *Kramer vs Kramer* Los Angeles première with Gene Simmons.

February, 1980-January, 1982

Cher's Las Vegas Residency

January 10, 1980: Cher resumes her residency at Circus Maximus Showroom at Caesars Palace in Las Vegas.

February 09, 1980: Cher and Les Dudek attend the *Xanadu* wrap party at General Studios in Hollywood, California, United States.

May 10, 1980: Cher takes her concert show over to Europe for a few dates, beginning in Monte Carlo, where it is filmed for broadcast.

June 05, 1980: Cher is back at the Circus Maximus Showroom at Caesars Palace in Las Vegas.

August 21, 1980: Black Rose's eponymous debut album is released in the US.

August 25, 1980: Spotted: Cher and Les Dudek sighting on Fifth Ave., in New York City.

September 19, 1980: Black Rose guest on NBC's *The Midnight Special*, performing *Never Should've Started*, *Julie*, *You Know It* and *Ain't Got No Money*.

"The New Cher – She's Got A New Guy And A New Image As Rock's Black Rose"

– Us Weekly, November 1980

296

January 10, 1981: Cher and boyfriend Les Dudek attend Rod Stewart's Birthday party.

February 24, 1981: Cher, along with sister Georganne and children Chastity and Elijah, attend the *The Rocky Horror Picture Show* After Party.

May 31, 1981: Celebrities including Cher – who takes along children Elijah and Chastity – play in the 9th Annual Riviera Las Vegas Celebrity Softball Classic in 1981 in Las Vegas, Nevada.

September 30, 1981: Cher appears on *The Tonight Show Starring Johnny Carson*.

November 22, 1981: Meat Loaf and Chers' duet *Dead Ringer For Love* enters the Official Singles Chart Top 75 at #63.

November 26, 1981: Cher takes her concert show to Australia for a few dates, beginning in Sydney.

January 15, 1982: Cher attends Liza Minelli's birthday party at Haston's Apartment in New York City.

January 17, 1982: *Dead Ringer For Love* by Meat Loaf and Cher makes a big jump from #26 to #7 on the Official Singles Chart Top 75, becoming Meat Loaf's first ever UK Top 10 hit. It is Cher's seventh overall UK Top 10 hit but her first since 1971's *Gypsies, Tramps & Thieves*.

February-November, 1982

Cher To Make Broadway Debut

"Big Apple, Beware! The First Lady Of Flash Moves To Manhattan With Her Kids And Takes On A Broadway Play"

– People Weekly, January 1982

February, 1982

01: Meat Loaf and Chers' *Dead Ringer For Love* is certified Silver by the BPI for shifting 250,000 copies.

07: *Dead Ringer For Love* by Meat Loaf and Cher spends its second week at #5 on the UK singles chart. It is Cher's fifth overall Top 5 hit in the country.

14: Cher takes part in a fashion show at the Night Of 100 Stars Gala, in which she dons a Bob Mackie wedding dress.

18: Starring Sandy Dennis, Cher, making her Broadway debut, and Karen Black, Broadway show *Come Back to the Five and Dime, Jimmy Dean, Jimmy Dean* débuts at New York's Martin Beck Theatre.

April-November, 1982

April 04, 1982: *Come Back to the Five and Dime, Jimmy Dean, Jimmy Dean* completes its run on Broadway, after 52 shows.

May 28, 1982: Cher releases her solo studio album, the pop-rock *I Paralyze*, on Columbia Records.

June 06 1982: Cher performs *My Heart Belongs To Daddy* at the 36th Annual Tony Awards.

June 09, 1982: Cher and date Val Kilmer attend the *Grease II* première party at The Red Parrot in New York City.

July 01, 1982: Che returns for a residency at the Circus Maximus Showroom at Caesars Palace in Las Vegas.

July 10, 1982: Cher performs *I Paralyze* on *Solid Gold*.

July 24, 1982: Cher performs song *I Paralyze* on *American Bandstand*.

September 02, 1982: Cher, son Elijah, and boyfriend Val Kilmer attend a performance of *Little Shop Of Horrors*.

September 30, 1982: The film adaption of *Come Back to the Five and Dime, Jimmy Dean, Jimmy Dean* starring Sandy Dennis, Cher and Karen Black has its U.S. première at the Chicago International Film Festival.

November 12, 1982: The film *Come Back to the Five and Dime, Jimmy Dean, Jimmy Dean* opens on a limited basis in just two theaters.

January-November, 1983

January 19, 1983: Cher gives a speech at the UCLA – the University of California, Los Angeles.

January 24, 1983: Cher appears on *The Tonight Show Starring Johnny Carson*.

January 26, 1983: Cher and David Geffen attend the LA première of *The Year Of Living Dangerously*.

January 29, 1983: Cher, date Val Kilmer, and her two children, attend the 40th Golden Globe Awards, in which Cher is nominated for Best Supporting Actress in *Come Back to the Five and Dime, Jimmy Dean, Jimmy Dean*.

January 30, 1983: Spotted: David Geffen and Cher outside La Scala Restaurant in Beverly Hills.

February 01, 1983: Spotted: Cher and David Geffen at Le Dome Restaurant in Hollywood.

February 02, 1983: Chastity Bono and mother Cher attend the grand opening of Sonny Bono's new restaurant, Bono's, in West Hollywood, California.

March 20, 1983: Cher and David Geffen attend the *Dreamgirls* opening night after party in Los Angeles, at the Shubert Theater in Century City. Cher poses for photos with Michael Jackson.

April 11, 1983: Cher and boyfriend Val Kilmer attend the 55th Annual Academy awards, during which Cher co-presents the music awards with Plácido Domingo,

April 21, 1983: *Cher: A Celebration at Caesars* airs on Showtime.

April 27, 1983: Cher, her mother Georgia Holt and daughter Chastity Bono attend Sonny Bono's restaurant in Hollywood, California.

August 24, 1983: Cher and David Geffen attend a "Welcome to Hollywood" party for Eddie Murphy at the Hard Rock Cafe in Los Angeles

September 16, 1983: Cher attends a performance of *La Cage Aux Folles* on Broadway

September 19, 1983: Spotted: Cher at Elaine's Restaurant in New York.

December, 1983-April, 1984

Cher Supports Streep In *Silkwood*

December 01, 1983: Cher attends the première of *Scarface* in New York.

December 14, 1983: *Silkwood* opens on a limited release in 257 theaters in the United States.

December 19, 1983: *Silkwood* ranks at #12 at the Box Office on its limited opening weekend of 16-18 December, grossing $1,218,322.

January 27, 1984: *Silkwood* has its wide release, in 816 theaters, in its seventh week of release.

January 28, 1984: Cher attends the 41st Golden Globe Awards, at which she wins the award for Best Supporting Actress for Silkwood.

January 30, 1984: *Silkwood* ranks at #1 at the Box Office on its wide opening weekend of 27-29, grossing $3,547,122:

January 27-29, 1984 Weekend

1. Silkwood; $3,547,122; 816 theaters

2. Terms of Endearment; $3,383,539; 903 theaters

3. Never Cry Wolf; $2,679,108; 491 theaters

February 07, 1984: Cher attends the *Footloose* première at The Academy in Beverly Hills, California, United States.

March 02, 1984: After 11 weeks at the US Box Office, *Silkwood* has grossed $31,764,738.

March 16, 1984: Cher and date Val Kilmer attend an American Film Institute Dinner at the Beverly Hilton Hotel.

April 09, 1984: In a floor-length pink dress, Cher attends the 55 Annual Academy Awards at the Dorothy Chandler Pavilion, Los Angeles with date Val Kilmer and her son Elijah. There, she is nominated for Best Supporting Actress for *Silkwood*, but loses out to Linda Hunt for *The Year of Living Dangerously*.

April 17, 1984: Cher attends the première of *The Bounty in LA*.

May, 1984-February, 1985

Cher's New Look

May 01, 1984: Cher débuts her dyed red hair as she attends the Los Angeles Stage Company Benefit for Sexually Abused Children.

May 29, 1984: Cher attends the *Streets Of Fire* première in LA.

July 08, 1984: With her real hair much shorter, and still red, Cher, and sister Georganne, attend *The Last Starfighter* LA première.

July 23, 1984: With her real hair having been cut very short and bleached blonde, Cher attends the *Grandview, USA* première at Samuel Goldwyn Theater in Beverly Hills, California, United States.

September 06, 1984: Cher attends the première of *Amadeus* at Westwood Theater in Westwood, California.

September 14, 1984: Cher attends a private party in LA hosted by Dan Aykroyd.

November 11, 1984: Cher and boyfriend Josh Donen attend the *Beverly Hills Cop LA* première.

December 10, 1984: Cher and Josh Donen attend the LA première of *Runaway*.

December 13, 1984: Cher and Josh Donen attend the *Passage To India* LA première.

February 01, 1985: Cher, boyfriend Josh Donen, and daughter Chastity, attend a *Heaven Help Us* screening at the Director's Guild in Hollywood, California, United States.

February 09, 1985: Cher attends the première of *The Sure Thing* in Beverly Hills, with her children, boyfriend Josh, and sister Georganne.

February 14, 1985: Cher is presented with the Hasty Pudding Woman of the Year award by the Hasty Pudding Theatricals society at Harvard University for having made a lasting and impressive contribution to the world of entertainment.

March-June, 1985

Cher Stars In *Mask*

March, 1985

05: Cher attends the première of *Mask* with Josh Donen in Los Angeles.

08: *Mask* opens in just 4 theaters in the United States.

14: Cher attends the *A Private Function* LA première with boyfriend Josh Donen.

22: *Mask* has its wide release, opening in 800 theaters across the US.

25: *Mask* ranks at #3 at the Box Office on its wide opening weekend of 22-24 , grossing $6,121,129:

March 22-24, 1985 Weekend

1. *Friday the 13th - Part V*; $8,032,883; 1,759 theaters

2. *Porky's Revenge (Part III)*; $6,207,507; 1,423 theaters

3. *Mask*; $6,121,129; 800 theaters

April, 1985

01: *Mask* rises to #2 at the Box Office on the weekend of 29-31 March, behind *Police Academy 2: Their First Assignment*, grossing $4,807,470.

09: Cher appears on *The Tonight Show Starring Johnny Carson*.

22: After spending three weekends at #2 behind *Police Academy 2: Their First Assignment* on the US Box Office, *Mask* finally slips to #4, so far grossing $29,823,069.

May, 1985

20: Cher attends the 38th Cannes Film Festival in France, in which she is presented with the Best Actress Award for *Mask*.

June, 1985

07: After 13 weeks at the US Box Office, *Mask* grossed $42,417,782.

21: Cher attends the *Cocoon* film première in LA with Josh Donen.

July-December, 1985

July 13, 1985: Cher joins in on the group performance of *We Are The World* at the Live Aid Stage in Philadelphia.

July 17, 1985: Spotted: Cher at China Club In New York City.

July 20, 1985: Cher attends the New York première of *Leader Of the Pack*, a musical starring old friend Darlene Love

July 28, 1985: Cher and boyfriend Josh donen attend the APLA Aids Benefit in LA.

August 05, 1985: Cher and *Mask* co-star Eric Stoltz attend the première of *The Bride* in LA.

August 16, 1985: Cher – in a big purple wig – and her boyfriend Josh Donen attend the wedding of Madonna and Sean Penn.

September 05, 1985: Cher with date Josh Donen and her daughter chastity attend The Palladium in New York. Cher is photographed with Darlene Love.

September 11, 1985: Cher and David Geffen attend a private screening of movie *After Hours*.

October 30, 1985: Trio of dyslexic celebrities Cher, Tom Cruise and Bruce Jenner each pick up the Outstanding Learning Disabled Achiever Award at the Lab School of

Washington, after visiting Nancy Reagan at the White House.

November 07, 1985: Cher attends the *White Nights* Los Angeles première at Samuel Goldwyn Theater in Beverly Hills, California, United States.

November 09, 1985: Cher and Chastity attend a *Saturday Night Live* party.

December 09, 1985: Cher and Bob Mackie attend Diana Vreeland's 14th Annual Costume Exhibit.

January-October, 1986

24: Cher and Josh Donen attend the 43rd Golden Globe Awards, at which Cher is nominated for Best Actress for *Mask*. The award goes to Whoopi Goldberg for *The Color Purple*.

27: Cher and Josh Donen attend The 13th Annual American Music Awards.

29: Cher and boyfriend Josh Donen attend the *Down And Out In Beverly Hills* film première in LA.

March-October, 1986

March 24, 1986: Cher attends the 58th annual Academy Awards at the Dorothy Chandler Pavilion in Los Angeles, where she presents the award for Best Supporting Actor, in a mohawk.

April 17, 1986: Cher attends the *At Close Range* première at Manns Bruin Theater in Westwood, California.

May 12, 1986: Cher attends the première of *Top Gun* in New York.

May 20, 1986: Cher accepts the Best Actress award at the Cannes Film Festival, for *Mask*.

May 22, 1986: Cher appears on Late Show With David Letterman, during which she calls him an "asshole".

June 12, 1986: Cher and Josh attend the *Legal Eagles* première In LA.

June 16, 1986: Cher attends an Eurythmics concert at the Roxy on Sunset Strip in West Hollywood, California.

September 07, 1986: Cher attends Whoopi Goldberg's wedding reception in Los Angeles, California, United States.

September 26, 1986: Josh Donen and Cher during the Toxic Waste Benefit at the MGM in Culver City, California.

October 09, 1986: Elton John and Cher perform on the first episode of *The Late Show* pose with star Joan Rivers.

June-October, 1987

The Witches Of Eastwick Hits Theaters

June 12, 1987: *The Witches of Eastwick* opens in 1,103 theaters across the United states.

June 15, 1987: *The Wtches of Eastwick* opens at #2, behind *Predator*, at the Box Office weekend of 12-14, grossing $9,454,238.

June 22, 1987: *The Witches of Eastwick* rises to #1 at the US Box Office for the weekend of 19-21, grossing $8,251,230. It is Cher's second #1 film after *Silkwood*:

December 3-5, 2010 Weekend

1. *The Witches of Eastwick;* $8,251,230; 1,123 theaters

2. *Predator*; $8,225,869; 1,636 theaters

3. *Beverly Hills Cop II*; $7,417,458; 2,326 theaters

August 07, 1987: After 8 weeks at the US Box Office, *The Witches of Eastwick* has grossed $57,985,869.

August 19, 1987: Cher and Rob attend the *Dirty Dancing* première in LA.

September 14, 1987: Cher and boyfriend Rob Camiletti attend the MTV Video Music Awards, at which Cher presents the Viewer's Choice Award.

October 23, 1987: Cher's second film of the year, *Suspect*, co-starring Dennis Quaid, is released in 1,029 theaters in the US.

October 26, 1987: *Suspect* ranked 3rd during its Box Office opening weekend of 23-25, grossing $4,152,015:

October 23-25, 1987 Weekend

1. *Fatal Attraction*; $8,046,843; 1,340 theaters

2. *Prince of Darkness*; $4,657,401; 1,239 theaters

3. *Suspect*; $4,152,015; 1,029 theaters

November-December, 1987

Cher Returns To Music

November, 1987

03: Cher's self-titled new LP is released in the States.

09: Cher attends the Mercer and the Movies Tribute to Johnny Mercer at the Waldorf Astoria in New York City.

14: Sonny Bono and Cher sing their hit song *I Got You Babe* for the first time in over 10 years, on *Late Night with David Letterman*, in New York. Cher also performs *I Found Someone*.

18: Cher and boyfriend Camiletti attend the *The Last Emperor* première in New York.

21: Cher enters the US Hot 100 for the first time since 1979 as *I Found Someone* débuts at #79.

22: Cher scores her first solo UK chart placement since 1974 as *I Found Someone* enters the Official Singles Chart Top 100 at #91.

December, 1987

01: Cher and Camiletti attend the New York première of *Moonstruck*.

05: Cher's new self-titled studio album, *Cher*, enters the Billboard 200 at #131 – her first placement on the chart since 1979.

07: Cher and boyfriend Camiletti attend the LA première of *Moonstruck*.

12: Cher takes part in the "Christmas Eve Dinner" program for the homeless in Washington.

18: *Moonstruck* has a limited release at 7 theaters in the US

January-February, 1988

Moonstruck Hits The Box Office

January, 1988

10: Cher's *I Found Someone* scores her 6th overall Top 5 UK hit as the song climbs to #5 on the the country's Official Singles Chart Top 100. Her self-titled new LP *Cher* is the week's highest new entry, at #63, on the UK Official Albums Chart Top 100, giving Cher her first UK hit album since 1966.

15: *Moonstruck* has its wide release in the US, at 635 theaters.

18: *Moonstruck* is ranked third at the US Box Office for its wide opening weekend of 15-17, grossing $5,069,508:

January 22-24, 1988 Weekend

1. *Good Morning, Vietnam*; $10,806,276; 1,194 theaters

2. *Three Men and a Baby*; $6,036,498; 1,813 theaters

3. *Moonstruck*; $5,069,508; 635 theaters

23: Cher and Camiletti attend the 45th Golden Globe Awards. Cher wins the Best Actress - Musical or Comedy award for *Moonstruck*.

24: *Cher* rises to the Top 30 of the UK Albums Chart, to #26.

25: Cher and Rob Camiletti attend the 15th Annual American Music Awards at the Shrine Auditorium in Los Angeles.

"The Ultimate Liberated Woman – Cher – She's Made *Moonstruck* A Megahit, Her Lover Is 23 & She's Tough Enough To Say: 'Mess With Me And I'll Kill You'"

– People Weekly, January 1988

February, 1988

04: Cher and Rob Camiletti attend the *Shoot To Kill* première at the Mann's Westwood Theater in Los Angeles.

08: For the fourth consecutive weekend, *Moonstruck* remains at #3 at the US Box Office, currently totalling $25,024,293.

March-August, 1988

Will Cher Win An Oscar?

March, 1988

05: Cher scores her eighth solo US Top 10 single as *I Found Someone* rises from #14 to #10 on the US Hot 100.

19: *Cher* becomes Cher's eleventh overall US Top 40 album as it rises from #44 to #40 on the Billboard 200.

24: Cher attends the Royal Film Performance of Steven Spielberg's *Empire of the Sun*, at which she meets Queen Elizabeth II.

April, 1988

09: Cher's *We All Sleep Alone* enters the US Hot 100 at #84.

10: *We All Sleep Alone* becomes Cher's 18th overall UK Top 50 hit single as it climbs to #47 on the UK Official Singles Chart Top 100.

11: Cher attends the 60th annual Academy Awards at the Shrine Auditorium in Los Angeles. She and *Moonstruck* co-star Nicholas Cage present the Best Supporting Actor Award, before Cher then wins the award for Best Actress, for *Moonstruck*.

24: *Cher* re-enters the Top 30 of the UK Official Albums Chart Top 100.

May-July, 1988

May 10, 1988: Cher's 1987 self-titled album is certified by the BPI for shipping 100,000 copies in the UK.

May 21, 1988: *Cher* spends a third consecutive week at #32 on the Billboard 200.

June 10, 1988: After 25 weeks at the US Box Office, *Moonstruck* has so far grossed $76,649,353.

June 11, 1988: *We All Sleep Alone* by Cher rises slightly from #16 to #14 on the US Hot 100.

July 28, 1988: Cher and her boyfriend Robert Camilletti hold a press conference in Los Angeles, where they plead Camilletti's case in which he was accused of trying to run down a photographer outside Cher's Benedict Canyon home.

July 30, 1988: *Skin Deep* enters the US Hot 100 at #90.

August 10, 1988: Cher promotes her new perfume Uninhibited in New York.

September-December, 1988

September 07, 1988: Cher attends the MTV Video Music Awards at the Universal Amphitheatre in Los Angeles, during which she performs *Main Man*, and presents Video of the Year. Cher's *I Found Someone* video is nominated for Best Female Video, but loses out to Suzanne Vega's Luka.

September 15, 1988: Cher and Josh Donen attend a cocktail party in honor of Michael Dukakis.

October 31, 1988: Dressed in an Egyptian-style outfit, Cher puts on a press show for her new perfume Uninhibited in Century City, Los Angeles.

November 04, 1988: Cher speaks during a rally for Gov. Michael S. Dukakis in Queens.

Cher and boyfriend Rob attend a performance of *Waiting For Godot* at Mitzi Newhouse Theater Lincoln Center in New York.

November 08, 1988: Cher leads a march of over 2,000 people across from the U.S. Capital Building in Washington, D.C., to demand that congress restore severe funding cuts in low-income housing.

November 17, 1988: Cher and Rob attend the *Scrooged* première in Los Angeles.

December 07, 1988: Cher and rob attend the première of Torch Song Trilogy in Los Angeles.

March-June, 1989

Cher & Peter Cetera Duet

March, 1989

11: Cher achieves her highest ever debut on the US Hot 100 as *After All (Love Theme From "Chances Are")*, a duet with Peter Cetera, enters the chart at #59.

12: Cher attends The 15th Annual People's Choice Awards, where *Moonstruck* co-star Olympia Dukakis presents her with the Favourite All Around Female Entertainer award.

29: Cher attends the 61st Annual Academy awards at the Shrine Auditorium in Los Angeles with date Rob Camiletti. Cher presents the biggest award of the night – Best Picture.

April, 1989

22: *After All (Love Theme From "Chances Are")* by Cher and Peter Cetera rises to #1 on the US Adult Contemporary Chart.

29: *After All (Love Theme From "Chances Are")* by Cher and Peter Cetera enters the Top 10 of the US Hot 100, from #15 to #9.

May, 1989

13: *After All (Love Theme From "Chances Are")* rises to #6 on the US Hot 100, and spends its fourth week at #1 on the Adult Contemporary Chart.

14: Cher and Peter Cetera's duet *After All (Love Theme From 'Chances Are')* enters the UK Official Singles Chart Top 100 at #84.

25: Cher is added to the KISS-108 party at the Great Woods Center for the Performing Arts on June 3. The concert is already sold out and features such headliners as Hall & Oates, Donna Summer, New Edition, Gloria Estefan and Al Green.

June, 1989

03: Cher performs in a black leotard with leather and metal belts at the KISS-108 party at the Great Woods Center.

21: Cher performs at the Pediatric AIDS Foundation benefit concert in Washington, D.C.

July-December, 1989

If I Could Turn Back Time Hits The Charts

July, 1989

08: Cher's *If I Could Turn Back Time* enters the US Hot 100 at #89. *After All (Love Theme From "Chances Are")* is still eight places higher at #81 in its twentieth week on the chart.

16: Cher's *Heart Of Stone* LP enters the Official Albums Chart Top 75 at #62.

22: *Heart Of Stone* enters the US Billboard 200 at #88 – Cher's highest ever debut on the chart.

September, 1989

09: Cher attends the MTV Video Awards in LA with date Richie Sambora. Cher performs her latest hit *If I Could Turn Back Time* completely live, donning the same controversial outfit as its music video.

Cher's *If I Could Turn Back Time* enters the Top 10 of the US Hot 100, from #11 to #9, to become her 10th solo US Top 10 single, and her 15th overall. Its parent album *Heart Of Stone* becomes her third ever solo Top 20 album as it rises from #25 to #20.

23: *If I Could Turn Back Time* climbs to #3 on the US Hot 100, to become Cher's first US Top 5 since 1974:

September 23, 1989 Hot 100

1. *Girl I'm Gonna Miss You*; Milli Vanilli

2. Heaven; Warrant

3. *If I Could Turn Back Time*; Cher

30: *If I Could Turn Back Time* spends a second week at #3 on the US Hot 100 for Cher, whilst climbing to #1 on the Billboard Adult Contemporary Chart.

October, 1989

14: *Heart Of Stone* becomes Cher's first ever US Top 10 album as it moves up one position from #11.

15: Cher achieves her ninth UK Top 10 single as *If I Could Turn Back Time* rises from #13 to #9 on the UK Official Singles Chart Top 100.

21: *Just Like Jesse James* becomes Cher's 43rd overall US Hot 100 hit as it enters the chart at #90. Album *Heart Of Stone* spends a second week at #10.

22: *If I Could Turn Back Time* reaches a new peak of #6 in the UK. Its parent album *Heart Of Stone* enters the Top 20 of the Albums Chart – Cher's first time there since 1966.

December, 1989-October, 1990

Heart Of Stone Spawns More Hits

December 16, 1989: *Heart Of Stone* becomes Cher's first ever studio album to score three US Hot 100 Top 10 singles as *Just Like Jesse James* jumps from #19 to #10.

January 07, 1990: Cher achieves UK hit singles in four decades as *Just Like Jesse James* débuts on the country's chart at #60.

January 13, 1990: Cher's *Just Like Jesse James* spends its fourth consecutive week at #8 on the US Hot 100. In that time, Cher has achieved solo US Hot 100 Top 10 placements in four decades. Its parent album spends a 19th consecutive week within the Billboard 200 Top 20.

February 01, 1990: Cher's album *Heart of Stone* is certified Platinum in the UK for shipping 300,000 copies.

February 10, 1990: *Heart Of Stone*, the single, enters the US Hot 100 at #92.

February 18, 1990: Cher's *Just Like Jesse James* climbs very close to the UK Top 10 by rising from #15 to #11. Its parent LP rises to #7 on the Official Albums Chart Top 75 this week – matching her previous highest peak on the chart with her debut *All I Really Want To Do* and Sonny & Cher's debut *Look At Us*, both hitting #7 in 1965.

March 31, 1990: Cher begins her *Heart Of Stone Tour*, in Dallas, Texas.

April 01, 1990: Single *Heart Of Stone* enters the UK's Official Singles Chart Top 100 at #67 to become Cher's fourth hit on the chart from the album of the same name.

April 14, 1990: *Heart Of Stone* enters the US Hot 100 Top 20 to become the fourth single to do so from Cher's album of the same name.

June 14, 1990: Cher begins her first of eight shows, during a six-night engagement, at The Mirage, Las Vegas.

July 05, 1990: Cher's album *Heart Of Stone* is certified Double-Platinum by the RIAA for shifting 2,000,000 in the US.

August 12, 1990: Cher's *You Wouldn't Know Love* is at #55 this week in the UK, becoming her fifth UK hit single from *Heart of Stone*, which is currently in its 47th week on the Albums chart.

August 29, 1990: Cher ends the North American leg of her *Heart Of Stone Tour*.

October, 1990

14: Cher begins the UK portion of her *Heart Of Stone Tour*, in Ireland.

21: *Baby I'm Yours* from the upcoming *Mermaids* soundtrack enters the UK Singles Chart at #89 to become Cher's fourth UK Top 100 hit this year.

23: Cher completes the sixth and final UK date of her *Heart Of Stone Tour*, in Birmingham, England.

24: Spotted: Cher at Heathrow Airport In London.

November, 1990-May, 1991

Cher: "It's In His Kiss!"

November, 1990

14: Cher begins the Australian leg of her *Heart Of Stone Tour*, in Adelaide.

24: *The Shoop Shoop Song (It's In His Kiss)* by Cher enters the US Hot 100 at #84.

28: Cher ends the Australian portion of her *Heart Of Stone Tour*, with its eleventh show in the country, in Melbourne.

December, 1990

02: Cher returns to The Mirage in Las Vegas for the last three dates of her *Heart Of Stone Tour*.

10: Cher attends the *Mermaids* première at Motion Picture Academy in Los Angeles, California.

17: *Mermaids* opens at #6 at the US Box Office for the weekend of 14-16, grossing $3,514,678 in 920 theaters.

January, 1991

09: Cher's *The Shoop Shoop Song (It's In His Kiss)* comes close to the Top 30 of the US Hot 100 by reaching #33.

February, 1991

02: Cher's *The Shoop Shoop Song (It's In His Kiss)* rises to #7 on the Billboard Adult Contemporary Chart.

08: *Mermaids* has grossed $31,391,628 after 8 weeks at the Box Office.

April, 1991

07: Cher visits fourteen-year-old Australian neurofibromatosis patient Marie Matejic as she undergoes facial surgery at Humana Hospital in Dallas, Texas.

Cher scores her 25th overall UK charted single as *The Shoop Shoop Song (It's In His Kiss)* from the *Mermaids* soundtrack débuts at #58 on the UK Singles Chart.

21: *The Shoop Shoop Song (It's In His Kiss)* makes a huge jump from #23 to #2 in its third week on the Official Singles Chart Top 75 to become Cher's highest-charting solo single ever in the UK. It is kept from the top spot by Chesney Hawkes' *The One and Only*.

Cher's 1989 album *Heart Of Stone* makes a return to UK Albums chart at #70 – its 61st week on the chart.

28: Cher earns her first ever solo UK #1 – and second overall after *I Got You Babe* with Sonny – as *The Shoop Shoop Song (It's In His Kiss)* rises to the top of the Official Singles Chart Top 75:

April 28, 1991 UK Official Singles Chart

1. *The Shoop Shoop Song (It's In His Kiss)*; Cher

2. *The One And Only;* Chesney Hawkes

3. *Last Train To Trancentral Ft The Children Of The Revolution*; KLF Featuring The Children Of The Revolution

May, 1991

21: *Music From the Original Motion Picture Soundtrack – Mermaids* is released in the UK.

26: Impressively, *The Shoop Shoop Song (It's In His Kiss)* by Cher enjoys its fifth week at #1 in the UK.

June-August, 1991

Cher Launches *Love Hurts*

June, 1991

01: *The Shoop Shoop Song (It's In His Kiss)* is certified Gold in the UK for shipping 400,000 copies.

06: Cher attends a music industry bash in Los Angeles, California.

15: *Love & Understanding*, the first single from Cher's LP *Love Hurts*, enters the US Hot 100 at #60 – her highest solo debut yet.

16: A re-issue of Meatloaf and Chers' 1981 duet *Dead Ringer For Love* enters the Official Singles Chart Top 75 at #53.

23: *Love Hurts* immediately becomes Cher's highest-charting album in the UK ever as it débuts on the Official Albums Chart Top 75 at #1. Its predecessor *Heart Of Stone* is still on the charts, at #57.

Cher's *The Shoop Song (It's In His Kiss)* enjoys its tenth week within the UK Top 10.

30th: *Love Hurts* remains at #1 in the UK.

July, 1991

01: *Music From the Original Motion Picture Soundtrack – Mermaids* is certified Silver by the BPI for shifting 60,000 copies in the UK.

06: *Love Hurts* enters the Billboard 200 at #81 – Cher's highest debut on the chart.

07: *Love & Understanding* immediately gives Cher her 18th overall UK Top 40 hit single as it débuts on the country's chart at #36. Predecessor *The Shoop Shoop Song (It's In His Kiss)* is just two places lower at #38 to give Cher two singles within the UK Top 40.

21: Cher achieves another UK Top 10 single with *Love & Understanding*. Love Hurts is still #1 on the Albums Chart.

27: *Love & Understanding* becomes Cher's 23rd overall US Top 20 hit as it rises to #20 on the US Hot 100. Its parent album *Love Hurts* moves into the Billboard 200 Top 50, to #49.

August, 1991

01: Cher's *Love Hurts* album is certified Platinum by the BPI for shipping 300,000 copies in the UK.

04: After six weeks at #1, *Love Hurts* finally slips down to #2 on the UK Official Albums Chart Top 75.

17: *Love & Understanding* spends a third consecutive week at #17 on the US Hot 100.

24: Cher's *Love & Understanding* climbs to #3 on the Billboard Adult Contemporary Chart.

27: Cher's album *Love Hurts* is certified Gold by the RIAA for shifting 500,000 copies in the US.

September, 1991-January, 1992

September, 1991

01: *Love Hurts* spends its 11th week within the UK Albums Chart Top 3.

04: Cher attends the record release party for Richie Sambora's new solo LP *Stranger In This Town* in Griffith Park, Los Angeles, California.

05: The 1991 MTV Video Music Awards are underway at the Universal Amphitheatre in Los Angeles. Cher attends the show with her guest Rob Camilletti. She presents the awards for Best Male Video and Best Female Video.

October, 1991

01: *Love Hurts* by Cher is certified Double-Platinum in the UK for shipping 600,000 copies.

06: Cher attends the Roast For Kenny Sacha at The Improv in Hollywood, Los Angeles, California.

13: *Save Up All Your Tears* enters the UK Top 40 at #37. Its parent album *Love Hurts* is at #21 on the Albums Chart.

19: Save Up All Your Tears enters the US Hot 100 at #92.

30: Cher is a guest on *The Sally Jesse Raphael Show* at NBC Studios in New York City, New York.

December, 1991

01: *Love Hurts*, the title track from Cher's latest LP, enters the Official Singles Chart Top 75 at #47. The LP is at #25 on the Albums chart.

21: *Save Up All Your Tears* enters the US Hot 100 Top 40.

January, 1992

01: Cher's *Love Hurts* album is certified Triple-Platinum in the UK for shipping 900,000 copies.

April-October, 1992

Cher's *Love Hurts Tour*

April, 1992

11: Cher performs *The Shoop Shoop Song (It's In His Kiss)*, with an onstage cameo by Mickey Mouse, at the inauguration of Euro Disney Resort.

12: Cher's *Could've Been You* débuts on the Official Singles Chart Top 75 at #32, giving the singer her highest debut on the chart since 1971's *Gypsies, Tramps & Thieves*. It also marks Cher's twentieth UK Top 40 hit single since her 1965 debut hit *I Got You Babe* with Sonny. *Could've Been You* is Cher's fifth charting single in the UK from her *Love Hurts* album, which is enjoying its 41st week on the charts.

15: Cher begins her *Love Hurts Tour* in Berlin, Germany.

May-June, 1992

May 17, 1992: Cher's 1989 album *Heart Of Stone* re-enters the Official Albums Chart Top 75 at #43 – its 81st week on the chart. *Love Hurts* is at #28 on the same chart.

May 27, 1992: Cher completes the European leg of her *Love Hurts Tour*.

June 30, 1992: Cher attends the *The Panama Deception* Los Angeles première at Director's Guild in Hollywood, California.

July, 1992

02: Chers' 1987 self-titled album is certified Platinum by the RIAA for shifting a million copies in the US.

04: *When Lovers Become Strangers* from *Love Hurts* rises to #15 on the Billboard Adult Contemporary Chart.

Video release *Extravaganza: Live At The Mirage* enters the Billboard Top Music Videos Chart at #3.

25: Cher's *Extravaganza: live At The Mirage* spends its fourth consecutive week within the Top 4 of the Billboard Top Music Videos Chart.

30th: Cher attends the *The Panama Deception* Los Angeles première at the Director's Guild.

August-October, 1992

August 1992: Christy Bono (Sonny's daughter from his marriage prior to meeting Cher) hosts the grand opening of her new restaurant the Yucatan Grill, in West Hollywood. Sonny, Cher and Chastity are all present at the event.

October 23, 1992: Cher begins the short North American leg of her *Love Hurts Tour*.

November, 1992-February, 1993

Cher's *Greatest Hits 1965-1992*

November, 1992

01: Cher completes the North American leg of her *Love Hurts Tour*.

08: *Oh No Not My Baby* by Cher enters the Official Singles Chart Top 75 at #33.

09: Cher's *Greatest Hits 1965-1992* is released in the UK.

15: *Greatest Hits 1965-1992* enters the UK Official Albums Chart Top 75 at #1, becoming Cher's second UK #1 album of the 1990's.

22: Cher's *Greatest Hits 1965-1992* slips to #2 on the UK Albums Chart.

December, 1992

01: Cher's *Greatest Hits 1965-1992* is already certified Double-Platinum by the BPI in the UK for shipping 600,000 copies.

06: Cher's *Greatest Hits 1965-1992* returns to #1 on the UK Official Albums Chart Top 75.

08: Cher attends the Billboard Music Awards.

January, 1993

01: Cher's *Greatest Hits 1965-1992* is certified Triple-Platinum by the BPI in the UK for shipping 900,000 copies.

10: Cher's live rendition of *Many Rivers To Cross* – her first ever concert-recorded single – débuts at #37 on the UK singles chart.

Cher's *Greatest Hits 1965-1992* spends its seventh week at #1 on the UK Official Albums Chart Top 75, beating the six weeks that its predecessor *Love Hurts* spent at #1. 1993 marks the seventh consecutive year, since 1987, that Cher has charted within the Top 30 of the UK Albums Chart.

February, 1993

01: Cher attends and presents an award at the Fashion designers of America Awards.

14: Cher attends the 8th Annual Rock & Rock Hall Of Fame ceremony in LA.

16: Cher flies to London to attend the 1993 Brit Awards but changes her mind upon arriving in London, deciding instead to make arrangement to travel to Armenia. However, she still makes it to the awards show, and accepts the award of Best International Solo Artist on behalf of Prince.

28: *Whenever You're Near* by Cher enters the Official Singles Chart Top 75 at #73.

April, 1993-December, 1994

Cher Winds Down The Work Hours

April, 1993

28: With support from the Armenian United Fund, Cher flies from London to Armenia with friends Paulette Betts and Rob Camiletti, manager Billy Sammeth, a media entourage, plus 45 tons of medical supplies, books, printing equipment, candy and toys.

30: Cher flies back from Armenia to London.

May, 1993-December, 1994

May 16, 1993: a re-issue of Sonny & Cher's *I Got You Babe* enters the UK Official Singles Chart Top 75 at #66.

"Cher – The Fittest Woman In Hollywood"

– Ms. Fitness, Summer 1993

October 15, 1993: Cher is photographed leaving themed restaurant Planet Hollywood in London.

December 04, 1993: *I Got You Babe* by Cher with Beavis & Butt-Head enters the US Bubbling Under chart at #8.

January 16, 1994: *I Got You Babe* by Cher with Beavis & Butt-Head is at #35 on the UK Singles Chart. It is Cher's third placement of the song on the chart following Sonny & Cher's 1965 #1 original and last year's #66 re-issue.

March 03, 1994: Cher makes a speech about recipient Jack Nicholson during an American Film Institute Lifetime Achievement Award ceremony.

March 22, 1994: Cher attends the D.A.R.E. Benefit In Los Angeles.

July 24, 1994: Cher records the entirety of a new album that she has written the majority of: *Born With The Hunger*; *Disaster Cake*; *Fit To Fly*; *Lovers Forever*; a track that is scrapped; *Our Lady of San Francisco*; *Runnin'*; *Sisters Of Mercy*; *Still*; *The Fall (Kurt's Blues)*; and *With Or Without You*.

October 11, 1994: Cher and Richard Berry attend the Katoucha Niane Spring/Summer 1994/1995 Ready To Wear Show at the Salle Wagram in Paris, France.

December 04, 1994: Cher rides a motorbike during the Happy Harley Days at Streets in Beverly Hills, California, United States.

December 07, 1994: Cher attends the 5th Annual Fire And Ice Ball To Benefit Revlon at the UCLA Women Cancer Center, taking son Elija Allman as her guest.

March-November, 1995

12: *Love Can Build A Bridge* by Cher, Chrissie Hynde and Neneh Cherry with Eric Clapton enters the Official Singles Chart Top 100 at #5. Whilst Cher's sole reason for involvement on the single was to raise money for charity Comic Relief, the #5 debut is monumental in that it is her highest ever debut on the UK chart, beating Baby Don't Go's #24 debut in 1965, and marks her 50th week within the chart's Top 10.

17: *Love Can Build A Bridge* by Cher, Chrissie Hynde and Neneh Cherry with Eric Clapton rises from #5 to #1 on the Official Singles Chart Top 100. It is Cher's third overall #1 on the chart:

March 17, 1995 UK Official Singles Chart

1. *Love Can Build A Bridge*; Cher, Chrissie Hynde and Neneh Cherry with Eric Clapton

2. *Don't Stop (Wiggle Wiggle);* Outhere Brothers

3. *Think Twice*; Celine Dion

May 14, 1995: Spotted: Cher in Beverly Hills.

June 18, 1995: Spotted: Shopping In Manhattan.

June 19, 1995: Spotted: Cher attends a performance of Hamlet in Los Angeles.

October 22, 1995: Cher's *Walking In Memphis* provides her with her highest ever solo debut on the UK Singles chart by entering at #11.

November, 1995

06: *It's A Man's World*, Cher's new studio album, is released in the UK.

07: Cher attends the Q Magazine Awards In London.

12: Cher's *It's A Man's World* enters the Official Albums Chart Top 100 at #28.

January-August, 1996

Cher Releases *One By One*

January, 1996

14: By entering the UK Official Singles Chart Top 100 at #7, *One By One* becomes Cher's first solo single to debut within the Top 10 of that chart. It is the second-highest debut of the week on the chart. Moreover, it makes its parent album *It's A Man's World* the fourth consecutive Cher studio album to yield a UK Top 10 single.

February, 1996

04: *It's A Man's World* rises to #10 on the UK Albums Chart to become Cher's sixth UK Top 10 Album. *One By One* by Cher spends its 4th week within the Top 10 of the UK Singles Chart.

21: Cher performs her song *One By One* at the Ariston theater in Sanremo on the Italian riviera.

April, 1996

05: *Faithful* opens at 803 theaters in the US.

08: *Faithful* opens at #15 at the US Box Office for the weekend of 5-7, grossing $967,956.

21: Cher bags another UK Top 40 hit with *Not Enough Love In The World*'s entry at #31 on the country's Singles Chart.

May, 1996

16: Cher attends the Cannes Film Festival In France, before attending an Aids Fund-Raiser At The Moulin De Mougins

23: Cher performs during the closing party at the Studio 54 club in New York.

June, 1996

01: Cher performs at a concert organized by Kiss FM in Boston

04: Cher attends a Details Magazine Party In NY.

08: Cher performs at a benefit concert Organized By Kiss FM, 'Kiss And Unite', at Irvine Meadows in Irvine, California.

15: *One By One* enters the US Hot 100 at #81 – Cher's first showing on the chart since 1991's *Save Up All Your Tears*.

July, 1996

11: Cher attends the Summer TV Critics Press Tour at Ritz Carlton Hotel in Pasadena, California, United States.

13: *One By One* nears the Top 50 for Cher as it rises to #52 on the US Hot 100. Meanwhile, its parent album *It's A Man's World* provides Cher with her highest debut yet on the Billboard 200, entering at #64.

20: *One By One* rises to #9 on the Billboard Adult Contemporary Chart.

August, 1996

06: Cher attends the European première of *Independence Day*.

11: Cher's *The Sun Ain't Gonna Shine Anymore* débuts on the Official Singles Chart Top 100 at #26. Impressively, Cher has scored UK Top 50 hit singles every year now for ten consecutive years, from 1987 to 1996.

September, 1996-December, 1997

HBO Presents *If These Walls Could Talk*

September, 1996

11: Cher and Demi Moore attend the Toronto Festival.

30: Cher joins co-stars Demi Moore and Sissy Spacek at the New York première of their new film, *If These Walls Could Talk*, at the Museum of Modern Art Monday.

October, 1996

01: Cher and Rob Camiletti attend the LA première *If These Walls Could Talk*.

11: Cher and her daughter Chastity attend the National Coming Out Day in Washington. This is the first time that Cher publicly acknowledged that her daughter is gay.

12: Cher addresses a crowd of several thousand that had gathered for an annual free two-day music concert at the Boston Common in Boston. The singer, who does not perform, offers words of support for a local radio station which is collecting donations for the Children's Advocacy Center of Suffolk County, Massachusetts.

13: *If These Walls Could Talk* airs on HBO.

"She's Been Scorned, Lovelorn, And Laughed At – Why It's Finally Fun To Be Cher Again"

November 06, 1996: Cher attends the première of *The English Patient*.

January 19, 1997: Cher attends the 54th Golden Globe Awards, at which she is nominated for the award for Best Supporting Actress – Series, Miniseries or Television Film, for *If These Walls Could Talk*. The award goes to Kathy Bates, for The Late Shift.

February 16, 1997: Cher makes a speech at Elizabeth Taylor's 65th Birthday Celebration.

April 14, 1997: Spotted: Cher shopping at Barney's New York, In Los Angeles.

May 11, 1997: Spotted: Cher looking at a site in Malibu to build a new house for herself.

June 04, 1997: Cher attends the Children's Craniofacial Association at Planet Hollywood, San Diego

September 14, 1997: Cher appears on *An Audience With Elton John* in London for ITV.

October 09, 1997: Cher attends the Spring-Summer 98 Ready To Wear Gianni Versace fashion show.

October 21, 1997: Spotted: Cher shopping at Bei Joseph in London.

November 24, 1997: Spotted: Cher at the construction site of her house in Malibu.

December 08, 1997: Cher, Madonna and Donatella Versace are amongst guests at a fund-raising gala honoring Donatella's brother, slain fashion designer Gianni Versace at New York's Metropolitan Museum of Art. Proceeds from the $2,000-a-plate dinner are to go to the museum's Costume Institute, which on Thursday will open an exhibition of Versace's work.

January, 1998-September, 1998

05 January, 1998: Sonny Bono dies in Nevada, aged 62.

09 January, 1998: Cher eulogizes Sonny at his funeral.

February 05, 1998: Spotted: Cher reportedly looking for her lost kitten among bushes in Los Angeles.

March 12, 1998: Spotted: Cher inspects the progress of her new house being built in Malibu.

March 23, 1998: Cher and son Elijah Allman attend the 70th Annual Academy Awards in Los Angeles. Cher then attends the Vanity Fair Oscar Party at Mortons.

April 19, 1998: Cher and daughter Chastity appear at the 9th Annual GLAAD Media Awards In Century City.

May 04, 1998: Cher appears on the International Television Awards in Milan.

May 10, 1998: Spotted: Cher shopping in Malibu.

May 15, 1998: Cher and Sonny's widow Mary Bono accept Sonny & Cher's star on The Hollywood Walk Of Fame.

June 26, 1998: Cher appears at a Children's Craniofacial Association event in Dallas, TX.

August 27, 1998: Cher's 1989 album *Heart Of Stone* is certified Triple-Platinum by the RIAA for having 3,000,000 copies shipped in the US.

September 19, 1998: In its 40th anniversary edition, Billboard magazine releases three lists of the most successful female artists on its charts – only Cher, Madonna, Diana Ross and Olivia-Newton John feature on all three lists:

Most #1 Hits By Female Artist

1. Mariah Carey (13)

[tie] 2. Whitney Houston (11)

[tie] 2. Madonna (11)

[tie] 4. Janet Jackson (8)

[tie] 4. Diana Ross (8)

6. Paula Abdul (6)

[tie] 7. Olivia Newton-John (5)

[tie] 7. Barbra Streisand (5)

[tie] 9. Cher (4)

[tie] 9. Donna Summer (4)

Most Top 40 Hits By Female Artist

1. Aretha Franklin (43)

2. Diana Ross (38)

3. Madonna (37)

4. Connie Francis (33)

5. Cher (32)

6. Dionne Warwick (31)

7. Brenda Lee (29)

8. Olivia Newton-John (27)

[tie] 9. Whitney Houston (24)

[tie] 9. Janet Jackson (24)

Most Charted Hits By Female Artist

1. Aretha Franklin (76)

2. Dionne Warwick (55)

3. Diana Ross (54)

4. Connie Francis (53)

[tie] 5. Cher (50)

[tie] 6. Brenda Lee (50)

7. Barbra Streisand (41)

8. Madonna (40)

9. Olivia Newton-John (39)

10. Linda Rondstadt (35)

October-November, 1998

October, 1998

15: Spotted: Cher in London, posing with a London red bus.

17: Cher performs *Believe* at London's Heaven Nightclub.

25: The entire Top 5 of the Official Singles Chart Top 100 is made up of new entries. And leading the pack with her first ever #1 debut on the chart is Cher, who is now the oldest female singer to achieve a UK#1 single, with *Believe*. She is the only female solo singer to achieve three UK#1 singles this decade:

October 25, 1998 UK Official Singles Chart

1. *Believe*; Cher

2. *Outside;* George Michael

3. *Sweetest Thing*; U2

30: Cher's single *Believe* is certified Platinum by the UK's BPI denoting sales of 600,000.

November, 1998

01: Cher's new album *Believe* enters the Official Albums Chart Top 100 at #8 to become her fifth consecutive – and seventh overall – UK Top 10 album. Cher performs *Believe* at the Le Queen nightclub in Paris.

09: Spotted: At Heathrow Airport, Cher Arrives in London From Spain.

11: Spotted: Cher at the Los Angeles International Airport.

13: Cher promotes *Believe* and her autobiography *The First Time* at a media event in NY.

18: Cher appears on the *Late Night With David Letterman Show*, to perform *Believe*.

23: Cher, in a flesh-colored Mackie gown and headpiece, arrives with her son Elijah Allman at the 70th Annual Academy Awards in Los Angeles.

24: Cher promotes *Believe* and *The First Time* at a media event in Santa Monica.

28: Album Believe enters the Billboard 200 at #139.

29: Cher answers questions from the media during a record store opening in Miami. Cher's *Believe* spends its sixth week at #1 on the UK singles chart, beating Cher's previous best of five weeks with *The Shoop Shoop Song (It's In His Kiss)*.

December, 1998-January, 1999

Believe Rules The UK Charts

December, 1998

07: Cher presents the Artist of The Year Award to Usher at the Billboard Music Awards in Las Vegas.

11: Cher performs at Celebration At KTU's "Miracle On 34th Street".

12: Cher appears at the Grand Opening Of The Virgin Megastore In Chicago. Single *Believe* tops the US Billboard Dance Club Songs Chart.

13: After a whopping seven weeks at the top, *Believe* by Cher is finally dethroned from the #1 spot in the UK as it moves down just one place to #2.

18: Cher's *Believe* album is certified Platinum in the UK for shipping 300,000 copies. Cher attends a Kiss-FM Radio event.

19: *Believe*, the single, enters the US Hot 100 at #99.

January, 1999

04: Singer Cher arrives at Heathrow Airport in London from Los Angeles. Cher is in the city to open the annual Harrods winter sale on Wednesday.

06: Cher attends a publicity event at Harrod's Store In Knightsbrige, London.

08: The UK's BPI certify Cher's single *Believe* Double-Platinum, for sales of 1,200,000.

09: Single *Believe* spends a fifth consecutive week at #1 on the US Billboard Dance Club Songs Chart.

11: Cher performs *Believe* at the 26th Annual American Music Awards In LA

25: Cher performs *Believe* at the Midem's Dance d'Or Awards in Cannes, France.

29: Cher attends a Hollywood Super Bowl XXXIII Press Conference

31: Cher performs *The Star Spangled Banner* at the Hollywood Super Bowl XXXIII.

February-March, 1999

Believe Heads Up US Hot 100

February, 1999

13: *Believe* leaps into the Top 5 of the US Hot 100, from #13 to #4, to become Cher's first US Top 5 hit single since 1989's *If I Could Turn Back Time*.

16: Cher attends the Brit Awards in London, at which she performs *Believe*.

23: Cher performs *Believe* on the stage of the Ariston theater in Sanremo, Italy during the opening night of the Italian song contest, Festival of Sanremo.

Cher's single *Believe* is certified Platinum by the RIAA for shifting 1,000,000 copies in the US.

25: Cher attends a press conference for her album *Believe* In Spain

27: *Believe* rises to #2 on the US Hot 100, to become Cher's highest position on the chart since 1974's #1 *Dark Lady*. Its identically-titled parent album becomes Cher's highest-charting solo album ever as it jumps from #12 to #7.

28: *Strong Enough* becomes Cher's fifteenth overall UK Top 10 single as it débuts at #5. Its predecessor *Believe* is still in the Top 40 in its nineteenth week on the chart.

March, 1999

06: *Believe* spends a second week at #2 on the US Hot 100.

11: Cher attends the Music Rockbjorn Awards in Denmark

12: *Strong Enough* is certified Silver by the BPI in the UK for shipping 200,000 copies.

13: *Believe* rises from #2 to #1 on the US Hot 100. It is Cher's fourth solo – and fifth overall – US#1, and her first since 1974. By hitting #1 in the US, the song becomes Cher's first solo Transatlantic #1 single ever, and makes her the oldest female solo singer to top the US charts:

March 13, 1999 US Hot 100

1. *Believe*; Cher

2. *Angel Of Mine*; Monica

3. *Heartbreak Hotel*; Whitney Houston Feat. Faith Evans

14: Cher's *Believe* album finds a new UK peak of #7 as it re-enters the Top 10 of the Official Albums Chart Top 100 in its twentieth week on the chart.

Lily Tomlin, Oscar nominee Dame Judi Dench, and former Oscar winners Dame Maggie Smith and Cher attend the the Royal Charity première of their new film *Tea With Mussolini* in London.

20: *Believe* remains at #1 on the US Hot 100.

26: Cher's *Believe* album is certified Double-Platinum by the BPI in the UK for shipping 600,000 copies.

27: *If I Could Turn Back Time – Cher s Greatest Hits* enters the Billboard 200 at #67.

April-June, 1999

Cher's *Believe* At #1 in The US

April, 1999

03: *Believe* spends a fourth week at #1 on the US Hot 100.

10: *Believe* slips to #2 on the US Hot 100. Album *Believe* spends its seventh week inside the Billboard 200 Top 10, currently at #7.

12: Cher talks at a press conference for *VH1 Divas*.

13: Singers Cher, Tina Turner and Elton John perform together during the *VH1 Divas Live/99* concert in New York.

16: Spotted: Cher outside the CNN Studios in Hollywood.

17: Cher's *Believe* album exits the Top 10 of the US Billboard 200.

24: Single *Believe* spends its ninth consecutive week within the Top 2 of the US Hot 100.

May, 1999

01: Cher's album *Believe* leaps from #12 to a new peak of #5 on the Billboard 200 to become her first solo US Top 5 album. *Strong Enough* tops the US Billboard Dance Club Songs Chart.

07: Cher performs at the World Music Awards in Monte-Carlo.

08: Cher's studio album *Believe* reaches a new peak of #4 on the US Billboard 200.

14: *Tea With Mussolini* opens at a modest 270 theaters across the US.

17: *Tea With Mussolini* grosses $1,633,183 and ranked #10 during its opening weekend at the US Box Office.

22: Cher scores her 50th overall hit on the US Hot 100 as Strong Enough débuts at #91 on the US Hot 100. Predecessor Believe is still in the Top 10 of the chart.

June, 1999

13: Cher's *All Or Nothing* enters the Official Singles Chart Top 100 at #12, making *Believe* Cher's first album to yield three UK Top 20 hits. The album re-enters the UK Top 40 at #36 during its 33rd week on the chart.

16: Cher begins her *Do You Believe? Tour*, with a sell-out show in Phoenix, Arizona.

26: Cher's *Strong Enough* spends its fourth consecutive week at #57 on the US Hot 100. *Believe* is still at #26.

July-December, 1999

July, 1999

22: Cher is presented with a Triple-Platinum certification by the RIAA for shifting 3,000,000 copies of her album *Believe* in the US.

September, 1999

17: *Tea With Mussolini* has grossed $14,083,206 during its first 20 weeks at the US Box Office.

October, 1999

02: *All Or Nothing* becomes Cher's third consecutive #1 on the US Billboard Dance Club Songs Chart.

15: Cher begins the European leg of her *Do You Believe? Tour*, beginning at the Wembley Arena in London, England.

20: Cher attends Hilary Clinton's 53rd Birthday Party At The Roseland Club.

31: *Dov'e L'amore* enters the UK Singles Chart at #21 to become the third Top 30 single from its parent album *Believe*.

November, 1999

14: Cher's *The Greatest Hits* becomes her second UK Top 10 hits package of the decade as it débuts on the country's Album Charts at #7.

17: Cher is handed the Most Played International Artist Music Control Airplay Award for *Believe*.

20: *VH-1 Divas Live/99* by Whitney Houston, Cher, Tina Turner & Brandy enters the Billboard 200 at #90.

December, 1999

04: Cher's *Live In Concert* enters Billboard's Top Music Videos Chart at #25.

16: Cher performs at the Venetian Hotel, California.

23: *Believe*, the album, is certified 4x Multi-Platinum by the RIAA for shifting 4,000,000 copies in the US.

30: Cher's *Do You believe? Tour* returns to North America, in Atlantic City.

January, 2000-October, 2001

January 15, 2000: Cher's *Live In Concert* rises to #6 on Billboard's Top Music Videos Chart.

January 24, 2000: *If I Could Turn Back Time: Greatest Hits* is certified Gold by the RIAA for shifting 500,000 copies in the US.

January 28, 2000: Cher's 1999 *The Greatest Hits* is certified Double-Platinum by the UK's BPI for shipping 600,000 in the country.

February 23, 2000: Cher wins the Best Dance Recording Award at the 42nd Annual Grammy Awards.

March 03, 2000: Cher ends her *Do You Believe? Tour* with a sell-out show in Boston.

March 26, 2000: Cher attends the 72nd Academy Awards at the Shrine Auditorium in Los Angeles to present the award for Best Original Song.

April 29, 2000: The video release of *VH-1 Divas Live/99*, starring Whitney Houston, Cher, Tina Turner & Brandy, enters Billboard's Top Music Videos Chart at #29.

June 26, 2000: Cher attends the *The Perfect Storm* première at Mann Village Theatre, Westwood, California.

July 26, 2000: Cher attends the première of *The Patriot* In Beverly Hills.

August 03, 2000: Cher attends Tony Bennett's Birthday celebrations.

August 12, 2000: Cher performs at the Gala Hollywood Farewell Salute to President Clinton.

August 17, 2000: Cher attends the Los Angeles première of *The Cell*.

September 08, 2000: Cher attends the Women In Film's 7th Annual Lucy Awards.

September 09, 2000: Cher attends the Face Forward Party In New York.

September 10, 2000: Cher attends the 52nd Annual Primetime Emmy Awards at the Shrine Auditorium in Los Angeles.

September 14 2000: Spotted: Cher at Heathrow Airport in London.

September 22, 2000: Spotted: Cher at The Nobu Restaurant In London.

October 24, 2000: Spotted: Cher at the Manhattan Hotel.

October 31, 2000: Cher speaks at an Al Gore Rally in Westwood In Los Angeles.

November 07, 2000: Cher speaks at Al Gore's Election Nights Party.

November 16, 2000: Cher appears in *Will & Grace* episode 'Gypsies, Tramps and Weed'.

November 08, 2000: Cher releases *Not.com.mercial*, an album of unreleased mostly-self-penned tracks from 1994, exclusively on the internet.

December 12, 2000: Cher performs *I Still Haven't Found What I'm Looking For*, *If I Could Turn Back Time* and *Believe* at the Democratic Committee Gala Concert.

March 29, 2001: Cher and her son Elijah attend the *Blow* première at Manns Chinese Theater, Hollywood.

May 18, 2001: Cher attends the Annual Race To Erase MS Dinner Gala.

July 18, 2001: Cher and Elijah attend the Stuff Magazine Takes Over Santa Monica Pier for 'Stuffland' event at Santa Monica

October 15, 2001: Spotted: Cher at London's Heathrow Airport.

October 29, 2001: Cher attends the Q Magazine Awards in London, UK.

November, 2001-February, 2002

Living Proof Hits UK Stores

November, 2001

04: Cher attends the première of *Harry Potter and The Secret Room* in London, UK.

11: *The Music's No Good Without You*, the first UK single from Cher's *Living Proof* album, enters the UK Official Singles Chart Top 100 at #8, meaning that Cher has had solo Top 10 singles in 5 consecutive decades in the country.

14: Cher hosts a media event for *Living Proof* in Madrid, Spain.

15: Cher attends the Bambi Awards In Germany.

25: Cher's *Living Proof* débuts at #46 on the UK Official Albums Chart Top 100.

26: Cher performs *The Music's No Good Without You* at the Royal Variety Dominion Theatre In London.

29: Cher performs *The Music's No Good Without You* at the Onda Music Awards In Madrid, Spain.

January-February, 2002

January 09, 2002: Cher performs *Song For The Lonely* at the 29th Annual American Music Awards.

February 14, 2002: Cher and R.E.M.'s Michael Stipes perform *I Got You Babe* during the First Annual Entertainment Industry Foundation 'Love Rocks' Concert, to Honor U2's Bono and to launch EIF'S National Cardiovascular Research Initiative at the Kodak Theatre in Hollywood, California.

February 16, 2002: Spotted: Cher leaving the Peninsula Hotel in New York.

February 26, 2002: Cher appears on *Late Night With David Letterman Show*.

March-May, 2002

Living Proof Hits Billboard 200

March, 2002

02: Cher performs US single *Song for the Lonely* from her new album *Living Proof* to a packed house at The Roxy in New York City.

07: Cher and her friend, jewelry designer Loreee Rodkin, attend a Fat Boy Slim listening party for his forth album *Live on Brighton Beach*, held in Beverly Hills, California.

16: Studio album *Living Proof* becomes Cher's 36th Billboard 200 hit and highest debut on the chart ever as it enters the chart at #9.

Cher speaks during the 4th Annual Costume Designers Guild Awards at The Beverly Hills Hotel

29: *Living Proof* is certified Gold for shifting 500,000 copies in the US.

April, 2002

06: *Song For The Lonely* enters the US Hot 100 at #85 – Cher's 51st overall hit on the chart. The song also tops the US Billboard Dance Club Songs chart.

14: Cher attends MTV Icon Honors Aerosmith event at the Sony Pictures Studios in Culver City, California.

369

20: Cher performs *A Different Kind Of Love Song* at American Bandstand's 50th Anniversary Celebration.

May, 2002

14: Cher and Bob Mackie attend the America Online Party Celebrates Launch of 2002 Celebrity *You've Got Mail* Campaign at The Highlands in Hollywood.

22: Cher rehearses for tomorrow's appearance on *VH1 Divas Las Vegas*.

23: Cher performs *Believe, Song For The Lonely, If I Could Turn Back Time* and *Heartbreak Hotel* at *VH1 Divas Las Vegas*, held at the MGM Grand.

June, 2002-October, 2003

Cher Embarks On Her Farewell Tour

June 14, 2002: Cher begins her *The Farewell Tour*, in Toronto, Canada.

August 31, 2002: Cher's *A Different Kind Of Love* Song becomes the second US Billboard Dance Club Songs Chart-topper from her Living Proof album.

September 07, 2002: *A Different Kind Of Love Song* spends a second week at #1 on the US Dance Club Songs Chart.

October 20, 2002: Cher performs at the The World Children's Choir event in Las Vegas.

November 09, 2002: Album *Divas Las Vegas* by Celine Dion, Cher, Dixie Chicks, Shakira With Anastacia & Stevie Nicks enters the Billboard 200 at #104.

December 09, 2002: Cher accepts a lifetime achievement award at the MGM Grand Hotel and Casino in Las Vegas during the Billboard Music Awards show.

April 05, 2003: *When The Money's Gone* becomes Cher's third Billboard Dance Club Songs Chart #1 from *Living Proof*.

April 08, 2003: TV concert *Cher: The Farewell Tour* airs on NBC, garnering over 17-million viewers.

April 19, 2003: *The Very Best Of Cher* becomes the singer's highest ever debut on the Billboard 200, and her fifth ever US Top 10 album, as it enters at #7.

1999 video release *Live In Concert* re-enters the Billboard Top Music Videos Chart at #7.

May 17, 2003: *The Very Best Of Cher* joins *Believe* as her highest-charting solo album, by reaching #4 on the Billboard 200.

June 15, 2003: Cher attends the Broadway play *Gypsy*.

June 21, 2003: After nine consecutive weeks within the Top 10, *The Very Best of Cher* falls to #12 on the Billboard 200.

July 26, 2003: *The Very Best Of Cher* rises back up the Billboard 200 from #18 to #10, for its tenth week inside the chart's Top 10.

August 26, 2003: Cher's video *Cher – The Farewell Tour* is released in the US.

August 30, 2003: Cher's *The Farewell Tour* video release enters Billboard's Top Music Video Chart at #17.

September 13, 2003: Cher's first solo live album *Live: The Farewell Tour* enters the Billboard 200 at #40 to become her 16th overall US Top 40 album. Meanwhile, *The Very Best Of Cher: Special Edition* enters the chart at #83. The standard *The Very Best Of Cher* is still on the chart at #34, giving Cher three albums on the chart simultaneously.

Furthermore, Cher's *The Farewell Tour* video release leaps from #15 to #1 on Billboard's Top Music Video Chart.

September 20, 2003: Cher's *The Farewell Tour* remains #1 on Billboard's Top Music Video Chart.

September 21, 2003: Cher wins the Emmy Award for Outstanding Variety, Music, or Comedy Special at the 55th Primetime Emmy Awards, for *Cher: The Farewell Tour*.

October 11, 2003: Cher meets the employees at the Walter Reed National Military Medical Center in Washington, D.C..

November, 2003-May, 2003

Cher Stars In *Stuck On You*

November 22, 2003: Cher speaks about new film *Stuck On You* during a press conference in New York.

November 28, 2003: *The Very Best Of Cher*, having been re-leased on the 24th, is certified Gold by the UK's BPI for having 100,000 copies shipped around the country.

December 08, 2003: Cher attends the première of *Stuck On You* in New York City.

December 11, 2003: Cher attends the *Stuck On You* pre-mière in Woonsocket, Rhode Island.

December 15, 2003: *Stuck on You* ranks at #3 during its opening weekend at the US Box Office, grossing $9,411,055:

December 12-14, 2003 Weekend

1. *Something's Gotta Give*; $16,064,723; 2,677

2. *The Last Samurai*; $14,087,074

3. *Stuck On You*; $9,411,055; 3,003

December 17, 2003: *The Very Best Of Cher* is certified 2x Multi-Platinum by the RIAA for shifting 2,000,000 copies in the US.

January 11, 2004: *The Very Best Of Cher* enters the Top 20 of the UK Official Albums Chart Top 100 to become the singer's 11th Top 20 album in the country.

February 19, 2004: *Stuck On You* tops the Australian Box Office, grossing $1,599,116 during its opening week there.

March 19, 2004: *Stuck On You* has grossed $33,832,741 at the US Box Office during its 14-week run.

May, 2004

08: Cher begins the European portion of her *The Farewell Tour*, in Dublin, Ireland.

28th: *The Very Best of Cher: The Video Hits Collection* is released in the US.

29th: Cher's 2003 video release of *The Farewell Tour* re-enters Billboard's Top Music Videos chart at #12.

30th: Cher's *Live – The Farewell Tour* enters the UK Official Albums Chart Top 100 at #79, as her *The Very Best Of Cher* sits one place lower at #80 in its 17th week on the chart.

July, 2004-December, 2005

Cher Completes Farewell Tour

July 02, 2004: Cher wraps up the European leg of her the Farewell Tour in Monte Carlo, Monaco.

July 10, 2004: *The Very Best of Cher: The Video Hits Collection* enters Billboard's Top Music Video Chart at #3.

July 23, 2004: Cher's *The Farewell Tour* resumes in North America, beginning in Canada.

August 23, 2004: Spotted: Cher wearing a face mask Los Angeles.

October 08, 2004: Cher plays the first of three dates in Mexico City on her The farewell tour.

October 16, 2004: Cher speaks during the Tour Of Duty: Americans Speak Out first day in LA

October 17, 2004: Cher speaks during the Tour Of Duty: Americans Speak Out second day In LA

October 22, 2004: Cher speaks at a MoveOnStudentAction.org 'Feel A Draft' Campaign rally at Crobar nightclub in Miami Beach, Florida.

November 04, 2004: Cher attends a Chrome Hearts party.

January 28, 2005: *The Very Best of Cher: The Video Hits Collection* is certified Platinum by the RIAAfor shipping 100,000 copies in the US.

February 01, 2005: Contactmusic reports that "The Farewell Tour has become the most successful US tour by a female artist, selling more than three million tickets and grossing over $200 million."

February 10, 2005: Spotted: Cher Shops at Horn in Beverly Hills.

February 20, 2005: Cher takes her farewell tour to Oceania, beginning with a New Zealand date.

March 06, 2005: Cher attends a performance of *The Lion King* during in Sydney

April 07, 2005: Cher's *The Farewell Tour* returns to North America, in Canada.

April 30, 2005: Cher completes her *The Farewell Tour*, at the Hollywood Bowl, in Los Angeles.

June 18, 2005: Cher's 2003 *Cher – The Farewell Tour* video release re-enters Billboard's Top Music Videos Chart at #24.

June 25, 2005: *Cher – The Farewell Tour* re-enters the Top 10, at #9, of Billboard's Top Music Video Chart.

December 26, 2005: Cher's 2003 video *Cher – The Farewell Tour i*s certified Triple-Platinum by the RIAA for shipping 300,000 copies in the US.

2006

Cher Enjoys Retirement

January 17, 2006: Cher attends a party for Rolex CEO Patrick Heiniger.

March 02, 2006: Spotted: Cher wearing a face mask in Los Angeles.

March 20, 2006: Cher attends Agent Provocateur Fashion Week in Los Angeles.

April 08, 2006: Cher attends a private viewing of Mark Seliger's *In My Stairwell*, hosted by Mary-Louise Parker at 401 Projects in New York City.

April 10, 2006: Cher attends the Chrome Hearts impromptu family party in New York City.

April 21, 2006: Cher attends a private art opening celebrating the launch of Visionaire's latest issue.

April 22, 2006: Cher attends a Scissor Sisters concert in New York

April 28, 2006: Cher attends the première of *The TV Set* in Los Angeles.

April 30, 2006: Spotted: Cher shopping in New York.

June 15, 2006: Cher sat in on the Congressional House Armed Services Committee meeting.

July 04, 2006: Cher attends a Chrome Hearts dinner party in Paris.

July 05, 2006: Cher attends the John Galliano & Christian Dior and Giorgio Armani fashion shows in Paris, France.

July 06, 2006: Cher attends the Chanel Haute Couture Fall-Winter fashion show in paris.

July 07, 2006: Cher and god-daughter Jesse Jo Stark attend the Jean-Paul Gaultier Fashion show in Paris.

July 12, 2006: Cher visits the Heaton Auditorium in Germany.

August 15, 2006: Spotted: Cher wearing a face mask in Los Angeles.

August 21, 2006: Cher attends a Deadsy record release party – the band of her son Elijah.

September 11, 2006: Cher attends the Focus Features première of *The Ground Truth*, in Los Angeles.

2007-2008

January 10, 2007: Spotted: Cher on a beach in Maui, Hawaii.

February 24, 2007: Spotted: Cher exercising in Malibu.

November 28 2007: Cher attends the LA première of *Love Sees No Color.*

October 02, 2007: Spotted: Cher with her mother Georgia in Los Angeles.

December 03, 2007: Spotted: Cher with daughter Chastity in West Hollywood.

December 20, 2007: Spotted: Cher Christmas shopping in Malibu.

February 10, 2008: Cher attends the 50th Annual Grammy Awards in Los Angeles, where she presents a performance by Tina Turner and Beyonce Knowles.

March 22, 2008: Spotted: Cher shopping in Los Angeles.

May 06, 2008: Cher begins a 200-date residency at Caesars Palace in Las Vegas, Nevada.

May 08, 2008: Special *Oprah* episode *Oprah, Cher and Tina Turner at Caesars Palace in Las Vegas* airs, on which Cher performs *Take Me Home*, and *Proud Mary* with Tina Turner.

"Cher – The Legendary Superstar Turns Back Time With Her Outrageous New Extravaganza At Caesars Palace"

– Casino Player, May 2008

June 12, 2008: Spotted: Cher at Foxtail Nightclub in West Hollywood

June 25, 2008: Spotted: Cher and boyfriend Tim Medvetz at Tootsies Orchid Lounge, and

a Merle Haggard concert, in Nashville, Tennessee.

June 28, 2008: Spotted: Cher at a race track in Ventura, California.

July 26, 2008: Spotted: Cher on Robertson Boulevard in Los Angeles.

August 01, 2008: Spotted: Cher leaving Beverly Hills Medical Center.

"Sultry Siren – Cher Sizzles At Caesars Palace"

– Events & Shows, September 2008

October 22, 2008: Cher attends the grand opening of Luau restaurant in Beverly Hills.

November 08, 2008: Spotted: Cher departs Los Angeles International Airport.

2009

January 18 2009: Cher attends a celebration to honor the inauguration of Barack Obama in Washington.

January 19 2009: Cher attends the inaugural party at Cafe Milano in Washington.

January 20 2009: Cher attends the RIAA and Feeding America's inauguration charity ball at Ibiza Nightclub in Washington, DC.

January 28 2009: Cher urges Los Angeles City Council members to halt the development of Los Angeles Zoo's new elephant enclosure and use the cash to move pachyderm Billy.

February 2 2009: Cher attends the *The Slumdog Millionaire / The Wrestler a*wards party In LA.

February 17, 2009: Spotted: Cher with goddaughter Jesse Jo Stark at Disneyland in Anaheim, California.

April 17 2009: Cher attends *CFC And Film Independent Presents A Tribute To Norman Jewison* in LA, and attends Kate Hudson's 30th birthday party.

May 9 2009: Cher makes an appearance at the *David Foster And Friends In Concert* event in Las Vegas.

September 05, 2009: Spotted: Cher attends a Malibu Fair.

October 18, 2009: Spotted: Cher at the Cirque Du Soleil's Kooza in Santa Monica.

October 31, 2009: Cher attends the Reach Out To Asia 3rd Gala Dinner

November 02, 2009: Spotted: Cher arriving at the Los Angeles International Airport.

November 11, 2009: Spotted: Cher at the Malibu Lumberyard Centre in California.

December 08, 2009: Spotted: Cher shopping at Barney's New York In LA.

January-September, 2010

January 17, 2010: Cher and Christina Aguilera present the Best Original Song – Motion Picture award during the 67th Annual Golden Globe Awards held at the Beverly Hilton Hotel, with mention of their upcoming movie *Burlesque*.

January 30, 2010: Cher attends the 62nd Annual Directors Guild Of America Awards in Los Angeles.

February 09, 2010: Cher is present at the Audi Celebrates The Academy Award Nominations party at La Vida restaurant in Los Angeles.

February 24, 2010: Cher attends a party at the The Kantor Gallery in Los Angeles.

March 24, 2010: Spotted: Cher at a Beverly Hill's Medical Center.

March 29, 2010: Spotted: Cher on holiday in Maui, Hawaii.

April 04, 2010: Cher at Del Rey Cafe in Los Angeles.

April 18, 2010: Cher makes an appearance at the The 45th Annual Academy Of Country Music Awards.

April 22, 2010: Cher attends the TCM Classic Film Festival *A Star Is Born* première

June 10, 2010: Cher appears at the 38th AFI Life Achievement Award, honouring *Silkwood*-director Mike Nichols.

June 27, 2010: Cher appears via satellite at the 37th Annual Daytime Entertainment Emmy Awards held at the Las Vegas Hilton.

July 02, 2010: Cher attends her son Elijah's art exhibition at The Madison Gallery

August 20, 2010: Cher and Ron Zimmerman holding hands during a walk in Los Angeles.

September 2010: Donned in a dress made entirely of meat, Lady Gaga accepts the award for Video of the Year from Cher at the MTV Video Music Awards in Los Angeles.

November 2010-March 2011

Burlesque Hits The Box Office

08: Cher attends the Glamour Magazine Honors The 2010 Women Of The Year event, at which she is presented with a Lifetime Achievement Award.

11: Cher appears on *Late Show With David Letterman*.

12: Cher appears at the MTV Video Music Awards to present the biggest award of the night: Video of the Year.

18: Cher stands in cement during a ceremony to put her hands and feet in cement in front of Grauman's Chinese Theatre in Los Angeles.

24: Cher and Christina Aguileras' movie *Burlesque* opens in 3,037 theaters across the US.

29: *Burlesque* opens at #4 at the US Box Office during its opening weekend, 26-28, grossing $11,947,744.

December, 2010

06: *Burlesque* moves up to #3 during its second weekend, 3-5, at the US Box Office, grossing $6,130,061:

December 3-5, 2010 Weekend

1. *Tangled*; $21,608,891; 3,603 theaters

2. *Harry Potter and the Deathly Hallows Part 1*; $17,018,475; 4,125 theaters

3. *Burlesque*; $6,130,061; 3,037 theaters

09: Cher attends the *Burlesque* première in Madrid.

10: Cher attends the 40 Principales Awards in Spain, where she is given the Lifetime Achievement Award.

12: Cher attends the *Burlesque* première in Berlin.

13: Cher attends the *Burlesque* première in London.

15: Cher attends the *Burlesque* première in LA.

25: Spotted: Cher on holiday with pal Kathy Griffin in Hawaii.

January, 2011

20: Cher attends *Elephants And Man, A Litany Of Tragedy* première in Los Angeles.

29: *You Haven't Seen The Last Of Me* from the *Burlesque* soundtrack becomes Cher's seventh #1 on the Billboard Dance Club Songs Chart.

February, 2011

09: Cher attends the opening night of *33 Variations* at the Ahmanson Theatre.

11: *Burlesque* has grossed $39,441,000 at the US Box Office during its 11-week run.

12: Cher attends a Pre-Grammy Gala & Salute To Industry Icons With Clive Davis event.

March, 2011

15: Cher is photographed at a private reception at The Boarder Grill.

29: Cher attends a party thrown by Vans for the launch of their collaboration with Jesse Jo Stark.

16: *Burlesque* has grossed $50,079,118 outside of the US, for a worldwide total of almost $90,000,000.

June, 2011-September, 2012

Cher Lends Her Voice To A Lioness

June 22, 2011: Cher attends a party for the Polyphony Foundation.

July 06, 2011: Cher and pal Kathy Griffin attend the Los Angeles première of movie *Zookeeper*, in which Cher voices a lioness.

July 08, 2011: *Zookeeper* opens at 3,482 theaters across the US.

July 11, 2011: *Zookeeper* opens at the US Box Office at#3 during the weekend of 8-10, grossing $20,065,617.

August 14, 2011: Cher attends the Annual Jen Klein Day Of Indulgence Summer Party in LA.

August 21, 2011: Spotted: Cher wearing face mask in Malibu.

September 08, 2011: Spotted: wearing a face mask in Los Angeles (08.09.2011)

October 28, 2011: *Zookeeper* has racked up $80,360,843 during its 16-week run at the US Box Office.

November 07 2011: *Zookeeper*'s gross outside the US stands at $89,491,916, bringing the movie's worldwide gross to almost $170,000,000.

January 11, 2012: Cher is photographed having dinner with friend Ron Zimmerman and author Michal Lemberger.

February 11, 2012: Spotted: Cher flying first class to Maui.

February 12, 2012: Spotted: Cher in Maui, Hawaii.

February 13, 2012: Spotted: Cher arrives at LAX Airport.

April 15, 2012: Spotted: Cher shopping in Santa Monica.

April 21, 2012: Cher presents son Chaz with the Stephen F. Kolzak Award at the 23rd Annual GLAAD Media Awards.

June 06, 2012: Cher, son Chaz, sister Georganne, and old friend Paulette Howell attend the LGBT Leadership Council Gala.

June 20, 2012: Cher attends the *The Magic Of Belle Isle* première In LA

August 19, 2012: Spotted: Cher leaving the Nobu restaurant in Malibu.

September 11, 2012: Cher takes part in the "Cycle For Heroes" Event On The Santa Monica Pier

September 12, 2012: Cher attends the *The Book Of Mormon* Hollywood opening night.

October, 2012-September, 2013

October 21, 2012: Cher attends a party celebrating ex-beau Val Kilmer's play *Citizen Twain*.

November 14, 2012: Cher attends the première of *American Masters Inventing David Geffen* at The Writers Guild of America, Beverly Hills, California.

December 10, 2012: Spotted: Cher departing on a flight at LAX Airport.

December 14, 2012: Cher performs a private concert at the Eurohall in Moscow, Russia.

March 25, 2013: Spotted: Cher at Charles de Gaulle Airport in Paris, France.

April 02, 2013: Cher attends Cavalia's *Odysseo* show in Burbank, California.

April 24. 2013: Cher attends the star-studded Target Presents AFI's Night At The Movies event.

April 25, 2013: Cher attends the fourth annual Turner Classics Film Festival in Hollywood.

May 29, 2013: Spotted: Cher Departing on a flight at LAX Airport, Los Angeles.

June 05, 2013: Spotted: Cher departing on a flight at Heathrow Airport in London, to Los Angeles.

June 28, 2013: Spotted: Cher enters the Z100 Studios in NYC.

June 30, 2013: Spotted: Cher rehearsing for a NYC Pride Performance.

July 06, 2013: Cher's *Woman's World* enters the US Bubbling Under chart at #25.

July 22, 2013: 1999 video release *Cher – Live In Concert* and 2003's *Cher – The Farewell Tour* are both certified Platinum by the UK's BPI for sales of 50,000 each.

August 10, 2013: *Woman's World* becomes Cher's eighth #1 on the US Billboard Dance Club Songs Chart.

August 11, 2013: Spotted: Cher at a party in Los Angeles.

September 23, 2013: Cher performs *Woman's World*, *I Hope You Find It* and *Believe* on NBC's *Today* show in New York.

September 30, 2013: Spotted: Cher arrives at LAX Airport in Los Angeles.

October, 2013-August, 2014

Cher Releases *Closer To The Truth*

October, 2013

01: Spotted: Cher arrives at the Berlin Airport.

05: Cher performs *I Hope You Find It* on German TV show *Wetten Dass...?* in Bremen.

12: *Closer To The Truth* enters the US Billboard 200 chart at #3, to become Cher's highest ever solo position on the chart, and her highest debut on the chart ever:

October 12, 2013 US BILLBOARD 200

1. *Nothing Was The Same*; Drake

2. *Mechanical Bull; Kings Of Leon*

3. *Closer To The Truth*; Cher

20: Cher's *I Hope You Find It* becomes Cher's 34th UK Top 40 hit single as it enters the UK Official Singles Chart Top 100 at #25. The entry makes Cher the oldest female singer to score a UK Top 30 hit with a new release.

Closer To The Truth enters the UK Official Albums Chart Top 100 at #4 to become Cher's highest-charting album since her 1992 #1 *Greatest Hits 1965-1992*. The album is also her second highest-charting studio album ever in the UK after 1991's *Love Hurts*.

November, 2013-August, 2014

November 02, 2013: Cher's *Closer To the Truth* spends its third week inside the Top 10 of the Billboard 200, at #8.

February 01, 2014: *Closer To The Truth* re-enters the Top 40 of the Billboard 200.

February 08, 2014: *Take It Like A Man* spends a second week at #2 on the Billboard Dance Club Songs Chart.

March 22, 2014: Cher's *Dressed To Kill Tour* opens in Phoenix, Arizona, with opening act Pat Benatar and Neil Giraldo.

April 12, 2014: *I Hope You Find It* rises to #17 on the Billboard Adult Contemporary Chart.

June 21, 2014: Cher's *I Walk Alone* spends a second week at #2 on the US Dance Club Songs Chart – her third Top 2 hit on that chart from Closer To The Truth.

August 01, 2014: Cher's 1998 single *Believe* is the first ever female single to be certified Triple-Platinum by the BPI in the UK, denoting sales of 1,800,000.

August 08, 2014: *Burlesque: Original Motion Picture Soundtrack* is certified Silver by the BPI for shipping 60,000 copies in the UK.

2015-2016

April 09, 2015: Cher attends the SP-Arte Gallery in Sao Paulo, Brasil.

April 10, 2015: Cher attends the 5th Annual AmfAR Inspiration Gala São Paulo in Brazil. She is honored with the amfAR Award of Inspiration.

April 18, 2015: Cher and son Chaz attend An Intimate Evening In Support Of Heidi Shink.

May 01, 2015: Spotted: Cher arrives at New York's The Public Theater to see the play *Hamilton.*

May 04, 2015: Cher appears at the China Through The Looking Glass Met Gala at the Metropolitan Museum of Art, Costume Institute in New York City.

May 16, 2015: Cher appears on the last ever episode of *Late Show With David Letterman.*

June 23, 2015: Spotted: Cher arrives at the Los Angeles International Airport.

June 29, 2015: Spotted: Cher at Club 55 in Saint Tropez, France.

July 02, 2015: Spotted: Cher holidaying in Saint Tropez, France

July 12, 2015: Spotted: Cher at LAX Airport.

August 23, 2015: Spotted: Cher at LAX In Los Angeles, California

September 09, 2015: Cher postpones her *Dressed To Kill Tour*: "Cher was diagnosed over the weekend with what the doctors termed 'acute viral infection' and has been required to be on full bed rest for several days."

November 12, 2015: Billboard list their "Greatest of All-Time Hot 100 Artists" – Cher is ranked at #43.

November 12, 2015: Cher's *Dressed To Kill Tour* is cancelled: ""With enormous regret, Cher has announced the cancellation of all remaining dates on her 'Dressed To Kill (D2K)' concert tour. Beginning in March, the multi-award-winning superstar completed 49 sold-out concerts to unanimous rave reviews before taking a scheduled break in July. Shortly before returning to the road in September, she was felled by an infection that affected her kidney function."

June 19, 2016: Spotted: Cher in Saint Tropez.

June 21, 2016: Spotted: Cher in Portofino, Italy.

September 17, 2016: Cher finishes two new songs in the recording studio.

October 18, 2016: Cher announces that she will be performing a residency show, *Classic Cher*, in Las Vegas and Washington, D.C. from February 2017.

October 20, 2016: Cher appears on *The Late Late Show With James Corden*, on which she performs an updated version of *I Got You Babe* with the host.

November 26, 2016: Forbes reports that Sonny & Cher's *I Got You Babe* is to be inducted into the 2017 Grammy Hall Of Fame.

2017-2018

January 22, 2017: *Cries from Syria*, a documentary film about the Syrian Civil War, premières at the Sundance Festival. It contains the Diane Warren-penned track *Prayers For This World*, sung by Cher and The West Los Angeles Children's Choir.

February 08, 2017: Cher embarks on her *Classic Cher* residency in Las Vegas and Washington, DC.

February 28, 2017: Cher appears on CBS's *The Talk* to promote *Classic Cher*.

March 02, 2017: *Edith+Eddie*, the short film, in which Cher is credited as a producer, debuts at the True/False Film Festival.

March 13, 2017: *Cries From Syria* airs on HBO in the US.

May 21, 2017: Cher is awarded the Icon Award at the Billboard Music Awards, at which she performs *If I Could Turn Back Time* and *Believe*.

August 11, 2017: *Chercophonie* airs – an episode of Netflix original series *Adventures with Tip & Oh*, in which Cher guest stars as the episode's titular character, performing two songs: *Ooga Boo* and *You Do You Boov*.

March 03, 2018: Cher headlines the 40th Sydney Mardi Gras' after-party in Australia, performing *All or Nothing*, *Strong Enough*, *Believe* and *If I Could Turn Back Time*.

April 25, 2018: Cher performs *Fernando* for the first time at CinemaCon.

May 7, 2018: Cher announces her Australian September-October *Here We Go Again Tour*.

June 12, 2018: *The Cher Show*, the Broadway play based on Cher's life, for which she also serves as Executive Producer, begins a small run in Chicago ahead of a fall debut on Broadway.

June 19, 2018: Cher guests on *The Late Late Show with James Corden*.

June 22, 2018: Cher appears on the UK's *The Graham Norton Show*.

July 20, 2018: *Mamma Mia: Here We Go Again* is due to be released in the UK and US. *BoxOffice Magazine* projects the film to gross $25–35 million in its opening weekend in the United States and Canada, and a final domestic total of around $105 million.

The Hits Of Cher

Noted for her outstanding longevity, numerous comebacks and countless reinventions, Cher has a longer span of US Hot 100 #1 hits than any other artist, has Billboard #1 singles in 6 consecutive decades and has 82 hit singles and 47 hit albums around the globe. She's the oldest female artist to hit #1 on the US Hot 100 and the Official UK Singles Chart (*Believe*, 1998), and is the oldest female artist to have a UK Top 30 hit single (with *I Hope You Find It*, 2013).

Trivia: Cher had already achieved 46 hit singles around the globe by the time that Madonna scored her first.

Cher topped the US Hot 100: before Barbra Streisand did; before Michael Jackson, Elton John, David Bowie and Rod Stewart were famous; and before Celine Dion and Mariah Carey were even born. She had solo hits before Tina Turner and Diana Ross did, and had reinvented herself multiple times (from folk-rock hippie, glamorous TV host, disco diva, rock chick to serious actress) before Madonna had even released her first single. Her music has been covered by a range of artists from Frank Sinatra to Stevie Wonder to Britney Spears. And she broke barriers in censorship and style to pave the way for generations of outlandish female starlets such as Cyndi Lauper, Christina Aguilera and Lady Gaga.

Highest-certified single

Believe – 1998, Diamond, France

Highest-certified album

Believe – 1998, 7x Platinum, Denmark

First hit single

All I Really Want To Do – July 03, 1965, US

First hit album

Look At Us – 21 August, 1965, US

Latest hit single

You Haven't Seen The Last of Me – last appearance: #91, October 21, 2013, Australia

Latest hit album

Closer To The Truth – last appearance: #70, August 16, 2014, US

First #1 single

I Got You Babe – 1965, Canada, UK, US

First #1 album

Heart of Stone – 1989, Australia

Latest #1 single

Believe – 1998, multiple charts

Latest #1 album

The Greatest Hits – 1999, multiple charts

First Gold single

I Got You Babe – 1965, US

First Gold album

Look At Us – 1965, US

Latest Gold single

Woman's World – 2013, Venezuela

Latest Gold album

Closer To The Truth – 2013, Canada

Most weeks spent on a singles chart

547 weeks – US

Most weeks spent on an albums chart

957 weeks – US

Most weeks on chart for a single

55 weeks – *Believe*, 1998, Canada

Most weeks on chart for an album

82 weeks – *Heart of Stone*, 1989, UK

Most weeks at #1 for a single

10 weeks – *Believe*, 1998, Denmark

Most weeks at #1 for an album

8 weeks – *Believe*, 1998, Denmark

Most hit singles in one country

51 – US

Most hit albums in one country

47 – Canada

Most #1 singles in one country

5 – US

Most #1 albums in one country

3 – Austria

Most Gold singles in one country

8 – US

Most Gold albums in one country

15 – US

Longest span on a singles chart

48 years, 2 months – UK

Longest span on an album chart

48 years, 6 months – US

Album(s) with most hit singles

Heart of Stone (5, 1989) & *Love Hurts* (5, 1991)

Trivia: Cher has scored 55 Top 40, 33 Top 10, 24 Top 5 and 12 #1 singles around the globe. She also has 30 Top 40, 14 Top 10, 9 Top 5 and 5 #1 albums around the globe.

Cher's #1 Singles Around The World

I Got You Babe (1965): Canada; UK; US

Baby Don't Go (1965): Canada

Sing C'est La Vie (1965): Belgium

Little Man (1966): Belgium; Netherlands; Norway; Sweden

Bang Bang (My Baby Shot Me Down) (1966): Italy

Gypsies, Tramps & Thieves (1971): Canada; US

Half Breed (1973): Canada; New Zealand; US

Dark Lady (1974): US

If I Could Turn Back Time (1989): Australia

The Shoop Shoop Song (It's In His Kiss) (1991): Austria; Ireland; Norway; UK; Zimbabwe

Love Can Build A Bridge (1995): UK

Believe (1998): Australia; Belgium; Canada; Denmark; France; Germany; Greece; Hungary; Ireland; Italy; Netherlands; New Zealand; Norway; Spain; Sweden; Switzerland; UK; US

Cher's #1 Albums Around The World

Heart Of Stone (1989): Australia

Love Hurts (1991): Austria; Ireland; Norway; UK

Greatest Hits 1965-1992 (1992): UK; Zimbabwe

Believe (1998): Austria; Canada; Denmark; Germany; Greece; New Zealand; Portugal; Zimbabwe

The Greatest Hits (1999): Austria; Denmark; Germany

Trivia: Cher once achieved 7 Canadian Top 10 singles in less than 9 months! Moreover, she has spent over 500 weeks on the Canadian single chart.

Sonny: The Early Years

Sonny Bono – born Salvatore Phillip Bono, 16 February 1935 – is most famous for his work in the music duo Sonny & Cher, and his later work in politics. However, Detroit-born Bono made numerous attempts to catch the public's interest before his big break with Cher.

In 1952, at around the age of 17, Bono – the son of Italian immigrants Santo Bono and Zena La Velle – already had his sights set on music. He co-wrote a song with friend J. Bloomfield called *Ecstasy*, and performed it on Los Angeles television music competition *Search For A Song* (a year before it went National and was renamed *The Peter Potter Show*). His performance won the highest "Audience Applause" ratings of the episode.

Bono then married girlfriend Donna Rankin on November 3, 1954. The following year, he recorded his contest-winning song *Ecstasy* for L.A.'s Dig record label – owned by "Original King of Rock & Roll" Johnny Otis. Unfortunately, the song failed to captivate the record-buying public in the same way it did the *Search For A Song* audience. In 1957, he co-wrote *You Bug Me Baby* with Speciality Records artist Larry Williams – the B-side of Williams' US#14 and UK#11 hit single *Bony Maronie* and a US #45 hit single in its own right. It was just the first of a number of B-sides that Bono wrote for the label's artists, although in 1958, he started to adopt the song-writing moniker of "S.Christy". It is certainly no coincidence that his first child, born 24 June 1958, happened to be named Christine A.K.A. "Christy".

Sonny's last B-Side composition on the label under the song-writing name "Sonny Bono" was on the Don & Dewey single *The Letter* and was called *Koko Joe*, which went on to be recorded by The Righteous Brothers in 1963. The following year, Bono co-wrote (with Roddy Jackson) The Larry Williams single *She Said Yeah*. Although a non-charter when released, it was revived by The Rolling Stones as the opening track of both the UK version of their late-1965 album *Out of Our Heads* (UK#2) and the U.S.-only album *December's Children* (U.S.#4).

Also in 1959, Bono resumed his singing ambitions, releasing self-penned track *Wearing Black* (with a self-penned B-side *One Little Answer*) as a single under the pseudonym "Don Christy" (a combination of Wife Donna and daughter Christy) on Speciality Records. The single failed to spark any interest. Before year's end, the label was closed and a subsidary label, Fidelity Records, was set up. Sonny used the fresh label to release another two singles – the festive novelty *Comin' Down The Chimney* under the name Little Joey & Little Tootsie, and a re-issue of *Wearing Black* (backed with *Don't Have To Tell Me*) as Don Christy. Both singles were unsuccessful, and the latter one was given a third shot with Satellite Records but again to no success.

1960 and 1961 saw Sonny repeatedly attempt – and fail – to launch a recording career under various names: *As Long As You Love Me* as Don Christy; *Don't Shake My Tree* as Ron-ny Sommers; *Shake Me Up* as Prince Carter; and *Little Miss Cool* as Daniel A. Stone (backed with *It Must Be Raining*). In 1962, the latter single was re-released (as a "Don Christy" record) on Rush, a new record label that Sonny launched with Sid Talmadge' – it, and Don Christy single *I'll Change*, failed to chart. The label quickly vanished.

Sonny and Donna separated in 1962, around the same time that the Sonny-penned *Every Day* ended up on the B-side of the minor hit single *Duchess of Earl* by The Pearlettes (US#96). In November, he met 16-year-old Cher...

From The Author

I became a Cher fan at a very young age. Even though I am only 27 years old now.

My father was a big fan of Cher – he had records, movies and concerts of hers, so I was always exposed to Cher my whole childhood. However, it was whilst watching Cher's performance of *We All Sleep Alone* on her *Live At The Mirage* video that I became really hooked – *I wonder why!*

I do not know where that moment fits into my timeline, but my first memory of being a "die-hard" Cher fan comes from after Sonny died. Cher was all over the newspapers, and I remember doing what many of us die-hards have done – cutting out her photos and making a scrap book. I was only 6 years old!

Cher plays a large part in my life. Me and my Dad bonded over our shared interest in music. I remember him buying *Believe*, the single, on cassette, and playing it excessively! Around this time, he bought me Cher's autobiography, *The First Time*, for Christmas. It was my first proper book – and I still have it today.

The first single I ever bought was *The Music's No Good Without You*. The first album I ever purchased was *Living Proof*.

I was not a privileged child or teenager – not by any stretch of the imagination. But I managed to get my hands on most of Cher's CDs and videos. I would visit a second hand music and video shop in my town centre almost every Saturday, and often come away with something that would make my week – a VHS of *Faithful* and the VHS of *Live At The Mirage* were my highlights.

In August 2011, I created *Cher News*. A fan site. I was 20 years old. I had no computer. I created the site on my cell/mobile phone. Looking back, I am not sure how I even achieved that. Later on, I managed to find an old (*very old!*) computer, which made running the site a little easier – however, I still did not have internet access other that that on my cell phone, so I had to get technical and connect the two devices. The site was a success. And many Cher fans even helped me out, giving donations – after all, it was costing me a bomb to run a Cher site through cell phone internet! In 2013, I got my first laptop – and proper internet access!

Fast forward to late 2016, and *Cher News* had over 500 articles – most of which were original articles – and had surpassed 2,000,000 page views.

In May 2016, I got the news that my Dad had died. I was working in a call centre at that time, and I went straight back to work, hoping that the news would not affect me. I got a caller named "Graham" on the phone – the same name as my Dad – and I broke down in tears. I was sent home. I did not want to face that job again. And I wanted time off work. Someone else offered me a job, I was unsure, but took it anyway. After a month, I wanted out. My head was not in a good place.

I could not face work nor people. Me and my Dad were not even super close. But his extremely unexpected death changed my life – in a bad way. I became a hermit. I stayed at home. But I had rent to pay. I needed to make money somehow. I needed to get out of this slump somehow.

Then a light-bulb appeared above my head – the idea to write an eBook, and dedicate it to Dad. That's what I did. I wrote about Cher. And released it. Luckily, Cher fans – mostly the faithful followers of *Cher News* – purchased it. A follow-up was destined.

When I was young, I owned a book about rock music, it was a huge book. And its entire contents was a massive timeline. Cher made a few appearances in it. Included, was a photo of Sonny & Cher in 1965 – naturally, I cut it out! For Vol. 2 of the The Cher Bible series, I knew I wanted to adopt the idea of a timeline of – not rock – but the lady that boasts hits across numerous genres, Cher.

2017, and more so 2018, have been active and exciting years for Cher — and her fans. With the success of *Classic Cher* and *Edith+Eddie*, and the announcements of *Mamma Mia! Here We Go Again,* the *Here We Go Again Tour* and *The Cher Show*, plus Cher receiving the Billboard Icon Award, it paved the way for updated versions of *The Cher Bible, Vol. 1: Essentials* and *The Cher Bible, Vol. 2: Timeline.*

"You know what? I'm kind of a warhorse.

Tina Turner and I are such... we just knew to do it.

You know, we just worked until the work was over.

And I got that kind of ethic from Sonny,

because he never wanted to stop working."

– Cher

Printed in Great Britain
by Amazon